Dialects in Schools and Communities

Dialects in Schools and Communities

Walt Wolfram
North Carolina State University

Carolyn Temple Adger
Center for Applied Linguistics

Donna Christian
Center for Applied Linguistics

LEA LAWRENCE ERLBAUM ASSOCIATES, PUBLISHERS
1999 Mahwah, New Jersey London

Lawrence Erlbaum Associates, Inc., Publishers
10 Industrial Avenue
Mahwah, NJ 07430

Cover design by Kathryn Houghtaling Lacey

Library of Congress Cataloging-in-Publication Data

Wolfram, Walt, 1941–
Dialects in schools and communities / Walt Wolfram, Carolyn Temple
    Adger, Donna Christian.
        p.   cm.
    Includes bibliographical references and index.
ISBN 0-8058-2862-1 (alk. paper). — ISBN 0-8058-2863-X (pbk. : alk.
    paper)
1. English language—Dialects—United States. 2. Language and edu-
    cation—United States. 3. Community and school—United States.
    4. Students—United States—Language. 5. Children—United
    States—Language. 6. Language arts—United States. I. Adger, Car-
    olyn Temple. II. Christian, Donna. III. Title.
PE2841.W654   1998
427'.973—DC21
                                                    97-47498
                                                        CIP

Books published by Lawrence Erlbaum Associates are printed on
acid-free paper, and their bindings are chosen for strength and dura-
bility.

Printed in the United States of America
10   9   8   7   6   5   4   3   2

Contents

Preface

Curiosity about language variation and the role that dialects play in society is natural. In education, concern with this topic has always been high, rising cyclically to extraordinary levels. The current awareness that students in the United States represent a rich array of linguistic and cultural resources brings this topic around again, with many of the related issues from the past still unresolved. In *Dialects in Schools and Communities*, we have addressed this natural interest and educational concern about dialects by considering some of the major issues that confront educational practitioners. This work is rooted in questions that have arisen in workshops, surveys, classes, and discussion groups with practitioners and teacher educators. The work thus intends to fulfill an important need in a range of educational and related service fields. No previous background in linguistics or sociolinguistics is assumed on the part of the reader.

Although the discussion has an empirical, research base, we do not give detailed documentation in the text. Instead, we synthesize current understandings and provide key references. In a sense, this is a kind of translation and interpretation work in which we attempt to bring together the practical concerns of educators and the vantage point of sociolinguistics.

This book was inspired originally by the response we received to our earlier work, *Dialects and Education: Issues and Answers*, by Walt Wolfram and Donna Christian (1989), but we have reconsidered and expanded our discussion of many of the issues raised in that earlier work in a completely revised format.

This volume is divided into eight chapters, with appropriate subsections in each. In the initial chapter, Language Variation in the United States, popular concerns with the nature of language variation are raised, and in chapter 2, Exploring Dialects, more specific issues about the characteristic structures of different dialects are considered. In the third chapter, Communicative Interaction, attention turns to various interactive patterns characteristic of groups.

Chapter 4, Language Difference Does Not Mean Language Deficit, looks at perceptions of declining standards for language and education and at some of the ways in which language differences can be construed as problems.

The particular educational impact of dialect on speaking, writing, and reading are considered in chapters 5 through 7. Chapter 5, Oral Language Instruction, takes up questions about teaching Standard English—whether to do it and how it might be more effective than in the past. Chapter 6 moves on to dialects and writing and chapter 7 addresses issues of dialect and reading. The final chapter, Dialect Awareness for Students, points to information about the value of understanding dialects as natural and normal language phenomena. It describes an antidote for the misunderstandings about dialects that contribute to inequity at school and elsewhere in the society. We include at the conclusion of each chapter some suggestions for further reading. We also include a catalogue of vernacular structures. This is not a complete inventory of any dialect or of vernacular features. It conveniently organizes and expands on structural descriptions discussed in the chapters.

This resource is intended for use by teacher interns and practicing teachers in elementary and secondary education, early childhood specialists, specialists in reading and writing, speech/language pathologists, special education teachers, and students in various language specialties. Most of these fields now consider information about dialects to be an important part of professional preparation, but they have had no available text that addresses the specific needs of practitioners. This volume also illuminates the language issues that arise as all of the content areas place increasing emphasis on oral and written language in learning.

Obviously, we do not have all the answers to practitioners' questions about dialect variation and education in this reexamination of dialects in schools and communities. We have, however, attempted to be honest in our response to practitioners' concerns and to admit where the research findings are limited or ambiguous. We offer the book as an updated, still-interim report on the state of language variation and education in the United States. We hope simply that we have faithfully represented the kinds of concerns that practitioners have brought to us in the past few decades, and we dedicate this work to those who have been willing to raise the kinds of concerns we address here. In the process, we have learned that there are few easy answers to the questions about language variation raised by practitioners.

Many colleagues and friends have commented on portions of this text, after reading our earlier work or drafts of this one. We thank each one heartily: John Barnitz, John Baugh, David Bloome, Ken Goodman, Yetta Goodman, Jacqueline Haynes, Susan Hoyle, Howard Mims, Joy Kreeft Peyton, John Rickford, Peg Steffenson, and Rose Marie Weber. Thanks especially to those with enough faith in us to experiment with parts of the text with their students. We deeply appreciate the gifts of those who have helped in these and other ways, including Lupe Hernandez-Silva, Quang Pho, Thom Raybold, and Vincent Sagart.

—Walt Wolfram
—Carolyn Temple Adger
—Donna Christian

1

Language Variation in the United States

ISSUES AND DEFINITIONS

Every language differs to some degree from place to place and from group to group. We use the term *language variation* to refer to the fact that a language is not uniform. Instead, it varies, corresponding to sociocultural characteristics of groups of people such as their cultural background, geographical location, social class, gender, or age. *Language variation* may also refer to differences in the way that language is used in different situations such as in the home, the community, and the school, and on different occasions such as telling a friend about a trip or planning a trip with a travel agent.

People who share important cultural, social, and regional characteristics typically speak similarly, and people who differ in such characteristics usually differ in language or dialect as well. The term *dialect* is generally used to refer to a variety of a language associated with a regionally or socially defined group of people. This definition of *dialect* is not a rigorous one, but it carries an important implication. Technically, as linguists use the term, the relative status of a dialect with respect to other dialects of the language (its social standing) does not make one dialect more valuable, or interesting, or worthy of study than another. The term *dialect* used this way is neutral—no evaluation is implied, either positive or negative.

For example, a difference in the use of *anymore* has been noticed in different English dialects. The patterns, or rules, of some dialects require that *anymore* be used only in negative sentences (those with *not* or some other negative) or in questions such as *Do you go there anymore*? In other dialects, it can also occur in affirmative sentences, such as *Houses in this neighborhood are expensive anymore*. This dialect difference usually corresponds to regional characteristics: Speakers using positive *anymore* are generally located in midland areas, running through Pennsylvania, Ohio, and westward. The important point is that neither use of *anymore* is linguistically right or wrong. They are only different: Some dialects include a restriction on *anymore* that others do not have. According to the technical meaning of *dialect*, one pattern is not better than another.

Variation is so much a part of every language that a person cannot speak a language without speaking a dialect of that language. Everyone is part of some group that can be distinguished from other groups, in part by how group members talk. If a person speaks the English language, that person necessarily speaks some dialect of the English language.

This chapter raises some basic issues for education and society that grow out of the contrast between differing perspectives on dialect: Research shows that dialects are all complete linguistic systems, and thus structurally equal, but social evaluation gives some dialects higher status than others. That is, views of the relative merit of a language variety are based on social, not linguistic, grounds.

Popular Meanings of Dialect

The term *dialect* is sometimes used in ways that contrast with the technical meaning just presented. One of the most common uses of the term carries a negative connotation, unlike the neutral, technical meaning. *Dialect* is sometimes used to refer to a particular social or geographical variety of English that is not the standard one. For example, a native Midwesterner hearing the speech of an African American from the deep South or a European American from rural Appalachia might say that the speaker uses a dialect. This use of the term assumes that only certain groups of people speak a dialect. Such assumptions are unwarranted, however, because everyone speaks some variety—or dialect—of their language. Some dialects may be more noticeable than others because of the social and political position of different groups and the linguistic salience of their distinguishing traits, but this does not mean that only some people use dialects.

Dialect is also sometimes used popularly as a synonym for *language*. For example, people sometimes refer to African or Native American dialects. In reality, many separate languages are spoken by Africans and Native Americans—and by Europeans and Asians. The equation of dialect with language tends to characterize situations that are unfamiliar and removed from the life of the observer.

Language specialists often object to the popular usage of *dialect* because of the different possible interpretations the term can have and because of the negative sense it may carry. They use instead the term *language variety* so that misinterpretations suggested by the different uses of the term *dialect* can be avoided. *Language difference, language variation,* and *linguistic diversity* are also used to avoid the negative connotations sometimes associated with the term *dialect*.

If everyone speaks a dialect, then how do we refer to the speech of people who do not speak a standard dialect? The most common labels are *nonstandard dialect, nonmainstream dialect,* and *vernacular dialect*. Although these terms can be used synonymously, and all are in common use, we use the designation *vernacular dialect* here. We prefer that term because it highlights the dimension of the indigenous communities associated with language varieties. This term also seems more neutral than the term *nonstandard* and leads to somewhat less confusion than the label *nonmainstream*, which has been used to refer to a range of groups considered outside of mainstream society for one reason or another.

Accent and Dialect

When it comes to language differences, the term *accent* is popularly used to refer to how people pronounce words. So, if a person pronounces *car* without the final *r*, as in "cah," or *creek* something like "crick," these pronunciations might be considered to be characteristic of a particular accent. References to accents may include differences other than pronunciation, but the focus is usually on pronunciation.

Situations in which someone might use the term *accent* can provide a basis for comparing what is commonly meant by *accent* with what may be meant by *dialect*.

1. A French waiter asks some diners what they would like to order. His question is English, but the pronunciation sounds as if he were using French rather than English sounds. The patron might remark, "That waiter has a very heavy accent."

2. Someone who grew up in northeastern New England visits Chicago. A native Chicagoan might observe, "You can tell where she's from the minute she opens her mouth—she really has a strong New England accent."

3. Someone originally from Chicago visits Northeastern New England. A New Englander might remark, "That person must be from Chicago. She says some words with a real accent."

The restaurant situation involves someone who presumably learned English as a second language and whose speech still shows influence from the native language. This is the classic foreign accent that might be more specifically labeled as a French accent, a Swedish accent, and so forth. The other two situations contain references to variation in a single language. In this respect, *accent* is closer to the term *dialect*. Of course, *accent* is more restricted because it refers primarily to pronunciation, and there are differences other than pronunciation among dialects. According to this definition, then, *accent* is one part of the broad definition of a dialect difference.

The term *accent* often carries some connotations like those for the popular use of *dialect*, although they are typically less severe. Despite the fact that each variety of English includes its own particular pronunciation pattern, the assumption is often made that only other people have accents. Thus, the native Chicagoan meeting someone from New England may think that it is only the New Englander who speaks with an accent—whereas the native New Englander may think that only the Chicagoan speaks with an accent. Of course, both of them have an accent, just as everyone speaks a dialect. Some accents (and dialects) are the subject of wider comment than others—including, for example, what people call a Southern accent, a Boston accent, a New York accent, and a British accent, all of which have stereotyped features that others recognize quite readily. Although negative connotations are sometimes associated with having an accent, there can be positive evaluations as well. For instance, many North Americans hold a British accent in high regard.

Kinds of Language Differences

Dialects may differ from each other at several levels in addition to pronunciation. One fairly obvious difference is in vocabulary items: for example, the use of a term like *tonic* in some regions of New England to refer to what in other regions is called *pop*, *soda pop*, or simply *soda*. The retention of the term *icebox* by members of older generations where the younger generation uses *refrigerator* also reflects this type of difference, as do the British forms *jumper, chemist*, and *boot* for American *sweater, drugstore*, and (car) *trunk*, respectively.

Dialects also contrast with each other in terms of the way words are composed and words are combined in sentences—the grammatical patterns of the language system. For example, in some rural areas of the South (reflecting an affinity with dialects of the British Isles), the plural *-s* may be left off of nouns of measurement as in *four mile down the road* or *sixteen pound of fish*. Other dialect areas would use the *-s* plural in these phrases. With respect to the combinations of words in sentences, an indirect question may be expressed as *He asked me could he go to the movies*, or as *He asked me if he could go to the movies*; negative patterns may be expressed as *He didn't do anything*, or as *He didn't do nothing*. In some dialects, both alternatives are used; in others, only one. Similarly, alternate responses to the question *Have you read that book?* illustrate a grammatical difference between British and American English: *No, but I should have done*, (British) versus *No, but I should have* (American).

Variation extends even beyond differences in pronunciation, vocabulary, and grammatical structure. There is also variation in how members of a group use particular language forms in social interaction. Thus, a Northerner and a Southerner may both use the terms of respect *sir* and *ma'am* but in contrasting ways that reflect different social and cultural conventions governing respect and familiarity. One social group may feel that it is appropriate to ask people what they do for a living, whereas another group may consider that question invasive. Some of these rules are explicitly discussed as children are socialized, but many are part of our unconscious knowledge about how to get along in the world through talking. Such differences in language use, often related to social and cultural group differences, may be hard to pinpoint but they can be highly sensitive areas of difference between groups and readily lead to cross-cultural communication conflict.

Speech communities—groups of people who share basic expectations about language use (Hymes, 1974)—also differ in the ways that they carry on conversation. For example, in some speech communities speakers overlap each other's talk enthusiastically in a good, satisfying conversation, whereas in others, a speaker is likely to stop talking when another one starts. Even what makes for a good conversational contribution can vary from group to group (Tannen, 1984). Garrison Keillor often refers humorously to what a good Minnesotan or a good Lutheran would say. One of his stories included a conversation in which a new boat owner responds to compliments by talking about the expense and time involved in maintaining the boat—as a good Minnesotan should, said Keillor—rather than saying how much fun it is (National Public Radio broadcast, July 1986). Speakers of

English from other backgrounds might find such a response to be inappropriate and even insulting.

SOURCES OF DIALECT DIFFERENCE

Language differences on all levels ultimately reflect basic, patterned behavior differences between groups of people. There may be diverse reasons underlying differences in language, but they all derive from this basic principle. When groups are physically or socially separated in some way, language differences can be expected. As a language changes—and languages are always changing—differences show up between dialects as groups of people follow different paths of language change (Wolfram & Schilling-Estes, 1998).

Physical, cultural, and social facts are responsible for the variation in U.S. English. Many of the regional differences can be traced to combinations of physical factors in the country's history and geography. Some patterns can be explained by looking at settlement history, which suggests the language patterns of the early settlers (Carver, 1987). The movement of the population, historically and currently, also has a bearing on the language of regions because people take their language practices with them when they move. Finally, characteristics of physical geography must be considered. Natural barriers such as mountains and rivers have historically cut people off from each other, creating a natural basis for differences to emerge and be maintained.

Social and cultural factors are also responsible for diversity in ways of speaking. Social status and ethnic distinctions in our society are often reflected in language differences, along with age and gender distinctions. We would certainly expect that the greater the social distance between groups, the greater the language differences. This principle does not always work exactly, but it is a reasonably accurate predictor of how language differences reflect group behavior differences (Labov, 1972; Wolfram & Schilling-Estes, 1998).

When we consider the general principle that behavioral differences between groups correlate with language differences, it seems reasonable enough to expect that a lawyer from Arkansas will speak differently from a Northern automobile factory worker, or a White Appalachian farmer in an isolated mountain area will speak differently from a Black California business executive, or a Native American artist in New Mexico will speak differently from an Italian police officer in New York. These characterizations include geographical, social, and cultural factors, all of which have been prominent in distinguishing groups of individuals from each other in American society. The same distinctions are important in understanding language differences.

Studies of various dialect groups generally indicate that regional dialects tend to be distinguished by pronunciation and vocabulary features, whereas social dialects show variation in these areas as well as in grammatical usage (Wolfram & Fasold, 1974; Wolfram & Schilling-Estes, 1998). We might guess that someone was from eastern Massachusetts if he or she pronounced the word spelled *idea* with an *r* sound at the end ("idear") in a phrase like *the idear of it* and dropped the *r* sound on a word like *car* ("cah"): *Take the car.*

Many pronunciation differences concern the vowel sounds in words. For instance, many Southern regional dialects vary from dialects in other parts of the country according to the way that speakers pronounce words with vowel glides, like *line* or *ride*. (A glide is a vowel quality that is attached to a main vowel. The vowel in *line* or *ride* consists of a main vowel, *a*, which flows into a vowel with the quality of *ee* or *y* [e.g., "layn," "rayd"].) People from Southern regional areas are likely to say something like "lahn" or "rahd," whereas people from Northern areas would pronounce these words with the glide as in "layn" or "rayd". Other pronunciation variants involve particular words rather than sets of words. For some people *route* rhymes with *boot*; for others, with *bout*. Similarly, *creek* is pronounced as "crick" in some Northern areas, but as "creek" elsewhere. These pronunciation differences are popularly referred to as accent, as we previously saw.

Regional dialects also differ in vocabulary. Depending on what part of the country you were in, for instance, you would need to order a *sub* (or a *submarine*), a *hoagie, grinder, hero*, and so forth, to get a particular type of sandwich. Water might be obtained through a *faucet*, a *tap*, or a *spigot*; and children would *favor* or *resemble* one of their parents. These alternative vocabulary items are readily noticed and commented on when speakers from different regions meet.

Social dialects not only show variation in vocabulary items and pronunciation features, they also have differences in grammatical structure. Some members of rural, working-class communities might say *You was right* and *I done it* whereas a middle-class office worker in a city might use *You were right* and *I did it* to mean the same thing. Variations in the verb are typical of grammatical differences between dialects. They affect the systems for relating subjects to verbs (i.e., agreement patterns) and for choosing a form of the verb for a particular tense.

People sometimes ask us how many dialects of English there are. Somewhat surprisingly, there is no agreed-on answer to this question, even after decades of research on differences in American English. We can discuss, as we have, the many differences in the speech patterns of different groups of people, but deciding where one dialect ends and another begins and then counting how many there are is a different matter. Dialects do not come in neat, self-contained packages; and many factors, of varying degrees of importance, must be considered in distinguishing them.

There have been a number of attempts to delineate dialect groups of English in the United States by region (Carver, 1987; Kurath, 1949; Labov, Ash, & Boberg, 1997). Linguistic geographers generally recognize several major dialect areas in the United States and a number of subareas in them. Although many cautions are given about the lines of demarcation and the importance of different lines, the map of dialects shown in Fig. 1.1 represents a fairly common delineation. This map, from Carver (1987), gives only a regional distribution, however, and it is based on vocabulary differences alone. In Fig. 1.2, a map based on pronunciation from Labov, Ash, and Boberg (1997) is superimposed on the map based on vocabulary in Fig. 1.1. Despite the difference in the level of language and a time lapse of a half century in terms of the collection of data for the maps, there is an amazing parallel in the regional dialect configuration. In and across areas, there are, of course, social, cultural, age, and gender considerations as well, which complicate the picture immensely.

LANGUAGE STANDARDS

There are numerous dialects that make up the English language. The first section of this chapter primarily concerned English in the United States. Imagine the range of variation if we included England, Australia, Jamaica, and other countries where English is spoken! Yet there is no one correct way to speak English, in the sense that one set of language patterns is inherently better than all the others. Certain language patterns are preferred over others, according to social norms (which may vary as well). These are often referred to in terms of the correct use of English, but correctness involves decisions based on social, not linguistic, acceptability.

Correct is a judgment that we make, typically based on some objective set of information. For example, the result of an addition problem, like 7 plus 3, has one correct solution (10), and all others are incorrect (11, 9, etc.). To compare arithmetic and language use, we must look for a set of objective

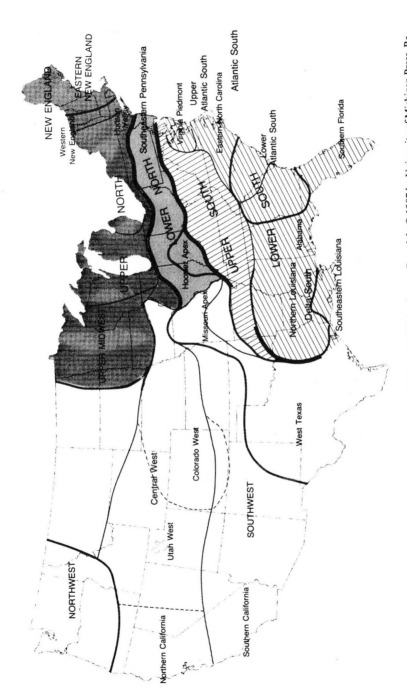

FIG. 1.1. Dialect map of the United States. From *American Regional Dialects* (1987) by Carver. Copyright © 1987 by University of Michigan Press. Reprinted with permission.

9

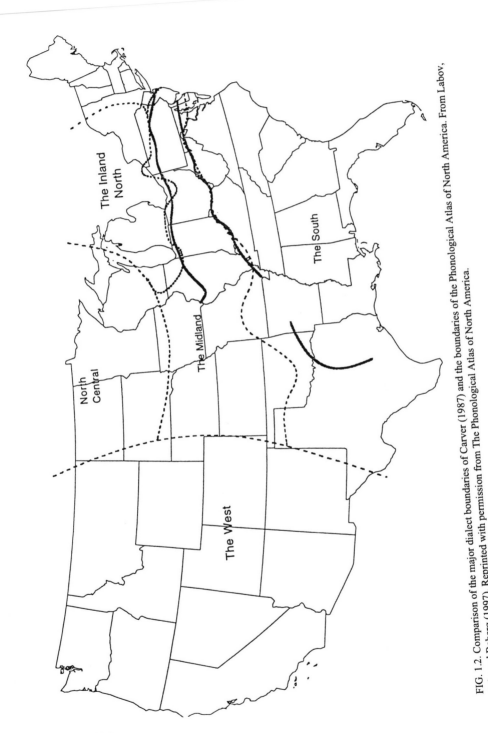

FIG. 1.2. Comparison of the major dialect boundaries of Carver (1987) and the boundaries of the Phonological Atlas of North America. From Labov, Ash, and Boberg (1997). Reprinted with permission from The Phonological Atlas of North America.

10

facts against which we might judge whether something in language is correct or incorrect.

One set of facts we might be able to depend on is our ability as proficient English speakers to decide what can and cannot count as English. So, for example, when we hear a sentence like "They will arrive tomorrow," we can observe that it is English and therefore in that sense correct. On the other hand, we would know that "Arrive will tomorrow they" or "Ils arriveront demain" are both incorrect as English sentences in that sense, although the latter would qualify for another language. Similarly, we would judge *pencil* to be a correct form of English but *tloshg* would not be accepted. In each case, we seem to be identifying things that speakers of English might say—as opposed to what they would not say—based on our knowledge of the English language. Here is one set of objective facts that we share as speakers of English.

When it comes to ways of saying things that are not shared by all speakers of English, however, the notion of correct becomes much more elusive and, at the same time, quite controversial. Consider two English sentences that may be used by native speakers of English: *I done it wrong* or *I can't see nothing*. It is clear that these are both possible sentences of English: When someone says a sentence like this, we would not want to claim that they were not speaking English. In this sense, then, these are both linguistically patterned English sentences, in contrast with non-English. However, if you ask someone about them, you may be told that they aren't good, proper, or correct English. Here, correctness is determined by social acceptability, rather than accuracy or intrinsic worth. There is no single basis, in terms of objective facts, for determining whether *I did it wrong* or *I done it wrong* is a better way to convey information. It is not possible, then, to identify just one way of speaking English as the correct way. The socially unacceptable forms, like *I done it*, are often termed *nonstandard*, to contrast them with *standard* forms or those that conform to social norms. These norms are based on judgments of social acceptability rather than technical assessments of linguistic patterning.

The value placed on a certain way of saying something is very closely associated with the cultural identity or the social status of the people who say it that way. This valuing is not an individual decision; it is the society's evaluation of different groups, including their ways of speaking. As we are socialized, we learn these attitudes, sometimes unconsciously, sometimes through expressed regulations and rules, just as we learn eating behavior. As children, we learn to eat peas with a fork instead of with a spoon or our fingers. The nutritional content of peas is the same regardless of how we eat them, and all three ways succeed in getting the peas into our mouths, but our society socializes us into viewing one way as proper or correct, and the other ways as unacceptable. In a similar way, the communicative effectiveness of *I done it* or *I did it* is identical, but we have been socialized into considering only one alternative as correct or proper and the other as incorrect or bad. In terms of social evaluation, then, correctness does not involve real, intrinsic linguistic value or assessment by any objective standard. What is acceptable according to the standards of the dominant group in society is considered correct; what is not acceptable to them will be looked on as incorrect.

Beliefs about language correctness are actually shared by most members of our society. Speakers from groups whose dialects are not highly regarded generally feel that their language is not as good as other people's. Those from groups who speak the favored dialects are likely to be aware of only some of the differences between their language variety and others, but to feel that their way of speaking is self-evidently preferable.

The U.S. situation is in no way unique in this regard. General acceptance of a standard language variety accompanied by negative attitudes toward the other language varieties is an unavoidable product of the interaction of language and society (Fasold, 1984; Preston, 1996).

Language and Logic

Like the notion of correct language, the idea that some dialects are more logical than others results from the social attitudes that surround language. Believing that standard forms of English are inherently better than others, many people will go on to maintain that certain linguistic structures are more logical than others, more systematic, and even more advantageous for cognitive development. There is no evidence, however, to support the contention that any language variety will interfere with the development of reasoning ability, or the ability to express logical concepts. All dialects and all languages adequately provide for the conceptualization and expression of logical propositions, but the particular manner of this expression may differ among language systems.

The use of so-called double negatives, or two negative forms in a single sentence, is often cited as evidence that a particular language variety is illogical. According to this argument, two negatives in a sentence like *They can't go nowhere* should cancel each other so that the meaning becomes positive (*They can go somewhere*). Because sentences like this are intended to have a negative interpretation, the claim is made that the structure is illogical. (According to this position, *Nobody can't go nowhere*, with three negatives, would have to be accepted as a negative sentence.) However, the natural logic of language users is not identical to formal mathematic logic, where for some operations (e.g., multiplication), two negatives do yield a positive. Natural logic allows both *They can't go anywhere* and *They can't go nowhere* to have a negative interpretation, depending on the language use conventions of the particular dialect community. Both are expressions of the logical concept of negation, but the singly negated form is socially acceptable whereas the doubly negated form is not.

It is interesting to note that multiple negation was an acceptable structure for English in the past. During the Old English and Middle English periods in the history of English, the only way certain negative sentences could be formed was through the use of double negatives (e.g., "There was no man nowhere so virtuous"; Pyles & Algeo, 1982). The change to favoring the use of a single negative in sentences like *They can't do anything* is a relatively recent development. Many other modern languages have extensive use of double negatives as a part of their standard grammar. In the French language, the use of two negative words (*ne ... rien*) is the current standard for making a negative utterance, as in *Je ne sais rien*, *I don't know nothing*. Similarly, in Spanish *no* and *nada*, as in *No hace nada*, *She or he isn't doing nothing*, is the standard form for making a negative utterance.

Another notion related to dialects with nonstandard features is the interpretation that these features simply reflect incomplete learning of the standard dialect. Common phrases used to describe certain language features reveal and reinforce this notion, such as "leaving off the endings of words," or "not using complete sentences." In some cases, the English speakers who are said to "leave off the endings of words" are really applying a pronunciation pattern that all English speakers use to a limited degree. For example, all speakers of English will, in casual speech, sometimes pronounce a word like *fast* as "fas'," leaving off the final *t* sound, as in "fas'break." If you listen carefully to the speech of those around you, you will probably notice this process in use to varying degrees. It is just one of the pronunciation rules of English that happens more often in casual speech.

This pronunciation rule of English is used somewhat differently in certain dialects, and it is often noticed by speakers of other dialects. One difference is that the rule is used more often in some dialects, and the higher frequency makes it noticeable. Another difference is in where the pronunciation rule applies. If *fast* is pronounced "fas'" in a phrase like "fas'" or slow," speakers of other dialects notice the absence of the *t* sound before the vowel at the beginning of the next word. The practice of "leaving off endings of words" is really a case of an English language rule of pronunciation that is used with minor, but noticeable, differences by different groups, but this practice is not restricted to any one group.

Similarly, all speakers of English use incomplete sentences. The following dialogue shows that we do not need to repeat in conversation what can be easily assumed:

Eva: When are you going to lunch?

Tom: Oh, about 12.

In fact, if Tom used a complete sentence in response, saying for example, *I'm going to lunch at 12 o'clock*, Eva might think that he was being ponderous or that he was annoyed.

The differences between dialects do not show that dialects are simpler or more complex versions of the same language. The differences show only that dialects are contrasting versions. Some of these differences may involve extensions or retractions of shared structures, but others reveal unique language forms that mark subtle but important meaning differences. As we shall see in chapter 2, verb forms in sentences such as *I liketa died, I done took out the garbage*, and *I be doing my homework* all encode meaning differences that are unique to nonstandard dialects. Standard varieties of English would have to use alternative phrasing to capture the precise meaning of the nonstandard forms. For example, to capture the exact meaning of *I be doing my homework* in Standard English, one would have to frame the sentence as *I always do my homework*, or to capture the specific meaning of *I done took out the garbage*, one would have to say something like *I have already finished taking out the garbage*. The relationship between standard and nonstandard forms in English obviously cannot be reduced to a matter of incomplete learning or language complexity.

Standard English

There is really no single dialect of English that corresponds to a standard English, although many believe that such a dialect exists in the speech of those who use so-called good English (Preston, 1993, 1996). This belief is actually close to the social truth: The speech of a certain social group of people does define what is considered standard in English. However, the norms for Standard English are not identical in all communities. Furthermore, there are two sets of norms—the informal standard and the formal standard.

The norms of language usage that members of a society consider to be acceptable constitute their informal language standard. This set of norms correlates to the way certain people actually speak and allows variation between speech communities in the society. It is fairly flexible and regionalized so that there is an *informal Standard American English* for the South, the Northeast, and so forth. It is also subjective in that different people may evaluate standards somewhat differently based on their background.

Formal Standard English, on the other hand, includes the norms prescribed in grammar books and is most typically reflected in the written language. For example, the formal standard dictates that certain distinctions should be made in the use of *lie* and *lay*, that one should avoid ending a sentence with a preposition, and so on. However, acceptable spoken language usage does not necessarily conform to these norms. Informal Standard English would allow sentences like *They're the ones you should depend on* with no stigma attached, despite the final preposition. In fact, an utterance like *They are the ones on whom you should depend* is probably less acceptable in social interaction in many circumstances because of its formality. Formal Standard English patterns that differ from the informal standard ones are often taught in English language arts.

If the formal standard is used as a reference point, it is unlikely that anyone speaks the standard language consistently. The formal standard is generally limited to the written language of educated people, and it is heard only in the most formal style of highly educated members of society. The informal standard is spoken, however, by those whose language usage sets the guidelines for what is acceptable in each community.

Two observations need to be made about the informal standard. First, because all speakers use a range of styles depending on the situation of speaking, someone who is considered a speaker of Standard English may at times use particular language patterns that are clearly not standard. For example, in an appropriate situation, a standard speaker might use *ain't* or double negatives. In fact, a president of the United States once said in a nationally televised address that *Washington ain't seen nothin' yet*. This usage did not indicate that the president had suddenly become a speaker of a vernacular dialect of English. Presumably, this nonstandard form was used to evoke a sense of toughness and resiliency, characteristic connotations of vernacular dialect forms.

Second, a number of different varieties qualify as informal Standard English. For example, a standard speaker from Maine and a standard speaker from Tennessee would have quite different pronunciation patterns and probably certain other differences as well. They would both be accepted as Standard English speakers in their own communities, however, and in most others as well, despite the fact that their accent might be noticed outside their home region. But although the informal standard for American English includes a range of language patterns, particularly in the area of pronunciation, there is a unified notion of what is not acceptable (unless used for effect as in the previous example).

The situation becomes quite a bit more complicated when we consider World Englishes—the varieties of English spoken in other countries. Just as in the United States, there are likely to be standard and vernacular English language varieties in countries that were colonized by English speakers, where English has become the mother tongue of most people (e.g., New Zealand) or a second language spoken by nearly everyone for certain purposes, like business and higher education (e.g., Nigeria). English is used for special purposes in many other countries as well, and local standards have developed. When English speakers travel abroad, they may find that speech considered standard in their own country may be considered difficult to understand, odd, even nonstandard according to the standards of the host country. Here again, Standard English is relative to the particular norms of the speech community. Standard Singapore English is very different from any version of Standard American English. Thus it is more accurate to speak of Standard Englishes.

In every society there are people whose position or social status makes their judgments about language use more influential than those of others including, for example, teachers and employers. These people decide who will get what placement in school and who will be hired. Their judgments about what is acceptable and unacceptable in language enter into evaluations made ostensibly on other bases, such as people's experience and achievement. Such judgments have more weight and more consequence than casual remarks about others' language in the course of daily life. These influential people are often looked up to by other members of their community whose opinions about matters like language are also typically respected. The speech habits of this social core are often admired and serve as a model of acceptability.

Standard American English, then, is a composite of the real spoken language of this group, generally professionals and others in the educated middle-class. Because members of this group in Chicago might sound quite different from their counterparts in Charleston, South Carolina, we need to recognize the existence of a number of dialects of Standard American English. For the most part, there is more shared structure in the grammar of Standard English speakers across communities than in pronunciation, but there are still some regional grammar differences that keep us from concluding that a single set of standard grammatical features exists. Different communities may have slightly different norms, and this informal set of norms is the one that really counts in terms of social acceptance. It is important, for this reason, to carefully distinguish between those norms that make up the formal standard and the informal, yet highly influential, norms of social acceptability that govern most everyday, interactional evaluations of standardness.

We use the term *Standard English* as a proper noun with a capital *s* on *standard,* but we intend it as a collective noun. Standard English is a collection of the socially preferred dialects from various parts of the United States and other English-speaking countries.

DIALECTS AND UNDERSTANDING

Given the differences among English dialects, it stands to reason that communication among speakers of different dialects might be occasionally flawed. But although problems in comprehension and interpretation can arise, the severity of these problems and their precise source is not always clear.

Certainly, there are Standard English speakers who claim not to understand vernacular speakers. To put this in perspective, however, we have to realize that this is a claim that one may also hear when a person travels through another region, such as a Northerner traveling through the South or a person from the mainland visiting a historically isolated island area in the Chesapeake Bay or the Outer Banks off of the coast of North Carolina. In most cases, such reports are exaggerated, based on a few items that may legitimately prove troublesome for an outsider to comprehend. An outsider in Appalachia for the first time may have difficulty comprehending certain *ire* words such as *fire* (pronounced much like *far*) or *buyer* (pronounced much like *bar*), or the use of a vocabulary item like *garret* for *attic* or *vittles* for *food*, unless there is sufficient context to interpret these items.

But such isolated problems would not usually result in a total breakdown of conversation. Adjustments may have to be made to comprehend certain pronunciations, grammatical patterns, and distinct vocabulary uses, but most speakers of Standard English seem able to do this with ease. Certainly, most English speakers who interact with speakers of another dialect on a regular basis do not encounter severe comprehension problems.

One of the factors that makes objective assessment of comprehension difficult relates to language attitudes. If speakers of a dominant, mainstream dialect feel that the vernacular version of the language is simply an unworthy approximation of what they perceive as the real language, then problems in comprehension are attributed primarily to vernacular speakers' inability to make themselves understood. In this interpretation, speakers of the mainstream variety may be unwilling to make the usual kind of language adjustments necessary to enhance comprehension across dialects. Studies of comprehension and social relations in other language contact settings have shown that the relative status of groups can play a very prominent role in the comprehension of language varieties (Fasold, 1984). Typically, the higher status group claims comprehension difficulties with the lower status groups, not the converse. In fact, the relative social status of groups may be a more important factor determining intelligibility than the actual language differences.

Vernacular speakers generally indicate less overall comprehension difficulty with standard varieties of English than Standard English speakers do with vernacular varieties. Vernacular speakers are typically exposed to Standard English varieties through educational and official institutions and the media, whereas Standard English speakers usually do not have comparable exposure to vernacular dialects. And, as we pointed out earlier, our society simply expects and assumes that vernacular speakers will comprehend standard varieties whereas the converse does not hold. Questions about comprehensibility have not been laid to rest, however, and additional research in this area would be helpful to educators.

The conclusion that vernacular speakers seem to comprehend standard varieties better than standard dialect speakers comprehend the vernacular does not, however, mean that comprehension of the standard dialect can be assumed to be equivalent for all speakers of English regardless of their dialectal background. In fact, people of different dialect and cultural backgrounds may comprehend particular constructions differently. For instance, there may be differences in literal or nonliteral interpretations of sentences: For example, *See you later* may be interpreted simply as a ritualistic way of taking leave or a commitment to return. Different inferences may be drawn from particular sentence constructions or word choices: Instructions in a testing situation to "repeat what I say" may be interpreted by students from some backgrounds as a request to paraphrase the test giver's words, and by those from other backgrounds as a request to repeat the utterance verbatim.

Subtle types of miscomprehension of standard language conventions by vernacular speakers can have an effect just as significant as more transparent cases of vocabulary comprehension difficulty. For example, standardized educational tests may assume that all students understand the Standard English directions for the task in exactly the same way. If, however, this is not the case, then the scoring of differential responses given by different groups of students as correct or incorrect may be called into question. Claims about Standard English comprehension by vernacular dialect speakers may have been overstated because of the preoccupation with obvious cases of literal word meaning. Only painstaking, detailed analysis of extended notions of comprehension can uncover such meaning loss, but these cases are extremely important in understanding the full range of potential miscomprehension across dialects.

DEFICIT VERSUS DIFFERENCE

We have been saying that in terms of how languages are organized, no variety of a language is inherently better than another. No speakers have a disadvantage in their fundamental ability to function cognitively and expressively as a result of the variety of the language that they acquire.

The realities of the social situation in this country cannot be denied, however. Members of some cultural and linguistic groups are at a disadvantage because of their less favored or stigmatized status in society. They are viewed as deficient in certain areas by members of the social groups that have more power and authority in our society's institutions and systems—education, government, health care, employment, and so on. Members of the powerful groups often believe that members of the stigmatized groups must change in order to be accepted. Success in school for children from these disenfranchised groups, for example, may depend on their changing aspects of their language and language use, and adapting to school norms—which are generally more like the norms of the powerful groups than those of the stigmatized groups. For members of a mainstream, powerful group, no change or adaptation is necessary. In this sense, children from some groups may be at risk for school failure although they are not intrinsically disadvantaged.

Two major schools of thought concerning groups that contrast linguistically and culturally with mainstream society have been referred to as the *deficit position* and the *difference position*. In terms of language, proponents of the deficit position believe that speakers of dialects with nonstandard forms have a handicap—socially and cognitively—because the dialects are illogical, or sloppy, or just bad grammar. Intelligence test scores and results of other standardized language measures may be cited as evidence for this position (Bereiter, 1965; Hernnstein & Murray, 1994) even though issues of test bias are typically not considered. On the basis of these test scores, recommendations may be made for remedial language and other educational services. The concept of compensatory programs evolved from this position. Educational programs were designed to fill in the gaps in language and other skills caused by the students' so-called linguistic and environmental disadvantages. According to this position, then, speakers of socially stigmatized dialects have a language deficit that can impede their cognitive and social development.

The contrasting perspective, and the one advocated here, is the difference position that views groups of speakers in terms of the differences among their language systems. Because no one linguistic system can be shown to be inherently better, there is no reason to assume that using a particular dialect can be associated with having any kind of inherent deficit or advantage. This perspective calls into question the evidence from test scores and school performance that is used to support the need for remediation. If educators assume that a particular dialect is best, if they formally accept and encourage only that dialect, and if they test ability and achievement only through the medium of that dialect, then it should not be surprising that students who enter school already speaking it fare better than those who use a different dialect. An understanding of the social attitudes and values concerning the dialects and their speakers is thus needed in order to deal with the differences.

From time to time, these contrasting positions, which have been discussed for decades now, produce acrimonious debate played out in a public arena. For example, in December, 1996, the Unified School Board of Oakland adopted a resolution that recognized Ebonics or African American Vernacular English as a language system to be taken into account in teaching school children Standard English. The resolution provoked wide comment, much of it scathing denunciation of vernacular dialect and the school system's acceptance of what was thought of as deficient language. Everyone had something to say—prominent persons in government, civil rights, entertainment, and education; ordinary citizens; national organizations concerned with linguistic research and language teaching (see Box 1.1); and many, many reporters and editorial writers. In fact, the debate even extended to a Senate subcommittee hearing on the topic. At the heart of the Ebonics controversy was the long-standing conflict between the deficit and the difference positions.

Taking the view that Ebonics, the language spoken by many of their African American students, is a legitimate linguistic system, different from the Standard English system, Oakland schools use students' knowledge of Ebonics in teaching Standard English. In this way, the schools respect and exploit students' linguistic competence as a resource for language development rather than a deficit. Their intention is neither to eradicate Ebonics nor to teach it, as some thought, but to help students add another language system.

Most educators are generally aware that dialect differences can interfere in education, but the Ebonics debate shows that the deficit position is still widely held, and that there is no consensus on how dialect differences ought to be accommodated.

Box 1.1.

The Linguistic Society of America Resolution on the Oakland Ebonics Issue

Whereas there has been a great deal of discussion in the media and among the American public about the 18 December 1996 decision of the Oakland School Board to recognize the language variety spoken by many African American students and to take it into account in teaching Standard English, the Linguistic Society of America, as a society of scholars engaged in the scientific study of language, hereby resolves to make it known that:

a. The variety known as "Ebonics," "African American Vernacular English" (AAVE), and "Vernacular Black English" and by other names is systematic and rule-governed like all natural speech varieties. In fact, all human linguistic systems—spoken, signed, and written—are fundamentally regular. The systematic and expressive nature of the grammar and pronunciation patterns of the African American vernacular has been established by numerous scientific studies over the past thirty years. Characterizations of

(continued on next page)

(Box 1.1 continued)

Ebonics as "slang," "mutant," "lazy," "defective," "ungrammatical," or "broken English" are incorrect and demeaning.

b. The distinction between "languages" and "dialects" is usually made more on social and political grounds than on purely linguistic ones. For example, different varieties of Chinese are popularly regarded as "dialects," though their speakers cannot understand each other, but speakers of Swedish and Norwegian, which are regarded as separate "languages," generally understand each other. What is important from a linguistic and educational point of view is not whether AAVE is called a "language" or a "dialect" but rather that its systematicity be recognized.

c. As affirmed in the LSA Statement of Language Rights (June 1996), there are individual and group benefits to maintaining vernacular speech varieties and there are scientific and human advantages to linguistic diversity. For those living in the United States there are also benefits in acquiring Standard English and resources should be made available to all who aspire to mastery of Standard English. The Oakland School Board's commitment to helping students master Standard English is commendable.

d. There is evidence from Sweden, the U.S., and other countries that speakers of other varieties can be aided in their learning of the standard variety by pedagogical approaches which recognize the legitimacy of the other varieties of a language. From this perspective, the Oakland School Board's decision to recognize the vernacular of African American students in teaching them Standard English is linguistically and pedagogically sound.

Chicago, Illinois
January 1997
Reprinted with permission of the Linguistic Society of America.

Language Improvement at School

Some aspects of schooling explicitly concern developing language skills. There is an emphasis on developing reading and writing across the curriculum, and in that sense everyone is expected to learn how to use language better. Students also may increase their repertoire of language styles in school. They may learn to critique each others' performance in unoffensive ways, to ask questions suggested by texts, to explain their thinking. They may also increase their vocabulary and develop other aspects of academic language in the content areas. Although these activities are not all a question of learning to use language better, there is certainly some development of language skills for educational and social purposes.

It is important to bear in mind that not all groups start from the same base in terms of the language and social habits that have been developed in the home community. For some groups, language socialization differs from that which schools typically require for various socioeducational functions (Heath, 1983). From the basically middle-class perspective of schools, these children may be viewed as not yet ready to learn. As they progress through a school curriculum, members of these groups must often develop a facility with certain standard dialect forms and ways of interacting with language. Thus, these students have an extra hurdle to overcome simply because they do not have the same background as others and because the school does not value some of their strengths.

Dialect differences between groups of students can affect the quality of education in at least two ways, in spite of sincere efforts to ensure equality of opportunity. One area that has been widely discussed is the possibility that a child's dialect may interfere with the acquisition of various skills (such as reading) and concepts on which later success might depend. More subtle, and perhaps more crucial, are the social consequences of being a member of a different dialect group. The attitudes of teachers and other educators, as well as other students, can have a tremendous impact on the education process. Often people who hear a vernacular dialect make erroneous assumptions about a speaker's intelligence, motivation, and even morality. This kind of dialect-based stereotyping can affect even those who value cultural difference and who pride themselves on treating everyone with respect because dialect prejudice can be very subtle and can operate on an unconscious level.

When a teacher or other school official reacts negatively toward a student's dialect, the result can be detrimental to students from nonmainstream backgrounds. Studies have shown that there can be a self-fulfilling prophecy in teachers' beliefs about their students' abilities (Rosenthal & Jacobson, 1968). It is possible that if a teacher underestimates a child's ability because of dialect differences, perhaps as a direct result, the child will do less well in that class. In some cases, students are tracked with less able students or placed in classes for students with disabilities largely because of their speech patterns. Obviously, children's self-concept may be injured if they encounter negative opinions about their dialect, and they may take up the negative stance toward their own dialect that they experience at school themselves. So educational and social equity may be directly affected by dialect differences.

Cultural Differences

Linguistic differences between groups are, of course, just one factor in the larger set of cultural differences. Members of society's various groups are defined by others and by themselves because they share a set of linguistic and other cultural characteristics. (*Culture* is used here in just this sense: patterns of behavior, including language behavior, shared by members of a social group.) Not only ways of speaking, but values, attitudes toward education, conceptions of politeness, and virtually all socially determined constructs can vary from one group to the next. Mainstream groups—roughly corresponding to the middle and upper class—are considered to exhibit socially acceptable behavior, both linguistically and culturally. As with language, their norms for behavior define a standard because they control access to attractive educational and work opportunities. Nonmainstream groups' norms tend to diverge to some extent from the mainstream norms on both counts—language and culture.

The classroom consequences of cultural differences are very similar to those caused by linguistic differences; and in fact, there is considerable overlap because cultural norms constrain how language is appropriately used. Cultural attitudes affect the interactions of students with teachers and fellow students. Research has reported numerous instances where behaviors have been misinterpreted because of a cultural difference between teacher and student. For example, Native American children in the Southwest have been labeled as passive or nonverbal and have had their level of intelligence misjudged because they seem unresponsive in the classroom to Anglo teachers (Erickson & Mohatt, 1982; Philips, 1993). According to the rules of their culture, however, they are behaving appropriately; active participation would be impertinent. Others report instances of culture clashes and misunderstandings in ethnically mixed classrooms. African American children sometimes get reprimanded for calling out an answer before being called on, or humming and making other noises while working independently (Delpit, 1995). Although these actions may reflect cultural patterns that are expected and valued in the community, a teacher with a different cultural background may see them as disrespectful and disobedient.

Heath has looked carefully at the language and culture patterns children bring to school with them from their home community. In a classic study of three communities—working-class White, working-class African American, and middle-class townspeople—Heath (1983) traced difficulties faced by both sets of working-class children in the middle-class oriented schools to home community differences. Although dialect patterns were involved, the differences she found extend to discourse. For example, the conception of what story and story-telling mean, certainly crucial in language arts instruction, turned out to vary from one community to another. For one group, the term was used in a narrow, and negative sense of an untrue account intended to deceive; in the other group, a story could include departures from fact, but with no intention to mislead the audience. Another revealing area concerned how and when reading and writing events occurred. For adults in both working class communities, reading and writing were used in restricted ways in the home and community (primarily in church-related activities) and played little or no role in their jobs. The perspective that children from these communities developed on the uses, and usefulness, of reading and writing skills influenced their approach to school tasks. Heath's studies point out that broad patterns of language and cultural beliefs and behavior, and subtle differences among groups, are relevant to children's success in the educational context.

Being realistic about the social situation, in terms of mainstream, institutional expectations, is important; and ignoring the difference that differences make, or pretending they do not exist, certainly is not in the best interests of children. All too often, education has avoided discussing differences frankly because these matters are considered too political. The specific course of action taken in response to the differences should depend on the beliefs and goals of the school and the community, and it is likely that disagreements will arise. Whatever decision is reached about policy and programs, the people involved should be well aware of the facts of the language and culture situation, as opposed to popular mythology, in order to make informed choices. This includes examining and acknowledging one's own and others' attitudes toward different varieties of English and culturally based discourse style.

DEALING WITH MULTIPLE DIALECTS

Three basic alternatives can be identified in terms of dealing with multiple dialects:

- accommodate all dialects
- require that a dialect of Standard English be learned and used, or
- identify a position somewhere between these two.

The first alternative, accommodating all dialects, is based on the knowledge that all dialects are inherently equal and no one should be penalized because of his or her dialect. This could mean that a conscious effort would be made to allow full use of a student's native dialect of English as the base on which education will build. Special programs might be implemented to lessen any interference that might come from the native dialect in the acquisition of skills and concepts in the school setting.

The other extreme position is to formally establish that a dialect of Standard English must be acquired and used to replace the vernacular dialect. Support for this position comes from the belief that such a variety is needed for success in mainstream education and society. Following this philosophy, special programs might specifically teach forms of Standard English, but other programs would not need to be changed. This position basically calls for the eradication of the vernacular dialect in schools in favor of Standard English.

The third alternative falls between these two extremes, and is undoubtedly the direction most often followed, often implicitly, in schools. The native dialect is accepted for certain uses, and a dialect of Standard English is encouraged or demanded for other uses. For example, in terms of mastering certain skills, a plan like the following might be formulated. In recognition of the fact that most written language uses a standard variety, a student would be expected to develop the capability to read and write a Standard English dialect. A student would not be required to eliminate the native dialect in classroom talk, but efforts would be made to work toward competence with the standard written forms of the language, both in reading and in writing. In this way, the two (or more) dialects of English would be used by the student for different purposes, much as people naturally use different styles of speaking for different situations. There are school situations other than those involving written language in which vernacular speakers do naturally shift toward Standard English. For example, we found in our observation of classrooms that vernacular speakers tended to use standard forms in place of vernacular forms when they adopted an authoritative stance toward what they were saying, similar to the teacher's customary stance (Adger, 1998). In explaining a complex process or in analyzing a piece of literature, vernacular speakers have been observed to use Standard English forms where in other contexts they might have used a nonstandard alternative (e.g., saying *The test tube doesn't contain any sediment* in reporting a science experiment, rather than *The test tube don't contain no sediment.*) Such natural shifting, which grows out of children's unconscious, community-based knowledge about norms of language use, can form a basis for exploring with them the natural functions of dialects in school and community.

This is just one example of the type of compromise that can be reached between the accommodation and the eradication positions. An advantage to such an arrangement is that the oral dialect in which children are expert when they come to school can be valued rather than tolerated. And an advantage to following a conscious policy concerning dialects is that children will encounter similar language expectations from classroom to classroom.

LANGUAGE ATTITUDES IN SOCIETY

The issues arising over language variation in education are just one reflection of dialect issues in the broader social context. The most pervasive issue concerns attitudes about language. A number of research studies focusing on language attitudes show that speakers of vernacular dialects are generally held in low esteem (Fasold, 1984; Shuy & Fasold, 1973). This view typically extends well beyond their language to other personal attributes, including their morality, integrity, and competence. Attitudes about language can trigger a whole set of stereotypes and prejudices based on underlying social and ethnic differences.

One of the interesting aspects of language attitude studies is the evidence about the young age at which such attitudes may be acquired. In fact, one study showed that children as young as 3 to 5 years of age were quite accurate in recognizing differences in language and made associations with other types of behavior on the basis of language differences (Rosenthal, 1977). Such findings are in line with research about the socialization of prejudice, which begins very early in life and manifests itself in many different details of behavior.

Some dialect differences are observed without prejudice in American society, of course. Many regional vocabulary differences are considered matters of curiosity alone, such as the different words for a paper container, *bag* and *sack* and *poke*, or the variant terms for submarine sandwiches noted earlier. Americans typically would not think a person uneducable, incompetent, or immoral simply because the person called a soft drink *pop*, *soda*, or *cola*. At the same time, however, the dialects spoken by members of particular class and ethnic groups are, in fact, subject to stereotypes related to intellectual capability and morality that are equally unjustified.

There are two possible ways of dealing with these inequities in the social dialects of English. One would be to eliminate the differences between dialects; the other would be to change the negative attitudes toward some dialects that are the source of the inequities.

Complete elimination of dialect differences is not a practical solution because variation is an inherent characteristic of language. Leveling in American English dialects may be happening in a limited way for certain language features, but most differences appear resistant to leveling forces. The existence of variation is a basic fact about language, and the use of variable features in oral language by members of different social groups is a basic fact about society. These principles are not likely to yield easily to efforts to change them.

The other possibility, eliminating the misconceptions about the significance of dialect differences, involves working on people's language attitudes. The set of attitudes about what is good and what is bad in language usage that children acquire with their native language develops into a set of opinions used to judge people by the way they speak. Language attitudes are generally shared by the members of a speech community, leading to a common evaluation of certain language patterns and the people who use them. Box 1.2 illustrates a common attitude toward vernacular and Standard English expressed in the response to an article on dialects.

Box 1.2

Speaking of Prejudice[1]

The job interview was going smoothly. And then the applicant wrapped a double negative around a regularized verb in the sentence *Nobody never growed nothing like that in this area.* The interview essentially ended at that point, the rejection of the candidate irretractably stamped. Was this a case of legitimate disapproval based on language or an instance of dialect discrimination?

(continued on next page)

_____

[1]Wolfram, W. (1993). Speaking of prejudice. *The Alumni Magazine of North Carolina State University, 65*(3), 44.

(Box 1.2 continued)

More than two decades of research on language variation and language attitudes in American society have led me to conclude that dialect prejudice remains one of the most resistent and insidious of all prejudices in our society. Public discrimination on the grounds of ethnicity, religion and social class differences is no longer acceptable; yet discrimination on the basis of dialect is still quite tolerable, even though many of the differences that serve as the basis for exclusion correlate with regional, class and ethnic variables. People who speak stigmatized dialects such as African American Vernacular English or Southern vernacular English continue to be rejected on the basis of their speech even when their dialects have nothing to do with their performance of job-related tasks and general competence.

Debate over language standards is hardly novel, but several studies and media reports during the past year have once again piqued interest in the role of language differences in multicultural education. I always find the treatment of language in such reports fascinating, but often because of what is left out rather than what is included. *A Time for Understanding and Action: Preparing Teachers for Cultural Diversity*, a report prepared by the North Carolina Professional Practices Commission (September, 1992), is fairly typical in its approach to language in multicultural education. The report urges teachers to learn another language. I applaud that. But the report is conspicuously silent in its acknowledgement of English dialects such as Southern, Appalachian, and African American Vernacular English.

Dialect differences represent one of the most commonly misunderstood and misinterpreted symbols of cultural diversity in American society. Popular myths view vernacular dialects as conceptually impoverished, linguistically unworthy approximations of Standard English that have no rightful place in English. In reality, vernacular dialects of English are intricately patterned linguistic systems, possessing a distinctive array of linguistic rules framed within a unique sociohistorical background. For example, "unconjugated" *be* in *Sometimes they be playing* and *done* in *They done finished the job* are more than stigmatized icons of English; *be* uniquely indicates a habitually occurring activity and *done* marks a completed or intensive action in the verb system of vernacular dialects. And the despised

(continued on next page)

(Box 1.2 continued)

"illogical" double negative was prominent in an earlier period of English that extended from Chaucer to Shakespeare, to say nothing of its use in the majority of the world's major languages.

If multicultural education is to be truly multicultural, then it cannot simply ignore or minimize dialect differences. Nor should it treat dialects as mere obstacles to be overcome in learning Standard English. Instead, dialect variation should be studied as a genuine resource that provides an essential and intriguing window into how language works, how it develops and how it reflects cultural traditions .... Teachers, students and the general public all have much to gain from a perspective that views dialects as an authentic sociocultural resource, not as an unjustified emblem of one's intelligence, competence and morality.

A Reader's Response[2]

It was with some disappointment ... that I read the comments of Walt Wolfram .... To tell a student [who] speaks bad English that he is merely suffering from dialect discrimination is so disingenuous and unfair as to be cruel. Initially, I thought the piece was some type of satire or parody, but it was so neat and concise in its silliness that I knew the author must actually be taking this seriously. To not know the forms of proper English usage is ignorance; to know them and then still not use them because of your desire to be "culturally diverse" is attempted murder upon the English language. Both conditions are apparently applauded by the author but seem to be strange "icons" in a center of learning [i.e., the university], which I had hoped was off limits to such sophistry.

---

[2]Fulghum, J. S., Jr. (1993, June). Letter to the editor. *The Alumni Magazine of North Carolina State University, 65*(4), 43. Reprinted with permission of *NC State* alumni magazine.

Language prejudices seem more resistant to change than other kinds of prejudice. Members of the majority culture, the most powerful group, who would be quite willing to accept and champion equality in other social and educational domains, may continue to reject the legitimacy of a dialect alternative. It is safe to say that dialect prejudice is one of the last prejudices to go. For example, in contemporary American society, the rejection of an applicant for a job based on gender or ethnicity would typically result in litigation of some type. Meanwhile, a person may be rejected ostensibly on the basis of speech without the same threat of litigation.

It should also be noted that dominant culture members are not the only ones who show language prejudice against vernacular dialects. In many cases, vernacular dialect speakers themselves hold vernacular dialects in very low esteem, at least with respect to values relating to occupational and social competence in mainstream society. Thus, it is not unusual to find a spokesperson for a minority group who exhibits the same kind of prejudice against the vernacular dialect as mainstream authorities do. Such minority members may decry prejudice in other spheres of behavior while reinforcing dialect intolerance. This attitude may make dialect prejudice seem more acceptable, but its consequences are no less severe. The high level of dialect prejudice found toward vernacular dialects by both mainstream and vernacular speakers is a fact that must be confronted honestly and openly by those involved in education about language and dialects.

The key to attitudinal changes lies in developing a genuine respect for the integrity of the diverse varieties of English. Knowledge about dialects can reduce misconceptions about language and the accompanying negative attitudes about some dialects. Informal attitude surveys before and after the presentation of information about dialects demonstrate that such attitudinal change does occur (Hoover, 1978). Because the educational implications of language attitudes are so great, developing a knowledge base in schools is especially important.

Change can begin through examining language myths. Collecting comments about dialects expressed in casual conversation or in the media can make clear just how vehement people can be about other people's talk. A close look at this evidence may suggest the nature of underlying language attitudes not only about language, but also about other attributes of individuals who use certain language varieties.

Another productive approach to combatting unwarranted language beliefs is teaching students to study language variation in their communities. Chapter 8 includes sample lessons from units on language variation that have been taught in English language arts, social science, and history classes. Students in both elementary and secondary classrooms find dialect study fascinating, partly because they can contribute their own knowledge to it. These lessons provide a model for developing further units on language variation, as well as interdisciplinary units on human variation.

DIALECT CHANGE IN THE UNITED STATES

One of the questions we are frequently asked about dialects concerns the effect of the media on their development. Most people simply assume that common exposure to the media is making us all talk more like each other. The precise effect of the mass media on dialect differences is difficult to determine, but a couple of points need to be made to counter this common assumption. For the most part, individuals are not prone to use media language, such as that of national newscasters or journalists, as a model for their own speech. (The one exception is certain phrases or words used by popular media figures.) People may recognize media language as different, and even as representing a prestige variety, but not as a model to emulate. This lack of general influence is partly due to the fact that people are not in direct social contact with the writers for the print media and the speakers in the broadcast media. Generally, people talk like those they identify with and whose approval they seek. There is little point in adjusting your speech to match that of television newscasters if they will never know you did it. This lack of direct social contact makes the mass media much less influential than peer group members whom a speaker interacts with frequently. The evidence suggests that on the whole, the influence of the media on language leveling has been exaggerated.

There are also aspects of media language usage that reveal the usefulness of dialect differences and may even reinforce them. Some personalities project a regional and/or ethnic dialect, or conversational style, as a positive attribute. When they are reported on in print or in the broadcast media, the dialect they use receives favorable attention. At the local level, the use of regional and ethnic dialects may be directly programmed to appeal to a local population. So the effect of the media on dialect differences is certainly not uniform.

We are also asked whether people in different areas of the country are not talking more similarly now than they were 50 years ago. The examination of dialect differences across different generations does show some leveling across dialects. Older representatives of different social, regional, and ethnic varieties tend to differ more in their speech than members of the younger generation. The exact cause of this age contrast is hard to determine, although increased education, increased accessibility to formerly isolated geographical areas, and expanded occupational opportunities have all played some role. Probably a combination of factors rather than one primary reason accounts for this leveling.

The fact that some dialect differences have lessened should not be taken to predict the extinction of English dialects in the United States. There is every reason to believe that different dialects will continue to be maintained, and even be enhanced in some instances. In the long run, these differences are a tribute to the various traditions and heritages that combine to make up the dialects of English.

FURTHER STUDY

Alvarez, L., & Kolker, A. (Producers). (1987). *American tongues.* New York: Center for New American Media.
This award-winning video (available in a 56-minute full-length version and a 40-minute secondary school version) is an invaluable supplement to any presentation of American English dialects. In a highly entertaining way, it presents a basic introduction to the nature of dialects and dialect prejudice. It can be used with a wide range of audiences representing quite different backgrounds (e.g., civic groups, professional development for educators, human relations seminars), and can be counted on to provoke a lively postviewing discussion.

American Speech. A publication of the American Dialect Society. Tuscaloosa: The University of Alabama Press.
This quarterly journal publishes articles on American dialects of all types, balancing more technical treatments with shorter, nontechnical observations.

Bauer, L., & Trudgill, P. (Eds.). (1998). *Language myths.* New York: Penguin.
The chapters in this book examine some strong and widely held beliefs about language use that are at odds with findings from research.

Carver, C. M. (1987). *American regional dialects: A word geography.* Ann Arbor: University of Michigan Press.
This work offers the most complete discussion available of all major regional dialects of the United States based on vocabulary differences, and includes summary maps of each region. Criteria for distinguishing regional varieties of English are also discussed. It is intended for dialectologists, but can be read by serious students in other fields as well.

Cassidy, F. G. (Chief Editor). (1985, 1991, 1996). *Dictionary of American regional English* (Vols. I–III). Cambridge, MA: Belknap Press of Harvard University Press.
Three volumes of this massive dictionary of American regionalisms are now available: Volume I, covering entries from A to C (Cassidy, 1985), Volume II, covering entries from D to H (Cassidy & Hall, 1991), and Volume III, covering entries from I to O (Cassidy & Hall, 1996). The front matter in the first volume

presents important background information about American dialects that is well worth reading for its own sake.

Ferguson, C. A., & Heath, S. B. (Eds.). (1981). *Language in the USA*. New York: Cambridge University Press.
This anthology covers a broad range of issues relating to English and other languages in the United States. It is divided into sections on 1) American English, 2) Languages before English, 3) Languages after English, and 4) Language in Use.

Lippi-Green, R. (1997). *English with an accent: Language, ideology and discrimination in the United States*. London/New York: Routledge.
Social attitudes toward accents are institutionalized in courts and perpetuated in the media and at work, so that people whose accents are not considered prestigious may suffer discrimination and job loss.

McKay, S. L., & Hornberger, N. H. (Eds.). (1996). *Sociolinguistics and language teaching*. Cambridge, England: Cambridge University Press.
Teachers in culturally diverse schools will find important background information in this collection of chapters on Language and Society, Language and Variation, Language and Interaction, and Language and Culture.

Miller-Cleary, L., & Linn, M. D. (Eds.). (1986). *Linguistics for teachers*. New York: McGraw-Hill.
This collection of articles covers a wide range of themes, including articles covered in this and subsequent chapters of this book. Topical areas covered are: History of English and Acquisition of Language; Language and Culture; Language and the Teaching of Reading and Writing; The Nature of Language and its Classroom Applications; and Teaching English as a Second Language. Many of the authorities relied on extensively in this book have articles in this collection.

2

Exploring Dialects

Because language plays such a central role in teaching and learning, educators often want to know more about the language patterns of the community from which their students come. Unfortunately, there are few resources that make careful descriptions of dialects accessible to those not specializing in linguistics, and those that exist cannot fully apply to every community in a broader dialect group. But teachers and practitioners have direct access to dialect data. They can learn about the local dialect norms by looking in detail at the actual speech of their students in the classroom, in the hallway, and on the playground.

This chapter provides direction for educators who recognize the importance of knowing what their students can do linguistically. Steps that sociolinguists follow in describing dialects are laid out. Then some contrasting patterns in pronunciation, grammar, and vocabulary are presented as examples of what teacher-researchers might notice in dialect research.

DIALECT STUDY

Certainly, investigating students' language patterns has not been among the tasks that teachers expect to do, and it is not easy. Not only does it take time, it also calls for some knowledge about language structure that may not have been part of a teacher's professional development. In addition, the scope of the task can be broad. Practitioners may need to look at language patterns in more than one speech community because fewer and fewer schools serve linguistically homogeneous populations.

There are, however, some resources that teachers can use for studying students' dialects. They can involve their students in scientific inquiry into language variation in their communities, along the lines of the dialect awareness lessons outlined in chapter 8. Schools can make dialect study part of school improvement plans. A number of teachers, working together, could integrate this work into community and parent involvement programs. At the school system level, the curriculum and instruction department might integrate dialect description projects into multidisciplinary curricula for students, ongoing professional development, speech/language assessment updating, and so on. Dialect description projects also fit well into standards implementation efforts because various national and state standards specify that students should understand dialect variation. Such projects offer teachers, administrators, and school systems a way to channel their concern for linguistic diversity into concrete, knowledge-building projects. Involving many educators and students lightens the work, creates a cadre of language resources, and signals that diversity is being taken seriously.

Dialect description is not beyond the reach of practitioners. We worked with a team of speech/language pathologists in Baltimore City Public Schools who conducted field work to describe the local vernacular dialects. Working with an inventory of vernacular features drawn from research, team members checked to see which features occurred in their students' speech. They also identified some previously undescribed vernacular features. As a result of their work, Baltimore's speech/language assessment procedures take into account the local language norms so that vernacular dialect speakers are not inappropriately labeled language disordered based on language variation (Wolfram & Adger, 1993).

Anyone can begin to explore dialects simply by listening more closely to speech in everyday life. In fact, most people are already good observers of language, in a selective way. That is, people notice features in the speech of others, but what they notice and how they interpret their observations is filtered through their attitudes and assumptions. For example, adults may notice that a child does what is popularly called dropping the g's at the ends of words like *going* or *running*, but will most likely fail to realize that they themselves sometimes do the same thing in informal situations. It is very hard to monitor your own casual speech, so you may assume your speech reflects what you feel is good (or bad) about language usage, and be unaware of what actually happens.

Scientific studies of community language patterns have shown the need to document both social and linguistic factors in order to understand the precise nature of language patterning. These factors cannot be overlooked even in a more casual study because a distorted view of the linguistic situation will result otherwise. Careful observation of the speech patterns of community members, taking into account important social factors, is the most important step in describing a dialect. When the speech of various groups is compared for similarities and differences, alternate patterns (i.e., where one group does one thing and the other group does another) can usually be found in each language area—pronunciation, grammar, vocabulary, and language use, or pragmatics. Patterns can be documented by examples from the speech of members of the groups involved.

Considering Social Factors

Formal studies of language differences have found significant variation among groups identified on the basis of age, socioeconomic status, gender, ethnic group membership, and geographical region (Labov, 1972; Wolfram & Schilling-Estes, 1998). For instance, speakers aged 40 to 60 may use certain language patterns that are different from those of a group of teenagers. In some cases, this contrast occurs because teenagers adopt some language patterns that are characteristic of their age level, and their use of these patterns diminishes as they get older. This pattern is referred to as *age-grading*. Slang words are a good example of this transitory state in an individual's language development, but there are age-graded pronunciation and grammar features as well.

In other cases, the differences between age groups stem from language patterns that individuals have acquired early and maintain more or less throughout life. These represent *generational differences* that signal language changes over time. In certain parts of the South, for example, members of the older age group were found to pronounce words like *water* and *war* without an *r* sound at the end of the word. The younger speakers, on the other hand, consistently used an *r* after a vowel (Myhill, 1988). Similarly, in rural Appalachia, older speakers use an *a-* form as in *He went a-hunting and a-fishing* where younger speakers and adolescents are much less likely to do so (Wolfram & Christian, 1976). Such age group differences point to changing language patterns in the community: The older group maintains the speech patterns they acquired as children, and the younger ones use the pattern that is being acquired currently. Age can be an important factor to consider when examining the language patterns of a community because differences typically do exist between age groups. This means that characteristics of children's language in a community should not be inferred from the speech of the adults. A balanced picture of the dialect should be based on listening carefully to the speech of members of different age groups.

The other social factors—socioeconomic status, gender, ethnicity—can operate in similar ways in a community. As with age, these social differences often correlate with linguistic differences. (Region as a social factor usually distinguishes between communities in different geographical areas. Its relevance to studying language in a single community is in differentiating individuals who are native to the area from those who moved there from some other area and in accounting for subregions in a community.)

In addition to social attributes of speakers, aspects of the context of speaking have significant influences on speaking. These factors, which are discussed further in chapter 3, must be considered in studying language behavior. Speakers have a range of options in their linguistic repertoires, and they make unconscious choices from this range depending on such factors as how formal they feel the situation is, their relationship with others in the situation, and what others have just said. With a close friend, someone might say something like *Watcha feel like doin'?* in a conversation about going out, and with a casual acquaintance it might be *What d' ya wanna do?* In a more formal context, it might be more like *What would you like to do?* Although these are not precise reflections of how the sentences would sound, they suggest that pronunciation, word choice, and grammar can all change according to the circumstances of speaking and that a change in one system can bring about change in another one. In the least formal style, for example, *do* disappears from the verb phrase as the speaker's pronunciation responds to the situation's informality so that *What do you feel?* sounds like *Whatcha feel?* In the most formal style, *would* occurs in the verb instead of *do*, perhaps because it mitigates the directness of the question.

So, in observing language patterns, it is important to keep in mind the social factors that link with differences in language forms. Although it will be instructive to sample a range of styles if that is possible, the natural language patterns of a community are clearest in the casual style. In a casual setting, people tend to use their language rules in their most natural way, thus avoiding shifts of overcorrection or irregular fluctuation of language items.

Examining Particular Patterns

The most reasonable approach to the investigation of dialect differences is a systematic, organized study of particular structures. As a rule, it is most effective to single out one or two features at a time for scrutiny because it is very difficult to keep track of multiple structures. The common technique used by linguists is to select a structure, investigate it in detail, and then move on to another structure. Although this approach imposes certain limitations in terms of an overall description of a language variety, it increases the potential for an accurate description of particular features.

The first steps in studying different language items are quite simple. Although linguists have had specialized training for investigating language structures and writing formulas to describe them, anyone can make significant observations about language patterns by following scientific principles concerning careful observation. The procedure begins with noticing an item in someone's speech (including our own). For example, in a Southern or Northern urban school setting, we may hear some children using forms like *He home today* or *You out*. We know that other speakers might use *He's home today* or *You're out* in these same contexts, and so we decide to investigate this structure further. We start listening to other children in natural speech situations, such as on the playground or in the hallway (in order to get a casual style of speech). Basically, we can listen for these structures anywhere that language is used in an unself-conscious way. We go to the grocery store; we stand in line at the movie theater and the motor vehicle bureau. Data gathered informally suggest that the forms that originally drew our attention are not just a slip of the tongue because they occur in the speech of many community members. This indicates that we are dealing with a language pattern that deserves a closer look. We start by filing (on 3-by-5 cards we carry around, in software data management systems, and so forth) the examples we hear in the natural use of language. It is particularly important to catalogue examples rather than rely on memory. This method allows us to look back at the data and to get some ideas as to the organization of specific patterns.

When we collect examples from real language use, we are likely to make two general observations. First, different people use the structure in different ways (i.e., there are alternate forms in other dialects). Second, the same speaker seems to use the structure at some times, but not at others. These observations raise basic questions that guide all linguistic analyses. In terms of language variation, the investigation focuses on (a) alternative forms that occur in other language varieties, and (b) when and where the form under study occurs. With this in mind, let's return to our examples, *He home today* and *You out*. With reference to alternatives in other dialects, we observe that the dialect in question does not use a verb form where Standard English uses *is* or *are*:

Vernacular English	Standard English
He home today	He's home today
You out	You're out

Our first study question, then, is answered fairly simply for this structure—the difference between dialects lies in the *presence* of certain forms of the verb *be*, as opposed to their *absence*. (In other cases, the alternatives are distinct items or sets of items, rather than a relationship of presence or absence.)

The second study question is a little more difficult because it requires looking at the language context surrounding this form. The question about the context for this dialect structure is this: Where can a speaker manifest the absence of *be*? We assume, as a starting point, that there are patterns of language structure that govern where a form is permissible and where it is not. In this case, there is a pattern as to where the *be* can be absent and where it must be present. It is this pattern that we are looking for. At this point, we turn to our examples and start figuring out exactly where the absence of *be* would **not** occur. Along the way, we make certain hypotheses that we check with the data. This involves coming up with ideas about how a pattern works, testing the ideas against the data, and revising them if necessary. Our own intuition can help if we use the pattern in our dialect, but only to a limited extent as previously discussed because we may not be totally aware of what we actually do in our casual speech. We can see how this analytic process works by looking at some data that might be found on our observation cards.

Absence of *be*

He in the army now	He at school
They messing around	They not here
We in trouble today	She taking medicine
She not home now	Y'll messing around now
You nice today	We in school—don't mess around
We playing around now	He gonna do it—I know he is

Our first impression from listening to the speaker(s) might have been that the verb *be* can be absent in their dialect wherever it is present in Standard English. When we start looking at the examples more closely, however, we find that the pattern is less extensive than that. Taking into account all of the different forms *be* can take, we may initially notice that absence occurs only where *be* would take a conjugated form in Standard English. That is, there are no cases where *be* is absent when the sentence is something like *He wants to be home* (i.e., no examples such as **He wants to home*) or *He* *should be here now* (i.e., no examples like *He should here now*) and many cases where the *be* is present as non-finite forms like *to be, should be,* and so forth. (The asterisk indicates that the sentence is ungrammatical according to the dialect's patterns.) We conclude that the pattern is limited to certain constructions, namely the conjugated forms of *be* (*is, are,* etc.). That conclusion provides a working hypothesis that we will target in our subsequent data collection until we are reasonably satisfied that the pattern holds.

Continuing to search for further restrictions, we notice that there are no examples of *be* absence where Standard English would use *was* or *were.* We have plenty of examples of past tense and all of them use *was* or *were*; meanwhile, we find no past tense sentences such as *We there yesterday.* We look at our data closely, checking out this hypothesis. This restriction turns out to be supported by the data. The absence of *be* thus appears to be limited to present tense, conjugated forms.

We look further. Are there more limits? We consider the subjects of the sentences. An examination of the data shows no cases of absence with the pronoun *I* as subject. Is this just an accident or is this a real pattern governing this rule? From our data, it appears that it might be a genuine pattern because we have no examples of *be* absence with *I.* But in order to verify that this is a pattern and not a matter of missing data, we will need to get examples with *I.* We start listening again, taking down examples with *I.* This time, we collect numerous examples of sentences with *I,* such as *I'm first, I'm taking it home,* looking for sentences where a form of *be* is absent. The fact that the verb form always appears when the subject is *I* leads us to conclude that absence of *be* can correspond to *is* or *are,* but not *am.*

This case demonstrates an important point about observing forms:

When looking for a pattern in language variation, you cannot look only at those cases that contrast with another dialect; you must look at similarities as well.

In order to get an accurate, comprehensive picture, you must look at similarities as well as differences between dialects. We found that *be* absence with *I* was impossible in both dialects. We had to look at all kinds of cases with *be* in order to find the pattern of *be* absence.

We could go on, and there are some more details of conjugated *be* absence that actually would be included in our final analysis. The important point here is demonstrating the data analysis process. We proceeded systematically, making a hypothesis and checking it with the data. One by one, we varied grammatical features in the linguistic context—conjugated versus bare form of the verb, tense, pronoun person and number. The rule must emerge from actual data—dialect items as used in a natural discourse context—rather than from our first impression. Invariably, questions do come up that were not anticipated in the original observations. That is why linguists often tape record speech. When we have extensive recordings, we can simply go back and note certain things we had not looked at previously. With observations made in other ways, we may need to collect more data. In our example with *be*, we needed to go back and look for cases with the pronoun *I* very closely to see if any absence of *am* occurred.

One way of getting additional data is to ask leading questions—questions that would raise the potential for certain structures to occur. For example, if we were trying to increase the potential for *I* to occur with a form of *be*, we might ask some personal questions that would probably be answered in the first person ("Tell me about your science project"). This strategy does not guarantee the use of certain structures, but it increases their probability and has been used successfully in a number of studies.

It is also possible to devise strategies to elicit certain forms quite directly. Word games have been created that utilize this technique. The idea is to set up a frame so that the response should contain one of the forms in question. For example, if we wanted to see what happens to *be* verbs when the subject is *I*, we might set up a simple task of changing a stimulus sentence with a nonfirst-person subject to a response sentence with a first-person subject. Speakers from the community can be oriented to the task with sample items unrelated to the forms you are interested in (e.g., "Here are some sentences that I want you to change: I will give a sentence like *He went to the store* and you say, *I went to the store, too*"). After they have learned the pattern, they are given stimulus sentences with the form being studied (e.g., Stimulus: *They going to the game*; Response: *I'm going to the game, too*). These games are not difficult to construct, and they can give access to some valuable forms for the description. However, it is important to use this kind of information only as supplemental data because word games do not always give the same results as ordinary speech. In combination with other data, however, this direct elicitation of structures can make an important contribution to our understanding of particular features.

Anyone undertaking analysis confronts the problem of deciding when there is enough data. Basically, you want enough data to get to the point where additional data does not add anything new to the understanding. As a guiding principle, some researchers use about 45 minutes to an hour of free conversation as an adequate sample of natural speech for one speaker, if the feature under scrutiny involves a fairly common structure such as the verb *be*. And a practical cut-off point of five speakers in a given social category (e.g., middle-class urban Italian-American teenage males, rural White Appalachian females over 60, etc.) is sometimes used as a basis for studying the social parameters of speech. Obviously, these amounts may not always be appropriate, but they are typical of databases that have resulted in valuable research.

Box 2.1

Steps in Describing Dialect Features

1. Identify a possible dialect feature for study.
2. Collect data.
   - Listen to casual talk in the speech community to determine that the structure is widely used.
   - Write down actual examples from casual talk.
   - Identify corresponding form(s) in other dialects.
3. Analyze data.
   - Develop hypotheses about the linguistic context in which the form occurs. Hunt for patterns in the data, considering:
      - Linguistic forms preceding and following the feature.
      - Various forms the feature can assume.
      - Etcetera.
   - Check the hypotheses against more data.
   - Accept hypotheses, reject, or refine.
   - Repeat the two previous steps, looking for both differences and similarities with other dialects and testing stereotyped explanations.
   - Stop when no new information appears.

VARIATION IN LINGUISTIC SYSTEMS

Patterned group-based differences show up in all the subsystems that make up a language. This section takes a closer look at what can vary and how.

Pronunciation Differences

Pronunciation differences occur in both regional and social dialects. Vowel pronunciation differences are particularly crucial in distinguishing regional dialects, and consonant pronunciation differences tend to be significant in marking the social dialects. (As chapter 1 pointed out, there is overlap between regional and social differences: In a social group, there will be regional differences, and in a geographical region, there will be social differences.)

Although dialect differences in pronunciation are widely recognized in our society, they are not always thought of in terms of rules of pronunciation. Instead, popular labels such as drawl, twang, nasal, and flat are sometimes used as cover terms for regional pronunciation patterns. In most cases, these labels are used to describe an overall impression rather than any particular pattern of pronunciation. Here we set out some rules that describe pronunciation patterns in terms of sound features.

Regional Dialects

Several different vowel patterns stand out in regional dialects. One prominent pattern involves the vowels in words like *time* and *ride*. In Northern dialects, what might be called the long *i* in *time*, *side*, and *pie* is actually a diphthong—the rapid production of two vowel sounds, one something like the vowel *ah* (dictionary *a*) and another something like the sound *ee* (dictionary *e*). The second vowel sound in the diphthong glides off the first, so that *time* is produced something like "tah-eem," *pie* as "pah-ee," and *side* as "sah-eed." In some Southern dialects (or dialects of Southern origin used in the North), the *e* gliding vowel may be eliminated. Pronunciations such as "tam" for *time*, "sad" for *side*, and "pa" for *pie* reflect this regional difference, although the quality of the *a* sound may vary considerably (from dictionary *a* of *bat* to *a* of *father*). On the islands of the Outer Banks of North Carolina and in the Chesapeake Bay (Smith and Tangier Islands), this vowel sounds something like a cross between *uh* and *oh* (as in *home* and *rope*) plus the *ee* sound. In this case, the first vowel of the diphthong is changed rather than the gliding of the second part of the vowel.

In the same way, the *y* glides of *boy* and *boil* may be reduced or even eliminated in some Southern dialects, giving a pronunciation like "bô" (*ô* in the dictionary; also called "open *o*" after the shape of its International Phonetic Alphabet symbol [ɔ]) and "bôl," respectively. The elimination of the glides following the *a* and *ô* vowels is a fairly well established characteristic of many Southern dialects of English, and one of the characteristics usually included by the term *Southern drawl*.

Another vowel pattern showing regional variation is the difference between the *i* sound (as in *bit*) and the *e* sound (in *bet*). Before a nasal sound such as *n*, these two vowels may sound the same in some Southern dialects. This means that pairs of words like *pin/pen* and *tin/ten* would actually be pronounced the same by these speakers.

The vowel differences just mentioned show variation along a Southern/Northern dimension, but vowels also show different kinds of geographic distribution. One of the vowels most sensitive to regional variation is the open *o* (dictionary *ô*) in items such as *fog, on, water, caught*. Pronunciation of this vowel ranges from the *a* of the vowel in *father* to the *o* of *boat*, or even the *oo* (dictionary *û*) of *book*, as in the Philadelphian pronunciation of *water* (something like "wûter"). In Baltimore, younger vernacular speakers use the schwa vowel sound, *uh*, in words like *dog* and *log*, so that they sound like *dug* and *lug*. This vowel is probably the most variable in American English regional dialects. The vowel *a* in items such as *bad* or *ran* is also quite sensitive to regional variation, although the range of pronunciation differences is somewhat more subtle than that for the open *o* of *fog*. The production of vowels before *r* is particularly likely to vary regionally, as indicated in how dialects differ in their pronunciation of words such as *Mary, marry,* and *merry*. Some dialects have identical pronunciation of all three items; some pronounce each item differently.

Other vowel patterns come from the influence of another language, such as those varieties of English influenced by the historical use of Spanish or a Native American language. A typical case of this kind of influence is the use of the *e* (*beet*) and *i* (*bit*) vowel pattern in some Latino communities in the Southwest. In these cases, the vowel of *bit* would be pronounced as the vowel of *beet*, so that there would be no contrast in the *e* and *i*. In such English varieties, pairs of words like *pick/peek* and *ship/sheep* are pronounced alike.

Social Dialects

Consonants are probably more prominent than vowels in distinguishing social dialects of English. However, there are some consonant contrasts between regional dialects and there are some vowel differences between social dialects. Moreover, regional and social dialect differences tend to interact with each other. Three areas of pronunciation difference relating to consonants have been widely described: the *th* sounds, *r* and *l*, and consonant blends or clusters. There are many other consonant differences as well. Some are listed in the Appendix. Works cited in Further Study at the end of the chapter can be consulted for more detail.

th Sounds.   Probably the most widely recognized social difference in consonant usage is the pronunciation of *these, them,* and *those* as the stereotypical "dese," "dem," "dose." At the beginning of a word, the *th* may be pronounced like *d,* a stop consonant. (Stop consonants involve briefly stopping or blocking the air stream coming through the mouth from the lungs.) The *th* sound of *think, thank,* and *throw* is different from the *th* of *these* (the *th* in *think* is voiceless [The vocal cords are not vibrating] whereas the *th* in *these* is voiced [The vocal cords are vibrating]). To test this yourself, touch your Adam's apple as you say the first sound of *think* and *these;* you will feel vibration differences in the two *th* sounds. In some dialects, the voiceless *th* may be produced something like a *t,* which is a voiceless stop, (*tink, tank, trow*) although it is not exactly the same. In general, the *d* for *th* in *these* is more common than the *t* for *th* in *think.* An interesting research finding about *d* for *th* at the beginning of a word is the fact that various social groups differ in how frequently they use this pronunciation, rather than not using it at all (Labov, 1966). Middle-class groups may use the *d* for *th* pronunciation to some extent in casual speech whereas working-class groups simply use it more often. This research finding counters the popular stereotype that working-class speakers **always** use *d* for *th* and middle-class Standard English speakers **never** do. A number of pronunciation differences are actually manifested in this way across social classes in our society.

In positions in a word other than the initial position, the *th* may take on different pronunciation characteristics. In the middle or at the end of a word, the voiceless *th* of *author* or *tooth* may be pronounced as *f,* as in "aufor" or "toof;" in words like *brother* and *smooth* with a voiced *th,* a *v* may occur ("brovuh," "smoov"). This pronunciation is most typically found in working-class African American communities and some Southern rural Anglo American communities, with the *f* pronunciation more common than the use of *v.*

r and l.   A number of regionally and socially significant pronunciations are also found in the *r* and *l* sounds. After a vowel, the *r* may be lost, and an *uh*-like vowel (schwa or dictionary *u*) may take its place. The "cah" or "fouh" pronunciations for *car* and *four* are typical of this variation. The *l* following a vowel may behave like *r,* so that words like *wool* and *Bill* may be pronounced something like "woou" or "Biu." In some instances, the *l* may be lost completely, including the *l* before *p* ("hep" for *help*) or *f* ("sef" for *self*). These *r* and *l* differences are linked for the most part with geographical region, and they tend to carry more social significance in Northern urban areas than in a Southern context.

Consonant Blends. One feature of pronunciation that has been studied fairly extensively in several communities concerns the blending or clustering of consonants at the end of words. Consonant blends in words like *west (st), find (nd)*, and *act (ct)* may be reduced to a single consonant, as in "wes'," "fin'," and "ac'." For all social groups, the final member of the blend may be absent when the next word begins with a consonant. Thus, many Standard English speakers will say things like "wes'side," "fin' time," or "ac' perfect" in casual speech. There is a considerable difference among groups in the loss of final consonant when the following word begins with a vowel, however. Structures like "wes' end," "fin' apples," and "ac' out" would be much more typical of working-class than middle-class speech. This consonant blend reduction is particularly prominent in working-class African American communities.

This reduction pattern does not affect all consonant blends at the end of a word. It is limited to those that end in a stop such as *t, d, k*, or *p*, and reduction only takes place with certain combinations of these blends. So it does **not** affect items like *sense* or *waltz*, which do not end in a stop combination (they end in an *s* sound); nor does it affect items like *colt, jump, thank*, or *gulp* where the first consonant is voiced—*l* or *m* or *n*—and the final member is voiceless—*t, k*, or *p*. Finally, it should be noted that this pattern affects words in which the consonant blend is formed by the addition of the *-ed* grammatical suffix indicating past tense, just as it affects words where the blend is a part of the base word. So, items like *missed*, formed with an *st* blend sound as in *mist*; and *talked*, actually pronounced as "tawkt"; and *banned*, pronounced "band," all would be affected by this rule, making them "mis'," "talk'," and "ban'."

As with the vowels, there are also regular consonant patterns in the English varieties used by some speakers from other language backgrounds. One kind of influence comes from differences between the sound system of English and that of the other language. A well known example occurs in the English of some Mexican Americans in California where a *ch* sound may be substituted for the *sh* sound (i.e., *shirt* may be pronounced as "churt"). The reverse pattern occurs as well in New Mexico, although it is not as remarked on ("shursh" for *church*) (Edwards & Doviak, 1975, cited in Wald, 1981). Another sort of difference involves extending the possible sequences of vowels and consonants in the other language into the English language. For example, many languages follow a consonant–vowel pattern in syllables so that consonants do not occur together in clusters, as in English *bread*. Speakers from those language backgrounds may insert a reduced vowel sound between the two consonant sounds (something like "buhread"). The restriction against certain types of clusters in the other language may also result in the insertion of a vowel before the cluster, resulting in the pronunciation of *star* as *estar*.

Another example involves the lack of contrast between the *n* sound and the *ng* sound at the end of words. In some Hispanic English and Native American English dialects in the Southwest, *sing* and *sin* may both be pronounced as "sin", whereas in other dialects they are both pronounced as "sing". This lack of contrast is related to the fact that the native language does not contrast these sounds as English does. Many of the pronunciation differences found in ethnic varieties of English are related to influence from the heritage language that has become part of the English variety.

Not all speakers from a particular language background follow identical English patterns. The English of Mexican Americans is different from that of Cuban Americans and Puerto Rican Americans, even though those groups share a Spanish language heritage. Moreover, there is variation in the English spoken in each one of these groups, depending on factors such as whether English is the first or second language, age at the time of immigration for nonnative speakers, and social class. Variability is also due to where an English language learner stands in the language learning progression from the first language to English. Thus the dialect situation for English speakers from other language backgrounds is quite complex. In fact, in diverse communities such as that of New York Puerto Ricans, individuals may need to be familiar with several varieties of English (standard and vernacular) and several more of Spanish (Zentella, 1997).

Beyond Consonants and Vowels in Pronunciation.   There are certainly other prominent differences in addition to contrasting consonant and vowel patterns. Some differences relate to aspects of pronunciation that affect a whole syllable. Syllables that are not stressed in a word may be eliminated. In casual speech, practically all speakers of English show this pattern to some extent, as indicated in pronunciations such as "'cause" for *because* and "'bout" for *about*. This rule may be extended considerably beyond these very common items, affecting items ranging from "'lectricity" for *electricity* and "el'phant" for *elephant* to "'tatoes" for *potatoes* and "'member" for *remember*. There are also cases where the number of syllables in a word is different for various dialects. For example, a word like *baloney* may consist of three syllables in one dialect ("bah-lo-ney") and two syllables in another one ("blo-ney"). In some Southern rural dialects, including Appalachia and North Carolina's Outer

Banks, words like *tire, fire*, or *liar* consist of one syllable (pronounced something like "tar," "far," and "lar," respectively) whereas they consist of two syllables in other dialects ("tai—er," "fai—er," "lai—er," respectively) (Wolfram & Schilling-Estes, 1997, 1998).

Popular discussions of social and ethnic differences in English dialects often include impressionistic references to characteristics such as voice quality, inflection, or lilt. More specific reference may include qualities such as voice raspiness, high and low pitch ranges, and general resonance. To a large extent, these qualities may be quite individualistic; however, some features such as voice raspiness may also be molded by community norms. For example, a stylized use of raspiness among African American males has been observed.

Several studies have suggested that the range between high and low pitch used in Black communities is greater than that found in comparable White communities (Tarone, 1973). This, of course, would be a culturally learned behavior and totally unrelated to biological race. Studies also suggest that women in American society typically have a greater pitch range in their sentences than do men (Brend, 1975). This kind of pitch distribution over a sentence is what is commonly meant by the popular reference to inflection, although linguists refer to this as *intonation*.

The rhythm or beats of syllables in a sentence can vary too. English typically gives extra prominence to the stressed words in a phrase and tends to run together the other syllables. So, in the phrase *He 'went to the 'store*, *went* and *store* usually get greater prominence than the other parts of the sentence (the marks preceding *went* and *store* indicate heavier stress). Other languages may give an equal beat to each of the syllables in the sentence, as in *'He 'went 'to 'the 'store*. This gives an impression of choppiness to those who have learned the conventional English timing system. Speakers of English whose pronunciation is influenced by a language with such a timing system may transfer this characteristic to speaking in English. Communities with historical or current influence from Spanish or a Native American language may have this quality.

Current knowledge of pronunciation is much more extensive with respect to basic consonant and vowel patterns than it is with respect to the other aspects of pronunciation such as rhythm and intonation. More research is needed in this area in order to come to firm conclusions about the exact role of these factors in dialect differences, but there is little doubt that they are a contributing factor in the construction of a dialect.

Grammar Differences

Dialects also contrast in aspects of grammatical usage. Grammar in this sense refers to the composition of words and the way words are combined in phrases and sentences. For example, the addition of -*s* to a verb form to mark agreement with certain types of subjects (*it walks* compared to *they walk*) is a grammatical process, as is the contrast in word arrangement that signals the difference between a statement and a question (*You are going* vs. *Are you going?*).

Differences between dialects on points of grammar are generally more subject to social evaluation than those in pronunciation. Nonstandard grammatical features more often carry social stigma than do pronunciation features, as pronunciation differences tend to be more readily tolerated, particularly in the form of regional accents. Many grammatical differences are more strongly associated with social groups than with regional dialects. These language evaluations match the general social evaluation perspective in which social class differences are less tolerable than are regional differences.

Suffixes

For the most part, the grammatical systems of all dialects of English are quite similar; there is a large common core. There are certain areas, however, where divergence is likely to occur. One of them is suffixes—short forms such as plural and past tense markers that attach to the ends of words. Over all, the language has a much more limited set of suffixes than it had earlier in its history, but there is considerable diversity among dialects in their use of the surviving English suffixes. These suffixes indicate certain grammatical meanings on verbs, nouns, and to a lesser extent, adjectives and adverbs. Incidentally, research on the history of English indicates that variation in the use of these grammatical markers is not a recent development: This kind of variation existed in England long before the settlement of the United States (Pyles & Algeo, 1982).

Verb Suffixes. Certain suffixes may be absent on verbs where they would be expected in Standard English. Less often, suffixes may be used in places where they would not be expected in Standard English. Such fluctuation can be explained more fully in terms of specific suffixes.

Several of the suffix fluctuations affect verbs in the Standard English grammatical system as well as the vernacular English system. One is the ***-ed***

suffix that is used to mark past tense on verbs (e.g., *they walked* and *they have walked*). This ending may be absent in speech, to a greater or lesser extent, depending on the dialect in question. As mentioned in the last section, this difference actually occurs in the area of pronunciation, but it affects a grammatical form. It has been found that all speakers occasionally omit this suffix in a sentence like *Yesterday they walk' by the park*. In some socially defined dialects, the suffix may be absent more frequently; and in cases like *Yesterday they walk' in the park*, where the *-ed* absence precedes a vowel sound, it is more noticeable. This higher frequency and wider distribution of *-ed* absence gives the impression that speakers of these dialects drop the endings of words, and it has even led to claims that speakers of these dialects do not know what past tense is! Research has amply demonstrated, however, that this suffix absence is typically an English pronunciation feature, not a grammatical one (Fasold, 1972). In some dialects, the process is used more frequently than in other dialects; but since the *-ed* past tense ending does occur in at least some instances, clearly the speakers know it.

The other suffix that affects verbs is the *-s*, used in the present tense to mark grammatical agreement with certain subjects (third person singular present tense *-s*), as in *the dog barks* or *the child plays*. This suffix may be absent in working-class dialects used in some African American communities, so that *he go* or *she have a car* may be used. Some absence of this suffix has also been noted for members of Native American communities, although suffix absence is typically more limited there than in African American working-class communities (Leap, 1993; Wolfram, Christian, Potter, & Leap, 1979). The absence is also prominent for speakers who learn English as a second language. For many, this absence may result from a lack of grammatical marking rather than a pronunciation rule.

One very widespread item related to the use of this present tense suffix is the form *don't*. In varieties of English that show no vernacular usage of the third person *-s* suffix, *don't* may be used with grammatical subjects that in standard use would call for *doesn't*. This results in sentences like *She don't know* and *He don't like it* (Christian, in press).

One further process concerns the use of the *-s* verbal suffix for the present tense. In some Appalachian and Southern communities, the suffix has been found on verbs occurring with plural subjects as well as with singular subjects, especially if the subject involves a collective noun: *People goes* or *A lot of them goes*. It also occurs frequently in these Southern dialects if the subject is a coordinate as in *James and Willis goes a lot*. The *-s* tends not to be used in these dialects if the subject is a pronoun (*they*), however (Hazen, 1996; Wolfram & Christian, 1976).

Other Suffixes.   Although the systems of verb endings show more extensive differences between dialects, other suffixes vary too. In the case of nouns, one of the suffixes affected is the **plural**. In working-class African American communities, absence of the plural suffix has been observed in phrases like *two card* or *all them book*. In some rural Southern or Appalachian dialects, the plural suffix may be absent with nouns that signify weights and measures, particularly when a numeral is used, as in *three pound* or *twenty mile*. Another pattern affects the irregular plurals in English, nouns that do not take a suffix but that form the plural in some other way (*feet, sheep*). Some members of working-class Southern and Black communities include these nouns in the regular pluralization pattern, so that they may say *two foots* or *many sheeps*, for example.

The other noun suffix that shows dialect difference is the **possessive -*s*** ending. Some speakers from working-class African American communities may omit the possessive -*s* ending, using *my friend book* as a correspondence for the standard *my friend's book*. A characteristic observed in some rural Southern speech in the Appalachian highlands and in isolated Southeastern island communities is the use of the forms *your'n* and *our'n* in places where the standard form is *yours* and *ours* (*his'n* and *her'n* occur as well), as in *This jacket is your'n* (Wolfram & Christian, 1976).

For adjectives and adverbs, the suffixes that have nonstandard alternate usages are the **comparative** (-*er*) and the **superlative** (-*est*) markers. In the standard pattern, these endings are used typically with words of one or two syllables (*stronger, friendlier*). For some words with two syllables, and all words with three or more syllables, the standard pattern uses *more* and *most* preceding the word rather than the suffix (*more efficient, more foolish*). This pattern differs across dialects. In some, the suffixes may be added to words that go with *more/most* in the standard patterns, resulting in forms like *beautifuler, awfulest*. Also, some irregular forms in the standard pattern may be treated differently (for example, *bad/worse/worst*). Forms built on the basis of analogy with regular form, like *baddest, gooder, worser*, have also been observed. Forms for comparatives and superlatives like the ones mentioned here have been documented in a wide range of dialects and are not restricted to any particular group.

Suffixes are particularly susceptible to dialect variation for several reasons. In the language system of English, many inflectional suffixes are redundant, so that they do not carry much meaning. For example, the -*s* on *he plays* adds little meaning to the present tense form. It shows that the subject of the sentence is third person, singular; but that information is already apparent from the subject itself (and English does not typically allow the omission of subjects as other languages such as Spanish do). When this kind of redundancy is found, a form is more susceptible to change. English present tense verbs have been losing different kinds of suffixes for centuries now. At one point, English had *I goe, thou goest,* and *he/she/it goeth*—a much more extensive set of suffixes than we have today (Pyles & Algeo, 1982). But the language has gradually been losing these forms, and the standard variety of English has preserved only the *-s* on third person singular forms. In some cases, vernacular varieties simply take to completion a process that has been happening to all dialects of English in one form or another.

Another reason for changes among suffixes comes from the pressure in the language to eliminate exceptions or regularize forms. Thus, a change from *oxen* to *oxes* or *sheep* to *sheeps* can be understood as a natural pressure to make exceptions or irregularities conform to majority patterns. From this perspective, the *-s* on third person forms (e.g., *he goes*) is an exception to the majority pattern in which all other present tense forms are not marked with a suffix (e.g., *I go, you go, we go,* etc.). Eliminating this exception makes the verb system more regular.

Other Differences in the Verb System

Three important kinds of patterned dialect differences in verbs relate to tense marking, agreement marking, and some special characteristics of the use of the verb *be*.

Irregular Verbs.   Earlier discussion focused on the role of the *-ed* suffix to indicate past tense. Irregular verbs form the past tense in a variety of other ways: For instance, the standard pattern for *know* is *knew* and *have known*; for *come*, it is *came* and *have come*. Many vernacular dialects do not follow the standard patterns. In many working-class communities, differences in the way irregular verbs form the past tenses have been noted, including the following patterns:

Vernacular Past Tense Formation *with Irregular Verbs*

Regularization: They *growed* a lot. (*heared, knowed*)
(The general pattern of English verbs is followed.)

| **Exchange of participle and** | I *seen* it. (*done, sunk*) I *have went* |
| **simple past forms:** | *already.* (*broke, saw*) |

(Simple past tense forms occur where the standard uses the past participle, and vice versa.)

| **Unmarked forms:** | I *give* it away already. (*come, eat*) |

(The plain verb form is used.)

| **Different irregular forms:** | They *brung* it. (*drug* for *dragged*) |

(The different irregular form is not part of standard dialects.)

Some of these forms occur with high frequency among speakers from working-class communities; others occur more rarely, or have been found to be more regionally concentrated (Christian, Wolfram, & Dube, 1988).

One restricted aspect of verb tense involves the **absence of the auxiliary verb *have***, especially before *been*, as I *been there before*. This grammatical pattern actually results from a pronunciation rule that removes the '*ve* after *have* has been contracted (or the '*s* of *has*, if that form is used). Another feature that has been found in Southern working-class communities is the additional use of ***done*** to signal completion of an action, as in I *done threw it away* or *They've done sold it*. It may also be used for emphasis as in I *done forgot it*. This *done* should not be confused with the past participle *done* of the verb *do* (e.g., I *have done it*). Even though the forms are identical, their functions are very different. The past participle is a main verb (I'*ve done it*), whereas the feature in question here functions as a so-called helping verb or auxiliary (I'*ve done sold it*). This structure shows that sometimes an additional distinction can be made in certain working-class dialects where there is no directly corresponding form in standard dialects.

Agreement Marking. We have already discussed agreement and the third person singular -*s*. Another area of subject/verb agreement involves the *be* verb forms. The standard pattern for *be* retains many agreement distinctions that other English verbs no longer use (I *am, it is, you/we/they are, I/it/was, you/we/they were*). In many working-class dialects, the agreement pattern allows the use of *is* and *was* with plural subjects (*the dogs is barking, they was barking*). This feature in the agreement pattern for *be* is quite common, and it has been observed in many communities. This adjustment is a kind of regularization where *is* or *was* is used throughout the paradigm (i.e., I/you/he, she, it/we/you (plural)/they was). Along the Outer Banks of North Carolina, we have found an interesting regularization in which *weren't* is used throughout the negative paradigm. Thus we get *I/you/he, she, it/we/you (plural)/they weren't*. In the affirmative, the regularization pattern is like that in other vernacular dialects, using *was* as the primary regularized form (*I/you/he, she, it/they was*).

Habitual be.   Other characteristics pertain directly to the *be* verbs. A use of the verb form *be* that has been noted in working-class African American communities signifies a meaning distinction in that dialect not found in other dialects. This use is found in sentences like *Sometimes they be acting silly*, where the verb form indicates an activity that takes place habitually (it happens at various intervals over a period of time). The use of habitual *be* must be distinguished from constructions that look similar but do not carry this meaning. Observations of language patterns have indicated that structures like *They be here tomorrow* and *They be here if they could* result from the absence of the auxiliary forms *will* and *would*, respectively. These structures are different from the habitual use of *be*. For the most part, the habitual use of *be* is limited to the speech of working-class African-American speakers (Fasold, 1972; Rickford & Green, 1998).

Another characteristic pertaining to *be* is the absence of a form of *be* in cases like *She not going* or *They nice*. The forms of *be* involved in this pattern are *is* and *are*. This feature was discussed in considerable detail in the previous section on describing language patterns, but one additional point is interesting. The patterned absence of *are* has been documented in many Southern White and Black working-class communities, whereas the absence of *is* has been found mainly in Black communities. That is, working class White Southerners would use sentences such as *We going to the game*, but not *She going to the game*, whereas working-class Black speakers may use both of these structures (Wolfram, 1974).

Other Grammatical Differences

There is a variety of other differences among English dialects that are socially significant. One area of difference is the variation associated with patterns of negation. The use of sentences negated in more than one place is widely noticed and frequently commented on. Most studies of dialects in working-class communities note the negative patterns in sentences like *We didn't go nowhere*, *They couldn't find no food*, and *It don't never run good*. These patterns have been compared to the standard pattern that allows only one negative to occur. In multiple negation, a negative form is attached to both the verb and the indefinites (*nowhere, no*) or adverbs (*never*) following the verb. In other words, the forms that can carry negation are made to agree with each other. In some Southern communities, inversion of subject and auxiliary in negation has been observed along with the more widespread pattern in which the negative indefinite word follows the verb: *Couldn't nobody see it* (a statement meaning *Nobody could see it*, not a question) and *Ain't nobody gonna do it*! have been noticed.

Another common but highly stigmatized feature of negation among working-class dialects is the use of *ain't*. This form is used to correspond to the Standard English negative version of *is*, *are*, *am*, *has*, and *have*, in cases like *They ain't here* and *I ain't found it*. In working-class African American speech, it can also be used for *didn't* as in *She ain't go yesterday*. An interesting pronunciation variation on this form is *hain't*, used by some rural Southern speakers. Despite the highly negative attitude often expressed toward *ain't*, it persists in widespread use in many speech communities.

In looking at the speech patterns of a community in terms of grammatical features, then, some important areas to check are suffixes, verb usage, and negation. These are areas of notable diversity among dialects of English, but any observation will undoubtedly yield many more potential differences for an inventory of a particular dialect. The list of dialect differences in the Appendix provides more detail.

Illustrative Dialect Samples

In doing dialect study, it is important to remember that not all speakers use all of the features of a dialect. Our discussions refer to a composite picture of some dialects rather than the dialect of any one person. To illustrate the actual occurrence of some variable structures in speech, we present two annotated passages taken from live speech samples. The first example, "An Appalachian Ghost Story," comes from an interview with an elderly White woman who lived her entire life in the southern part of West Virginia. The second passage is from a conversation with an 11-year-old African American from Baltimore, Maryland. For these samples of vernacular speech, dialect features are noted and described following the samples. Odd-numbered superscripts refer to pronunciation differences and even-numbered superscripts refer to grammatical differences. We have chosen to use regular spelling for the most part, so that the majority of the pronunciation differences are not indicated in the spelling. The punctuation roughly reflects the pausing and intonation patterns in the flow of speech, rather than written language conventions. For frequently occurring features such as *d* for *th* and *n'* for *ng*, we only mark the first five instances of the feature in the typescript.

Appalachian Ghost Story

I was always kindy[1] afraid to stay by myself, just me, you know, it was gettin'[3] about time for me to get in, so Ingo, he'd[2] went[4] over to this man's house where we carried our water from, and to get some water, and, ooh, the moon was so pretty and bright, and I thinks[6], heck, hit's[5] dark, I hear him a-talkin',[3,8] a-settin'[3,8] over there in the field where the spring is, I'll just walk down the road and meet him, you know, ooh, it was so pretty and light. I got down there and I hearn[10] something shut the churchhouse door, but I didn't see a thing, and the moon, oh the moon was as pretty as daylight, and I didn't see nothin'[3,12]. And he come[14] on the walk, pitty-pat, pitty-pat, and I just looked with all my eyes, and I couldn't see a thing, come out that gate, iron[7], slammed it and hit[5] just cracked, just like a[9] iron[7] gate, it will just slam it there. And all at once, something riz up[10] right in front of me. Looked like it had a white sheet around it, and no head. I liketa[16] died. That was just a little while before Florence was born. I turned around and I went back to the house just as fast as I could go, and about that time, Ingo come[14] along and he says[6], "I set the water up," and he said, "I'm going down the churchhouse," he said, "I hearn[10] somebody go in", he said, "They went through that gate." And he walked across there and he opened the door and he went in the churchhouse. And they had him a-lookin'[3,8] after the church, you know, if anybody went in, he went down there. He seen[18] something was the matter with me, I couldn't hardly[20] talk. I told him, I said, "Well, something or other, I hearn[10] it, I seen[18] it, whenever I started over to meet you, and I couldn't get no[12] further." So he went down there and he took his lantern, of course, we didn't have flashlights then, took his lantern, had an old ladder, just spokes, just to go up beside of the house, he looked all behind the organ, all behind every bench, he went upstairs and looked in the garret, not a thing in the world he could find. Not a thing. Well, it went on for a right smart little[32] while and one day Miss Allen was down there. Her girls come down there very often and sweep the church and clean it. So one evenin', they come[14] up the house, you know, and I's[11] tellin' them. They said, "Honey, don't feel bad about that," she said, "Long as you live here, you'll see something like that," said, "they[34] was, in time of the war, they[34] was a woman, that somebody'd cut her head off and they'd buried her in the grave down there." And they said there'd been so many people[24] live in the house we live in, would see her, and said "That's what it was," said, "it just had a white sheet wrapped around it." And we didn't live there very long cause I wouldn't stay. He worked away and aw heck—I's[11] just scared to death but still Miss Allen told me, she said, "Don't be afraid because hain't[5,26] a thing that'll hurt you."

Wild Life

Boy: And th[13]en I went home. And th[13]en I was watchin'[3], um, Wild Life, about animals.

Interviewer: And which animal did you see.

Boy: And a[9] elephant and a rhino was[22] fightin'[3]. The elephant kicked th[13]e rhino down. And th[13]en it start[30] grabbin[3] its whole body with[23] its, with[23] its.

Interviewer: Tusk, trunk.

Boy: Yeah, thr[15]ow him but he couldn't get him up but it ran. And th[13]en it was this little dancin[3] chickens, that do like this, like Indians, so they were jumpin'[3] up and down doin'[3] a dance.

Interviewer: Why.

Boy: I don't know.

Interviewer: Were they mad at each other?

Boy: No, they was[22] dancin'.

Interviewer: They were happy. Did they have music (makes sound of music)?

Boy: Yeah, with[23] they[36] mouth[23], they go uh uh uh uh and stuff. It[34] was a whole lot of them doin' it. And then the Indians'll come out and do it with[23] them.

Interviewer: And then the Indians would dance with the chickens. Wow!

Boy: And then we saw a movie with, uh, lions, uh uh cheetah, and um gorillas on it, and they said a, a dog[17] bit the baby and it died.

Interviewer: Bit a real baby?

Boy: (Nods yes)

Interviewer: Oh.

Boy: And then that man had another tiger, a po[21]lice came to the house and shot that one and they got another one.

Interviewer: This is all on Wild Life?

Boy: (nods)

Interviewer: With the elephant and the rhinoceros? All this happened on Wild Life?

Boy: (Nods)

Interviewer: Wow.

Boy: And then another one came on about the, uh, white lions and stuff. Don't you know them[38] white ones?

Interviewer: White lions?

Boy: Tigers I mean.

Interviewer: White tigers. Tigers are orange with black stripes, thank you.

Boy:	No, they[40] white too. Uh huh. They got white—they got white, then they got white, I mean, black stri[25]pes goin' down.
Interviewer:	That's a zebra.
Boy:	Um uhm, it's[34] another one, that's a snow tiger.
Interviewer:	Oh, the snow tigers, oh, okay.
Boy:	And then that man had one. Then, we went to a black, a black panther. It wasn't[27] no[12] black panther, it was something, black what you call em, I don't know.
Interviewer:	Um huh.
Boy:	And then, it[34] was a um, we was[22] lookin' at monkeys jumpin' up and down, had—
Interviewer:	Monkeys are funny, huh.
Boy:	And they were hittin' each other—and then it[34] was one that went to the doctor's and he was uh (makes noises). Cause—
Interviewer:	A monkey went to the doctor?
Boy:	[29]Cause he ain't[26] want to get his shot. Went in his leg. And he said (noises) and he got a needle shot in his leg and he say[6] (noises). And then the man gave him a peppermint so he could suck on it. And then he was bitin' his glasses. Then he put them on and was lookin' at the camera. And then when he got home he said that lady said he don't[28] like to say no so he had bang[30,42] on the table and all that. And then that lady gave him a sucker and he was suckin' on it.
Interviewer:	Just like a little kid, huh.

Boy: And then he had diapers on, had a little jumper.

Interviewer: (laughs) She kept him in her house? Oh, so it was like her pet monkey. Or was it a monkey out in the jungle. Oh.

Boy: And then they'd take him places with em, like a diner and all.

Interviewer: Don't you think the monkey will run away?

Boy: He won't run away.

Interviewer: Did they have him on a leash? Like they do a dog?

Boy: No. And then when they got him home, they were jumpin' on a big trampoline.

Interviewer: All three of them?

Boy: No, just one.

Interviewer: Oh, just the monkey.

Boy: Yeah.

Interviewer: The lady wasn't jumpin' on the trampoline too?

Boy: No, she was watchin' them [29]cause they was[22] jumpin' up and down, walkin' around.

Notes on Transcripts

Pronunciation.

1. In an unstressed, final syllable of a word, the schwa sound [ə] can be changed to the high vowel *ee* of *beet*, as in *sofy* for *sofa* or *kindy* for *kinda*.

3. The *-ing* form in a final unstressed syllable may be changed from an *ng* sound to an *n* sound.

5. Before the items *it* and *ain't* an older English *h* may be retained, resulting in items like *hit* for *it* or *hain't* for *ain't*.

7. The sequence *ire* in items like *tire*, *fire*, or *iron* may be collapsed in a single syllable, resulting in pronunciations such as *arn* for *iron*, *tar* for *tire*, *far* for *fire*, and so forth.

9. The form *a* may be generalized to occur before items that begin with a vowel (e.g., *a apple*, *a iron*) as well as those that begin with a consonant (e.g., *a pear*).

11. Initial *w* sounds may be deleted when in an unstressed syllable, resulting in forms like *young 'uns* for *young ones* or *we's* for *we was*.

13. Voiced *th* becomes *d* in initial position.

15. Following a consonant, *r* may be deleted before *oh* and *u* so that *throw* becomes "th'ow" and *through* becomes "th'u."

17. Open o is centralized to schwa so that *dog* and *Doug* sound the same.

19. When the suffix *-ed* is realized by a stopped consonant (*t* or *d*) following another consonant, thus creating a consonant blend or cluster, the final consonant may not be pronounced—so that *happened* (pronounced *happend*) may be pronounced as *happen*.

21. Stress shifts in certain words, and a change in vowels results. *Police* is stessed on the first syllable, and the vowel of the stressed syllable is *oh* instead of schwa.

23. When it occurs in a medial or final position of a word, the voiceless *th* sound may be pronounced as *f*, as in *deaf* for *death*; and the voiced *th* sound may be pronounced as *v*, as in *mover* for *mother*.

25. The consonant cluster *str* is pronounced as *skr*. *Street* becomes *skreet* or *stream* becomes *skream*.

27. Before nasal sounds (*m*, *n*, and the sound spelled *ng*), certain consonants can be altered. Voiceless *th* may become *t* (*nothing* becomes *not'n*); *z* may become *d* (*wasn't* may become *wadn't*); and *v* may become *b* (*seven* may become *sebm*).

29. Unstressed syllables may be deleted. *Because* may be rendered as *'cause; remember* as *'member.*

Grammatical Differences.

2. A pronoun form may be used after a subject noun, as in *My mother she ...* or *The man in the middle, he ...*

4. The past form of an irregular verb may be generalized as the past participle form, as in *he had went* or *she had did.*

6. Present tense forms may be used in animated narratives of past time events, including an -s on nonthird person forms, as in *I says* or *we goes.*

8. An *a-* prefix may attach to verbs or adverbs ending in *-ing* as in *He was a-hunting* or *He makes money a-building houses.*

10. Different irregular verb forms may be used in past tense forms as in *brang* (for *brought*), *hearn* (*heard*), or *tuck* (*took*).

12. Multiple negatives may include a negative marker in the verb phrase and a negative indefinite form following the verb, as in *I didn't see nothin'* or *She ain't goin' nowhere.*

14. A present tense root of an irregular verb may be used in past tense forms as well, as in *She come late yesterday* or *Last year he run in the race.*

16. The special modal form *liketa* is used to mark a significant event on the verge of happening that does not actually take place.

18. The past participle form of an irregular verb may be generalized to a simple past tense form, as in *He seen it* or *She done it.*

20. Multiple negation may involve negative marking in the verb phrase and an adverb following the verb, as in *They don't hardly eat* or *She shouldn't never go.*

22. The conjugated forms of *be* may be regularized to *is* in the present tense, as in *We is here now* or *was* in the past tense, as in *They was there.*

24. Relative pronoun forms can be absent if they are the subject of a relative clause, as in *That's the dog bit me.* In standard dialects, these relative pronouns can only be absent when they are the object of the relative clause, as in *That's the house he was building.*

26. The form *ain't* can be used for *be + not, have + not,* and *did + not,* as in *He ain't here, She ain't done it,* or *He ain't go.*

28. The third person singular present tense form *-s* may be absent from the verb, so that forms such as *she go* or *He don't* may occur.

30. The past tense maker *-ed* may be deleted: *After the movie, we want to go to that restaurant, but it wasn't open.*

32. The adverbs *right, right smart,* and *right smart little,* are used to intensify attributes, such as *She's right tall* or *He took a right smart little while.*

34. For the expletive use of *there* in Standard English (e.g., *There's a new boy in my class*), vernacular dialects may use *it* (e.g., *It's a new boy in my class*) or *they* (e.g., *They's a new boy in my class*).

36. The subject form of the third person plural pronoun *they* can serve the possessive function: *Let's go to they house.*

38. The demonstrative pronoun *those* may be replaced by *them* to get *Them dogs was barking all night long.*

40. The copula may be omitted, as in *She crazy.*

42. Past participle may occur in place of the simple past: *They went to the game and they had yelled at the umpire.*

Vocabulary Differences

Most Americans can readily cite cases where the word for an item in one region differs from that used in another. When travelers return home from a visit to New England talking about how *frappe* and *cabinet* are used where other regions might use the term *milkshake*, or when Northerners mention that a Southerner uses *carry* in the sense of accompanying, as in *He carried her to the movies*, they are referring to basic vocabulary differences in regional dialects. Vocabulary differences can affect all classes of language structures, including nouns (e.g., *hoagie/grinder/submarine/hero sandwich*), verbs (e.g., *press/mash the button*), prepositions (e.g., *sick at/to/in my stomach*), adverb/adjectives (e.g., *very smart/right smart fella*), and adverbs (e.g., *fell plumb asleep*). *The Dictionary of American Regional English*, which has been in the making for more than three decades, has more than 50,000 vocabulary entries for regional words (Cassidy & Hall, 1996).

A few examples from recent investigations into the language variety used in Ocracoke, one of the islands of North Carolina's Outer Banks, suggest something of the complexity inherent in regional vocabulary differences. There are several kinds of relationships between the Ocracoke vocabulary and that of other dialect areas. First, the Ocracoke dialect, called the *brogue*, includes some words that have not been found elsewhere, even on other Outer Banks islands. This is a very small set of words, perhaps no more than a few dozen, which includes terms for locations or geographic features such as *up the beach*, meaning off the island to the north; *down beach*, meaning off the island to the south; and the *ditch*, meaning mouth of the harbor. These Ocracoke-specific words also include terms for games and activities, such as *meehonkey* and *whoop and holler* for local versions of hide-and-seek; *call the mail over* for bring the mail from the mainland; and *scud* for car ride. Although the set of words that are unique to Ocracoke is very small, and some words may even be restricted to particular groups in the island community, they cannot be ignored because some of them are used fairly frequently in everyday speech. *Going up the beach*, meaning going off the island to the north, is a fairly common activity that islanders often mention in conversation. If listeners are not thoroughly familiar with what this phrase means, they might inappropriately expect someone who had gone up the beach to return shortly from a nearby sandy spot. The islander going *across the beach*, meaning to the shore along the sea, may be back in a short while, but not the one who is going *up the beach*. Even though they are relatively few, the vocabulary words that are found only in Ocracoke are critical to understanding and participating in the daily routines of island life.

Many common vocabulary words are shared by Ocracoke and other Outer Banks communities, including some of those on the coastal mainland areas immediately adjacent to the Outer Banks, but they are not known to occur elsewhere. This set of words includes items like *mommuck* (hassle), *slick cam* (very smooth water), *dingbatter* (nonislander), *quamish* (upset stomach), and *hard blow* (strong wind).

Some Outer Banks words show regional distribution in the Outer Banks. *Bankers* is an older term apparently used more in northern areas of the Outer Banks than in the southern islands. Similarly, *dingbatters* may not be used in all areas of the Outer Banks. On Harkers Island, *dingbatter* alternates with the term *dit-dot* for outsiders, which used to occur more frequently than *dingbatter*. Despite this variation in the Banks, some of the Outer Banks words have taken on symbolic significance in distinguishing Outer Banks residents from the rest of the world.

Most of the distinctive vocabulary words in Ocracoke are shared with dialect areas throughout the South, including the Appalachian region and the Atlantic South, as well as the Piedmont area that lies between the mountains and the lowland Atlantic South. This list of shared vocabulary is quite extensive and includes many terms popularly associated with the South, such as *fixin' to* (about to), and *reckon* (suppose).

Unlike grammatical differences, most vocabulary differences in regional varieties of English are considered neither good nor bad—they are typically viewed as quaint curiosities. There is little social value associated with saying *spigot* versus *faucet*, *pail* versus *bucket*—these are simply accepted as part of the normal regional variation of English.

Malapropism

Some vocabulary uses that are negatively evaluated are related to *malapropism*, as in *I found the discussion very interesting and enervating* (for *energizing*) or *I caught ammonia* (for *pneumonia*). Such uses come about when two words sound reasonably similar. In some cases, a less familiar word (*enervating*) replaces a more familiar word with the same stem (*energizing*); in other cases the less familiar word may be replaced by a more familiar, similar-sounding but unrelated word, as in *old timer* for *alzheimer* as in *She's got old timer's disease*.

Some malapropisms may be stimulated by a situation in which a person feels the need to use more formal, educated language. The classic example is someone from a working-class background who attempts to use a more formal, middle-class, educated style of speech—one with which the speaker is not entirely comfortable. Although such uses have been stereotyped as humorous, they arise in natural language situations. The negative evaluation they receive is related to the fact that the speaker is attempting to appear educated but not succeeding at it. Middle-class, educated people also use malapropisms (The sentence with *enervating* was heard at an annual meeting of a professional organization) or they adopt those that have some currency: *There were some incidences of looting* for *incidents of looting*. The motivation seems similar to that of working-class people—the desire to sound educated and erudite. These vocabulary (mis-)uses are different from uses that are shared by a group of speakers.

What About Slang?

The term *slang* seems to be used popularly in several senses, as typified in the following examples:

  a. Those people don't speak Standard English: They just use slang.
  b. People today use a lot of slang words, like *way scary* for *very scary* and *chill* for *calm down*.
  c. Basketball players have their own slang, like *rebo*, *jumper*, and *chucker*.

In some instances, *slang* is used to refer derogatorily to any variety of English that is not Standard English. In the Ebonics debate of 1997, African American Vernacular English (AAVE) was often inaccurately called slang and broken English. This sense is illustrated in sentence (a) just shown.

Slang is also used to refer to certain words or phrases that have a strong connotation of informality, particularly as compared with the words they replace ([b] earlier). This sense of informality is conveyed by using *man* or *girl* as a term of address, in place of a person's name, or saying *No problem* instead of *You're welcome* in response to someone's "Thank you." Many of these uses have a short life span, arising quickly and falling just as quickly into disuse. Most slang items are associated with the teenage and early adult years in a person's life. Other slang items actually last fairly long and become stabilized as a kind of national slang (e.g., *cool*). This interpretation of *slang* is probably the most widely used one and certainly cuts across different dialects. However, those dialects that are associated with informality would probably be expected to have more slang items than dialects that carry a more formal connotation.

Finally, *slang* is sometimes used to refer to a specialized vocabulary associated with a particular field of activity, a profession, or a trade. Reference to a specialized vocabulary such as that used by computer specialists or athletes typifies this usage. In some cases, it may refer to secret vocabularies, such as that of drug dealers or prostitutes. This is the usage illustrated in (c), which most linguists refer to as *jargon* rather than *slang*.

Linguists restrict the use of the term *slang* to the sense illustrated by (b). Even here, however, there can be disagreement over what words should be designated as slang. Although there may be near consensus on some words (e.g., *freaked* [stressed]; *phat* [excellent]), there are many other items where the classification is much more indeterminate (e.g., *bucks* for *money*, *fired* for *terminated*). It appears that there is a set of characteristics for classifying slang rather than a single definition (Dumas & Lighter, 1976). Furthermore, there seems to be a slang scale because some items appear to be more slangy than others. Like other words, terms that fall somewhere in the indeterminate category of slang may differ regionally and socially. Part of the appeal of these words for young people is the fact that they highlight the boundary between the peer group and other age groups (Eble, 1996). Despite its reputation as linguistically marginal, slang shows complex and interesting sociolinguistic properties.

This section has considered the broad categories of dialect difference—pronunciation, grammar, and vocabulary—where linguistic processes show distinctive social and regional patterning. There are many more than those mentioned here. Linguists' expanding descriptions of dialects can inform educators about the details of particular varieties. Sociolinguistic methods of describing dialects can be used to extend existing dialect descriptions so that teachers gain fuller understanding of the regularities in students' English language varieties.

The next section concerns a particular variety of English that has received more attention by far in the discussion of dialects over the last several decades.

African American Vernacular English

Even before the Ebonics debate, the dialect called *African American Vernacular English* or *Black English*, was certainly one of the most prominent vernacular dialects of U.S. English. Part of its prominence is due to its difference from Standard English. But other U.S. dialects also contrast remarkably with Standard English. For example, there are some isolated dialects on the Southern seaboard, such as Tangier Island and Smith Island in Virginia and Maryland, and Ocracoke and Harkers Island on the Outer Banks of North Carolina, that are probably more difficult to comprehend in natural conversation for speakers of other varieties than African American Vernacular English. AAVE is certainly the most prevalent native English vernacular dialect in the United States in terms of numbers of speakers. Furthermore, this dialect has received considerable attention in the media, focusing on everything from teenage rapping to rap music to, most recently, Ebonics and Standard English instruction. Often AAVE has been misrepresented. In fact, it is a variety of English that has combined a number of vernacular English forms in a unique way. Its uniqueness lies not so much in the distinct language forms that are found only in that dialect, although there are a few, but in the particular combination of forms that make up the dialect.

In the 1960s this language variety typically was called *Nonstandard Negro English* and *Negro Dialect*. The term *Black English* then replaced these terms for a couple of reasons. First, there was a precedent for designating dialects with color terms; for example, the terms "Black Bobo," "Red Thai," and "White Russian" are used for distinct varieties of these languages. Second, the name change reflected the change in the ethnic label from *Negro* to *Black* that was taking place in American society at the time. Finally, the name change was motivated by the desire to throw off the pejorative stereotypes of terms such as *substandard*, *nonstandard*, and even *dialect*. The ethnic designation should never be misinterpreted for a racial one because there are certainly African Americans who do not use this dialect at all or to any great extent. In addition, Whites who learn their language in the context of a Black working-class community may learn this dialect.

The modifier *vernacular* was added to the terms Black English and African American English in order to avoid the stereotype that all African Americans spoke this variety, so that it became known as *Black English Vernacular* or *Vernacular Black English*, and *African American Vernacular English*. Alternative labels such as *Ebonics*, *Afro-American*, and *Afram* were selectively used in some circles over the past few decades, but these terms have not been widely adopted by linguists. The label *African American Vernacular English* (AAVE) was used by African American linguists in the early 1990s, in keeping with the general shift from the label Black to African American in American society.

Names and labels can be a tricky business. Often they become symbolic tokens of sociopolitical stances. We can be assured that whatever label is used, it will be somewhat controversial. The articles, "'What is Africa to Me?': Language, Ideology, and *African American*," by Smitherman (1991), and "The Politicization of Changing Terms of Self-Reference Among American Slave Descendants," by Baugh (1991), consider these labeling issues in depth.

The history of AAVE may be somewhat different from that of some other British-derived dialects of English; and this history, combined with the social conditions under which African Americans have existed in American society, accounts for the uniqueness of the dialect. According to some linguists, what we call AAVE today probably started out as a *creole* language something like the creoles, or so-called mixed languages, of the Caribbean (e.g., Jamaican Creole). When two groups of speakers do not have a language in common, they often create an intermediary language for communication with a drastically altered grammar and a modified vocabulary taken from one of the primary languages. This type of language often develops under special social conditions, such as the need to communicate for trade or business purposes. This situation is what probably happened originally on the West Coast of Africa as Europeans from various countries, including the British Isles, developed trade routes along the coast of West Africa. Over time, this intermediary language (a *pidgin*) became an established means of communication (a *creole*). The pidgin or creole that was first developed along the West Coast of Africa was then brought to the Americas along with the importation of slaves. In the American South, it mixed further with Southern White varieties of English, but the change from the prior creole was neither instantaneous nor complete. AAVE today is not a creole like the Caribbean creoles, but it still has some traces of its creole past combined with many features of Southern English. The different historical origin, the addition of Southern features, and the fact that the dialect developed in a largely segregated society have resulted in a unique dialect of English.

Although the history of AAVE has been hotly disputed in the 1990s (Bernstein, Nunnally, & Sabino, 1997; Mufwene 1996; Schneider, 1989), most linguists conclude that current-day AAVE is a distinctive vernacular variety. Linguists who do not accept the creolist hypothesis point to the social conditions that have segregated Black and White Americans and a sense of ethnic solidarity as the basis for developing and maintaining a distinct variety of English among some African Americans.

The question of who speaks AAVE is a difficult one. Certainly, not all African Americans speak it. Furthermore, some speakers use some of the forms associated with it without using others. And the definition of who speaks it depends on what forms are considered to be central to the dialect. Although there are varying opinions as to what forms define the dialect, typical inventories usually include nonstandard grammatical forms such as suffix -s absence (e.g., *She like school*), the use of habitual *be* (e.g., *Sometimes my ears be itching*), and copula absence (e.g., *He nice*), along with a set of pronunciation features that are largely Southern English. Certainly, the African American working-class population is more likely to use these forms than the African American middle class, just as the White working class is more likely to use vernacular forms, but this is a statistical trend that cannot necessarily be applied to an individual speaker.

The Changing State of AAVE

The recent course of change in AAVE has also been debated. In a study done among the urban African American working class in Philadelphia, Labov (1987) reported that AAVE was becoming *more* different from other vernacular dialects of English, rather than converging with them. As linguistic evidence for his position, he cited some forms that had not been highlighted in the earlier studies of AAVE; as sociological evidence, he cited the increasing pattern of de facto segregation among urban African Americans that might promote divergence among dialects because social or physical segregation tends to promote divergence.

Labov's contention that AAVE is diverging from other vernaculars, rather than converging, has been contested by some of his fellow linguists who also study AAVE. Some linguists think that, if anything, AAVE is leveling its differences with other dialects rather than diverging from them. Linguistically, they note that the forms Labov offered as evidence have been in existence all along, and that his analysis of their diverging use in African American English is not justified. Sociologically, they cite the increasing educational levels of African Americans, and note that general education trends are probably more closely related to change in AAVE than segregation (Fasold, 1987). Certainly, the final word on this issue has not been spoken. At this point, we can only say that AAVE is certainly not dying out; whether it is diverging or converging with other dialects of English is still an open question.

Dialect, Language, and AAVE

Although the criteria used to distinguish a dialect from a language are sometimes debated by linguists, the kinds of differences that distinguish African American Vernacular English and Standard English are those that typically characterize dialects rather than separate languages.

When the linguistic characteristics of African American Vernacular English and Standard English are placed side by side, we find many more shared language features than distinctive ones. Dialectologists tend to focus on the differences between dialects rather than their similarities, and our discussion here has largely concerned differences. However, African American Vernacular English and Standard English dialects share a large common core of structures and vocabulary. A similar comparison of French and English, or Spanish and English, or even Spanish and Italian would make the differences between African American Vernacular English and Standard English seem trivial. (Compare the degree of difference, for example, in *They're talking, They talkin'*, and *Ils parlent*.) Most linguists, then, conclude that the kinds of language differences found between vernacular and standard varieties of English set apart dialects of the same language rather than separate languages.

The level of intelligibility between speakers of Standard English and African American Vernacular English also suggests a dialect rather than a language difference. For the most part, vernacular speakers understand what Standard English speakers are saying, and speakers of Standard English who have some exposure to vernacular dialects comprehend what vernacular speakers are saying. This generalization does not rule out some minor problems in understanding each other, but any difficulty in comprehension does not match that found between speakers of different languages.

FURTHER STUDY

Mufwene, S., Rickford, J. R., Bailey, G., & Baugh, J. (Eds.). (1998). *African American Vernacular English*. New York: Routledge.
This collection brings together a set of articles by leading researchers on the history and current state of AAVE. Authors consider both historical and descriptive issues pertaining to AAVE.

Peñalosa, F. (1980). *Chicano sociolinguistics*. Rowley, MA: Newbury House.
This overview considers Spanish-English contact in the Southwest United States. Although not treated in the present discussion of dialects, this language contact situation is a major sociolinguistic issue to be reckoned with in a number of educational contexts.

Schneider, E. W. (Ed.). (1996). *Varieties of English around the world: Focus on the USA*. Philadelphia: John Benjamins.
This book is intended for language scholars, but it may be interesting to others who want to know how U.S. dialects came to be and what they look like now in various locales.

Smitherman, G. (1986). *Talkin and testifyin: The language of Black America*. Detroit: Wayne State University Press.
A readable discussion of language in the Black community that includes the consideration of dialect functions as well as dialect forms. A lively presentation format incorporates dialect into the text at times, as Smitherman integrates a personal community perspective with her discussion of empirical facts.

Wolfram, W. & Schilling-Estes, N. (1998). *American English: Dialects and variation*. Oxford, England: Basil Blackwell.
This description surveys the social and linguistic factors that account for dialects and the functions that dialects serve. It introduces students and a general audience to the principles underlying language variation. The discussion attempts to limit technical terminology, but provides an extensive glossary to assist readers.

3

Communicative Interaction

Dialectologists usually focus on regionally and socially based pronunciation, grammar, and vocabulary differences. But there are also important differences in the way groups of people use language for social purposes. Interacting through talk is, in a very essential way, a kind of cultural behavior. As with other aspects of cultural behavior—such as eating and showing emotion—competence involves knowing what to do, how to get along, and what to expect from others.

To understand the communication processes in a particular cultural group—a group that shares expectations about appropriate ways of interacting—researchers investigate what kinds of communicative behavior are considered appropriate in what situations. This may involve the use of particular linguistic forms, such as when people use each other's first names and when they use last names, or more general rules for interacting, such as when to keep quiet and when to talk. For example, one cultural group's unwritten rules for appropriate behavior may favor greeting strangers in most situations. If unacquainted people pass each other in a public place, perhaps a courthouse or hospital hallway, then it would be considered inappropriate according to the norms of their culture not to exchange greetings. In a speech community that shares this norm or rule, greeting a stranger is expectable and unremarkable; but not greeting a stranger is remarkable. (As with dialect features, the term *rule* applied to culturally based behavior refers to observable regularities rather than prescriptions for deportment.) Someone who follows the rule but is not greeted in return may conclude that something is wrong with other people—that they are rude or uncaring or so deep in thought as to be oblivious to others. If the nongreeting person obviously comes from a different cultural group, then the lack of a greeting may evoke a stereotype about some people's lack of manners; but if the person seems to come from the same group, the lack of a greeting is more likely to be interpreted as a temporary lapse in behavior. We might be more inclined to rationalize some apparently inappropriate communicative behavior coming from someone of our own cultural group, and more likely to attribute bad intentions, moral turpitude, or social ineptness to someone from another group.

CULTURES AND DIALECTS

There are certain distinctions between a cultural group and a dialect group. As previously mentioned, *culture* generally refers to the shared ways of doing things associated with a group of people. It includes language(s) and norms for language use, but it extends beyond language to include nonlinguistic behavior, as well as values and beliefs about the nature of the shared world. People belonging to a cultural group are likely, but not certain, to identify themselves as members of a group—as Armenians, women, teenagers, Moslems, Cherokees, Byrd High School faculty, Hoosiers, and so forth. No single set of variables defines people as members of a cultural group; but cultural group members share ways of doing things that set them off from other cultural groups. When culture is defined this broadly, individuals may be members of several groups, each with some unique conventions for using language together. The term *cultural group* emphasizes the common expectations about language behavior that underlie successful communication. As the term *dialect group* is being used here, those who belong to a group might not necessarily identify themselves as a cultural group. Speakers of the Midland dialect would probably not call themselves that.

There is significant overlap between dialect groups and cultural groups, particularly when social dialects are considered. Cultural groups can use dialect to highlight solidarity and to resist assimilation. In fact, an anthropologist found that in the high school where she did field work, African American students used AAVE as one way of refusing to comply with culturally alien aspects of schooling (Fordham, 1998). A similar phenomenon was found among middle-aged native islander men on Martha's Vineyard off the coast of Massachusetts and on the Outer Banks island of Ocracoke off the coast of North Carolina. These men, feeling challenged by tourists from outside the island, highlighted and heightened dialect features as a kind of resistance to outside social forces (Labov, 1963; Wolfram, 1995).

Language as a form of cultural behavior and as an identifying feature of cultural groups goes beyond the basic questions of dialect diversity. The two are, however, inevitably intertwined in producing differences in language behavior between groups and in contributing to the social attitudes toward those differences.

This chapter outlines some important dimensions of language use for social purposes, emphasizing that cultural groups may display unique patterns. Such contrasts between groups can be perplexing to students and teachers alike. As with dialect differences, teachers may find that research into interaction in their classrooms will help them and their students to see the regular patterns associated with cultural groups.

APPROPRIATENESS

How people show consideration for others is very much a matter of cultural background. Tannen (1984) found that people show consideration for each other in two quite different, general ways, and that cultural groups place different values on these consideration principles. One kind of considerateness stems from the desire for **interpersonal involvement,** which motivates speakers to show friendliness and enthusiasm for each other's talk. Some groups do this by talking fast and loudly, by giving a lot of nonverbal and verbal feedback while the other person is talking—"Yeah, yeah, yeah"; "Uh huh"; "Right"; "I'm telling you"—by hooking their talk immediately onto the previous speaker's or overlapping with talk that extends the topic. They respond to another's story by offering one of their own on the same topic.

The other kind of considerateness is **deference**-based. Following this principle, speakers maintain some social distance to avoid trampling on each other's conversational toes. Speakers in high deference groups generally leave somewhat longer pauses between turns at talk. For them, overlapping is interrupting. They stop talking if another person overlaps them, or they mark the overlap as competitive by outshouting the speaker who appears to be usurping their turn. They ask leading questions to evoke coconversationalists' stories.

Although individuals observe both principles at different times, their cultural group may generally encourage one kind of considerateness over the other. In studying Thanksgiving dinner table talk among friends and acquaintances, Tannen (1984) found that those who shared a New York Jewish background also shared a high involvement conversational style, and that guests from cultural groups favoring deference-based talk felt interactively crowded by the high involvement speakers who showed interest by firing what Tannen (1984) calls machine gun questions at them while they were talking or just as they finished.

Variable turn-taking behavior in classroom discourse is not all due to members' cultural backgrounds, but some patterns are rooted in different traditions. The pace of talk in whole-group instruction may be relatively slow when only one person speaks at a time, but it picks up when more than one person responds. Some African American teachers occasionally engage students in overlapping and unison talk that is reminiscent of the call and response style of gospel meeting (Smitherman, 1986). This highly engaging interaction is structured by the teacher in terms of topic, but the students participate in determining who will talk (Adger & Detwyler, 1992; Foster, 1989). What constitutes appropriate language behavior, then, depends to a great extent on one's cultural background.

Conversational Politeness

Social interaction is similar to driving in that there are some basic, underlying rules that individuals must follow if the social enterprise is going to work. Even though drivers are individually more or less considerate of each other, what people do behind the wheel must be responsive to what others are doing, as well as to such basic conventions as driving on the right or the left side of the road. The important thing is not the side of the road we drive on but the fact that group members have to follow the same pattern. Many of these patterns are culturally influenced, and some are fairly universal. Many rules of the road are taught, but others are tacit: Drivers may not realize the extent to which their driving patterns respond to others.

A universal principle has been suggested for social interaction: People tacitly agree to talk in a way that will save face for themselves and others (Brown & Levinson, 1987). Politeness boils down to maintaining others' face so that they will be kindly disposed toward maintaining our face—as people take turns merging from two lanes into one, letting one car go ahead in the expectation of getting the next turn to merge. Face has two sides: negative face, including the needs people have for territory and freedom; and positive face, including needs to be approved of. Both are respected in conversation.

Although people generally take into account each other's face, they sometimes have to say things that are inherently face-threatening. A request or command, for example, threatens hearers' negative face because it imposes on them—their freedom to act is compromised. When this happens, there are trade-offs between communicating directly and preserving the other's face. For example, if someone steps on your toe, you can issue the direct command, *Get off my toe*. However, by speaking so directly you risk threatening the offender's negative face. In addition, if you grimace in making the demand, you also threaten the person's positive face by showing disapproval of the action. You might mitigate your statement by appealing to the offender's positive face: *Hey, you're on my toe* said with a laugh that shows friendliness and no hard feelings. You could use an indirect strategy aimed toward negative politeness (putting your own negative face at risk), such as *Excuse me, would you mind moving your foot?* posing the message as a question rather than a command. Even less direct is *Oh, my toe!* In determining what to say, you unconsciously weigh the social relationship between yourself and the offender, along with how face threatening the message is.

On top of these general principles for interacting with politeness, there are cultural differences with respect to what constitutes face and threats to face. These can make interactions across cultures difficult. For example, teachers concerned with preserving students' face might say *I like the way Antoine is working* as an indirect demand, a hint, that others get to work. As long as teacher and students have a common basis for interpreting talk, the former statement can convey something like the latter message.

However, if students come from a cultural background where authorities are expected to issue direct messages and indirectness is viewed as weakness, then the effort to preserve their face is worthless. Not only is the basic politeness system subject to cultural variation, but people do not necessarily know how others intend their words to be taken.

Sometimes people tell each other to "just say what you mean." But saying what you mean turns out to be a Pandora's box. People have been led to believe that they can make themselves understood by being clear and logical when they talk and write, as if a message in one person's brain could be fully encoded into language, heard or read, and then decoded in the other person's brain. According to that explanation, people would only need to speak the same language in order to understand each other. Conversational experience suggests otherwise. We often have misunderstandings, or at least conversational rough spots, with other English speakers.

In order to be understood, we say and do things that will get others to recognize our communicative intentions, but we hardly ever spell out fully what we want to communicate—and we can't really. Hearing what we have said, others fill in the rest, using their store of general information and beliefs about the world and assuming that the speaker is following culturally based rules for conversation.

Making Meaning

Philosopher H. Paul Grice (1975) contended that conversations are meaningful because conversationalists cooperate with each other to get meanings conveyed. Each participant in talk is entitled to assume that everyone is following certain conversational maxims as they speak:

1. Quantity—Be as informative as is required by the conversation, but not more so.
2. Quality—Be truthful, and do not say anything that you are not sure about.
3. Relation—Be relevant.
4. Manner—Be clear in expressing yourself, brief, and orderly.

Conversationalists either follow these maxims, or they flout them in principled ways. A speaker who is clearly not following a maxim intends that others will recognize that fact and figure out why. In the segment of conversation in Box 3.1, the second speaker follows all of the maxims except Relation. Saying "OK, I'll call Ann," in response to "It's snowing in Dayton" flouts the Relation maxim because telephoning is not relevant to snow. Here, the second speaker signals to the first to fill in the missing information that would make that turn relevant. To understand the second turn as a coherent response to the first one, considerable background knowledge is necessary. If the speakers made explicit all of the assumptions listed in Box 3.1, the conversation would be absurd and tedious, and both speakers would feel insulted at being told the obvious.

Box 3.1

Ellipsis in Conversation

The following segment introduced a long distance telephone conversation:

John: It's snowing in Dayton.
Carolyn: Okay, I'll call Ann.

To interpret this talk as cooperative and meaningful, the participants drew on background information from previous conversations and shared history, as well as general knowledge about the world, such as the following:

- John is in Dayton, and Carolyn is not.
- John is about to get on an airplane.
- Airplanes sometimes get delayed by snow.
- Because John's plane might be delayed, he might not get home as planned.

(continued on next page)

(Box 3.1 continued)

- Carolyn is going out for the evening.
- Carolyn and John have a baby, Jake.
- If John does not get home, no one will be available to take care of Jake.
- Friends sometimes help with child care in emergencies.
- It is reasonable to ask their friend Ann to stay with Jake because Carolyn and John sometimes care for Ann's baby.

Although this list is not completely detailed, it suggests that speakers appeal to a broad range of unspoken information when they speak and when they interpret each other's talk.

The fact that interaction is so elliptical, that meaning isn't fully specified, opens the way to misunderstandings. Add cultural background differences to that basic vagueness and the fact that people do manage to communicate most of the time becomes remarkable! Conversationalists have to share a vast set of assumptions about the nature of the world to interpret each others' talk.

Not only do we not say everything that we mean; we often say things that are not intended literally. Everyone uses figurative language, and we all recognize not only conventional figures of speech ("It's just a stone's throw from here.") but novel ones as well (said of an organization's e-mail access to the Internet: "We've got a little dirt path out to the information highway," Q. Pho, personal communication, July, 1995). Here again, there are culturally based differences on various levels of language use. For example, whereas European Americans may say that someone has recently passed away, African Americans may say that someone has passed. Conventions regarding literal meaning can vary even in cultural groups. Goodwin (1990) noticed that preadolescent African American girls criticized each other for bragging whereas African American boys of the same age frequently referred to their abilities and actions in exaggerated terms. In some groups, any mismatch between word and deed is expected to be understated rather than overstated because value is placed on projection of personal humility about physical capabilities. So underlying cultural values often enter into the determination of situational appropriateness concerning literal and nonliteral meaning.

The Functions of Talk

"Saying what you mean" suggests another pervasive myth about language: that its primary purpose is to communicate information. Teachers and parents of teenagers know that much of young people's talk is for purposes other than conveying information. When people of any age say that they are just shooting the breeze or just talking, they are referring not to some secondary use of language but to language use for vital recreation and relationship-maintaining purposes. After a long, satisfying conversation with friends or family members, one may be hard pressed for an answer if someone asks what was said. The talk itself is more important than the topic.

Tannen (1986) emphasized the fact that metamessages, which concern the relationship of the speaker(s) and hearer(s) and how the message is intended to be taken, always enter into verbal messages in the choice of phrasing, facial expression and other nonverbal behavior, and vocal elements such as intonation and word stress. In a phone conversation, the voice quality and intonational pattern on "'Bye" alone often gives a metamessage showing how the speaker feels about the other person and their relationship.

The social relationship element of language use is really a constant part of communication, and for that reason social appropriateness in language use is an important criterion. It is not something we think about most of the time, but it is something that consistently underlies the unconscious choices we make in talk.

Language Rituals

Although different groups have their own implicit standards about what makes for appropriate or satisfying conversation, there are also certain situations that call for particular language forms and interactional patterns. Sometimes the connection is so predictable as to constitute ritual. For example, in many cultures, there are ritual-like behaviors that are appropriate responses to death—what people say and do to console family members, how they conduct ceremonies that mark the event, and so on. Common everyday occurrences such as greetings are also ritualized. That explains why people would be taken aback if the greeting *How are you?* were responded to with detailed information about a person's health, and why sick people sometimes respond with *Fine* to this question when it is part of a doctor's greeting. Conventions for ritualistic communication may be passed on orally to younger members of the group, or in some cases written down.

Other clearly established routines of daily life may be so ritualistic in nature that they have been given labels by members of the community. Very specific rules may govern how the language forms are put together. For example, a form of verbal behavior among members of certain African American communities that has been widely described is known as sounding (e.g., Labov, 1972). This game of insults, also known in some places as signifying, joning, or playing the dozens, usually involves groups of young males and builds from a fairly low-key exchange at the start to a point of considerable verbal creativity by the contestants. The insults traded usually include slurs on the opponent and the opponent's family. Real proficiency in this verbal game is a valued ability among members of the cultural group. Other examples of stylized language use can be found in various procedures used in storytelling among different groups. Distinctive styles of telling stories may characterize the verbal art tradition of a community. These varieties of speech events are often easy to identify because of their ritualistic qualities.

Other rituals of everyday life do not have labels but do include highly predictable interactional patterns. Rituals that develop in families, to become part of that small group's unique shared interactional pattern, are likely to have a cultural basis. For example, in many middle-class families, children are expected and invited to talk about their day at school over dinner, at length or briefly. Although they may have little to say, the topic is raised day after day because it is part of the family's culturally based patterns. This kind of ritual reinforces the notion that the child's education is an important family concern. It also serves a practical function. By providing the occasion for children to participate in discussion with adults, an interactive activity that schools value, the ritual encourages development of skills for that function.

Classroom Rituals

Schools observe rituals too, of course. Like families, which may have their own version of a general cultural pattern, classrooms may develop their own routines, or their own versions of pervasive school routines such as opening exercises and early arrival seat work, written activities that children do until time for opening exercises in elementary schools, and checking the homework assignment or reviewing for a test in secondary schools. All of these routines are likely to include some highly predictable interactional patterns and even recurring phrases and specific terms, although details of these elements may well differ from classroom to classroom. Students come to know these rituals and the special meanings connected with them. When a teacher says, "I want you to be responsible for the material on page 243," or a student says, "Do we have to know the perfect numbers?" special meanings are conveyed concerning what may appear on a test. Participating appropriately in the test review ritual requires understanding these special meanings.

Not every situation is ritualized, of course, but unconscious norms and subsequent judgments about appropriateness guide interaction nonetheless. In less predictable situations, people make appropriate conversational contributions based on what they think is going on. Doing this requires instantaneous, unconscious assessments of subtle modulations in topic and context. Some features of context may remain constant throughout a conversation—perhaps the setting and the speakers—but others can change from moment to moment. A serious conversation can be punctuated with humorous remarks. Or there may be some change in how new speakers enter the discourse. For example, teachers often expect students to raise their hands for a turn at talk, but at other times they welcome spontaneous student talk. Clearly, something in the context modifies the way in which speakers are selected so that on some occasions it is appropriate for students to speak voluntarily, and on others it is not.

Contextual Factors in Appropriateness

Context is not easy to pin down because potentially it includes all of the elements that people could take into account in making meaning in conversation, including their general knowledge. Hymes, a linguistic anthropologist whose work on language use and culture has been very influential, devised a basic outline of contextual elements that could well be important to any interaction (Hymes, 1974). These elements, organized under the mnemonic acronym SPEAKING, are useful for investigating communication patterns:

> S—Setting or scene.
> P—Participants.
> E—Ends (purpose).
> A—Acts of speaking.
> K—Key (the tone or participants' feelings).
> I—Instrumentality (the language or language variety).
> N—Norms.
> G—Genre.

The first letter of the mnemonic refers to aspects of the **Setting**. The very fact that talk is happening at school rather than at home or in the doctor's office favors some potential meanings over others; but focusing more narrowly in the school setting, talk in classrooms has a different context from talk in hallways, even when the speakers remain the same. The social identity of the **Participants** constitutes an important feature of context for any talk, so that their status will probably be important for figuring out meaning, especially speakers' relative status and their particular relationships to each other. For example, when a teacher says *Jeffrey* in a classroom, it is highly likely that Jeffrey is being called to respond to a question already on the conversational floor, or to do something, or to pay attention. The same word spoken by a peer in a different setting, such as during a basketball game, might carry some of the same meaning potential. It might be a call to pay attention, but it would probably not be a way of recycling a question, as it is when spoken by a teacher in a classroom.

Other potentially important contextual elements are the **Ends** of the interaction—its purpose(s), its goals—and, of course, what is being said—the talk or communicative **Actions**. Each turn at talk becomes a context for the next one. This is what discourse analysts call the contingent nature of talk (Schiffrin, 1994). What can come next is predicted to some extent by what was just said—the act or action that was accomplished through speaking. The teacher's saying *Jeffrey* counts socially as nominating him to speak. We can expect that when Jeffrey hears the teacher call his name, he will be the one to respond, and others will wait for him to do so or else accept criticism for not waiting. Moreover, what he says must constitute an act of responding. For example, if a question or direction is already on the floor (e.g., "Let's see whether people had trouble with the homework."), then Jeffrey is expected to respond with a statement (e.g., "I couldn't do the last one."), a question (e.g., "Is the first answer 2x - y?"), or some other act that is relevant in that moment.

Key refers to the psychological or emotional state prevailing in the situation: If participants are excited, perhaps the one-speaker-at-a-time rule can be temporarily over-ridden, allowing students to call out responses without being called on. **Instrumentality** is the language or language variety being used—for example, whether a standard variety, a vernacular variety, or a fairly formal language register or style, as opposed to a casual one. **Norms** refers to the underlying interactive rules in play—for example, whether or not overlapping talk is appropriate; and **Genre** is the type of interaction—for example, faculty room chat. Thus it is important to determining meaning in the "Jeffrey" example to know that it occurs in a lesson, not on a basketball court. The acronym SPEAKING does not cover every possible facet of context in a specific way, but because it refers generally to a broad range of contextual elements, analysts have found it a useful tool.

The importance of context is referenced when people claim that their talk has been taken out of context, or when people try to tell about an incident that seemed funny or striking in some way, and the telling falls flat on its face. *You had to be there* is the stock response, because if you had been there you would have sensed the contextual elements at play. Context is not just out there, a fringe on the tapestry of verbal interaction: Aspects of the context form the very warp and woof as people weave conversational meaning together.

Cultural groups may see the meaning of contextual factors somewhat differently, foregrounding some dimensions and disregarding others. Differing perspectives on context can result in quite different interpretations of a single behavior. Delpit, an educational anthropologist and a teacher, reported an anecdote involving some White teachers who felt that a Black teacher in their school was very authoritarian (Delpit, 1988). Talking loudly and using direct commands rather than indirect suggestions (e.g., *Talk louder, Paula*, direct; rather than *I don't think people can hear you, Paula*, indirect), this teacher struck her colleagues as unfairly emphasizing her power, rather than striving to create a democratic environment as they would have done. Delpit pointed out that the African American teacher was following a different set of interactional norms than the White teachers expected.

In that teacher's community, authority is not assumed by virtue of status; it is created or at least simulated in the give and take of institutional life. Teachers from this cultural group act out their authority status in concert with their students, said Delpit, creating and maintaining a social structure that they lead and that casts children as students. These teachers are authoritative leaders, not authoritarian dictators. Judging from their own cultural perspective on appropriate teacher talk, the colleagues had misconstrued the social identities that the teacher was assembling with her students, the purpose of her talk, aspects of her oral language, the key being created, and perhaps even the genre of talk.

Culture creates lenses or frames for viewing interaction as having certain meaning potential. When our frame is different from that of other participants, results can range from feeling that something is slightly out of kilter to gravely misjudging the meaning of events and participants' intentions.

CULTURAL STYLES IN THE CLASSROOM

When teachers and students come from different backgrounds, they bring different expectations about language use that can cause interactional difficulties. Unaware that a problem could be due to cultural differences, teachers may infer students' incompetence or lack of interest in education. Because schools generally align with the cultural traditions associated with the middle class, educators may perceive the interactional patterns of students from nondominant groups to be deviant rather than based in a different cultural tradition and history. Such judgments can place students at risk for failure or make them candidates for referral to special education. The excerpt in Box 3.2 comes from an early, classic sociolinguistic investigation into the ways in which institutional practice may fail children.

Box 3.2

Excerpts from "The Logic of Nonstandard English," by William Labov (1969)

In the past decade, a great deal of federally sponsored research has been devoted to the educational problems of children in ghetto schools. In order to account for the poor performance of children in these schools, educational psychologists have attempted to discover what kind of disadvantage or defect they are suffering from. The viewpoint which has been widely accepted and used as the basis for large-scale intervention programs is that the children show a cultural deficit as a result of an impoverished environment in their early years. Considerable attention has been given to language. In this area, the deficit theory appears as the concept of "verbal deprivation": Negro children from the ghetto area receive little verbal stimulation, are said to hear very little well-formed language, and as a result are impoverished in their means of verbal expression: they cannot speak complete sentences, do not know the names of common objects, cannot form concepts or convey logical thoughts.

Unfortunately, these notions are based upon the work of educational psychologists who know very little about language and even less about Negro children. The concept of verbal deprivation has no basis in social reality: in fact, Negro children from the urban ghettos receive a great deal of verbal stimulation, hear more well-formed sentences than middle-class children, and participate fully in a highly verbal culture; they have the same basic vocabulary, possess the same capacity for conceptual learning, and use the same logic as anyone else who learns to speak and understand English.

(continued on next page)

(Box 3.2 continued)

The notion of "verbal deprivation" is a part of the modern mythology of educational psychology, typical of the unfounded notions which tend to expand rapidly in our educational system. In past decades linguists have been as guilty as others in promoting such intellectual fashions at the expense of both teachers and children. But the myth of verbal deprivation is particularly dangerous, because it diverts attention from real defects of our education system to imaginary defects of the child; and … it leads its sponsors inevitably to the hypothesis of the genetic inferiority of Negro children which it was originally designed to avoid. …

Verbality

The most extreme view which proceeds from this orientation—and one that is now being widely accepted—is that lower-class Negro children have no language at all. … On many occasions we have been asked to help analyze the results of research into verbal deprivation in … test situations.

Here, for example, is a complete interview with a Negro boy, one of hundreds carried out in a New York City school. The boy enters a room where there is a large, friendly white interviewer, who puts on the table in front of him a block or a fire engine, and says "Tell me everything you can about this." (The interviewer's further remarks are in parentheses.)

[12 seconds of silence]
(What would you say it looks like?)
[8 seconds of silence]
A space ship.
(Hmmmmm.)
[13 seconds of silence]
Like a je-et.
Like a plane.
[20 seconds of silence]
(What color is it?)
Orange. [2 seconds] An' whi-ite. [2 seconds] An' green.
[6 seconds of silence]
(An' what could you use it for?) (continued on next page)

(Box 3.2 continued)

[8 seconds of silence]

A je-et.

[6 seconds of silence]

(If you had two of them, what would you do with them?)

[6 seconds of silence]

Give one to some-body.

(Hmmmm. Who do you think would like to have it?)

[10 seconds of silence]

Cla-rence.

(Mm. Where do you think we could get another one of these?)

At the store.

(Oh ka-ay!)

We have here the same kind of defensive, monosyllabic behavior which is reported in [a psychologist's] work. What is the situation that produces it? The child is in an asymmetrical situation where anything he says can literally be held against him. He has learned a number of devices to *avoid* saying anything in this situation, and he works very hard to achieve this end. ... If one takes this interview as a measure of the verbal capacity of the child, it must be as his capacity to defend himself in a hostile and threatening situation. But unfortunately, thousands of such interviews are used as evidence of the child's total verbal capacity, or more simply his "verbality." ...

The view of the Negro speech community which we obtain from our work in the ghetto areas is precisely the opposite from that reported by [psychologists]. We see a child bathed in verbal stimulation from morning to night. We see many speech events which depend upon the competitive exhibition of verbal skills: sounding, singing, toasts, rifting, louding—a whole range of activities in which the individual gains status through his use of language. We see the younger child trying to acquire these skills from older children—hanging around on the outskirts of the older peer groups, and imitating this behavior to the best of his ability. We see no connection between verbal skill at the speech events characteristic of the street culture and success in the schoolroom.

Anthropologists of education and sociolinguists have investigated contrasting language behavior in multicultural classrooms, discovering how mismatched language use patterns produce discord and also how groups learn to accommodate some of their differences. Discussions of school problems in various Native American communities, for example, have indicated that the children do not participate in the classroom as White teachers expect them to. Investigators who have examined this situation from the community perspective have noted that there appear to be different rules of language use that are in conflict. Mohatt and Erickson (1981) noticed that in an Odawa community, turns at talk in groups were not controlled by one person. White teachers, however, were accustomed to controlling the flow of students' talk as integral to teaching. The cultural mismatch between student and teacher meant that Native American students remained silent or responded in ways which struck the teacher as awkward when they were called on. In group work, however, Odawa children spoke to each other about the academic task with ease. Philips (1993) found that in classrooms on the Warm Springs Indian Reservation, teachers faulted students for not asking questions or interrupting to get the floor. But in the community, children who asserted themselves were viewed as pretentious and bold.

Patterns of verbal participation that have been learned in the cultural context of the home community may account for much of children's interaction in the classroom. This behavior is often misinterpreted by those who do not share the cultural background of the children.

Often when things go wrong in an interaction, people recognize that there has been a misunderstanding and do some repair work so that they can proceed. For example, consider the following exchange:

Molly: The movers are coming next weekend.

Vanessa: But I won't be here. You know that I'm going to the beach Friday.

Molly: No, not this weekend—next weekend.

The misunderstanding in this exchange results from differences in using *next* to signify the first weekend or the second one from the time of speaking. Such a misunderstanding can lead to considerable inconvenience, but it seems just as likely to get cleared up as it is here because many people are aware of language use differences that are not culturally based.

Misunderstandings are not always identified easily and immediately. Often, people realize that something has gone wrong somewhere in the conversational flow, but they do not know what it is and they do not know how to repair it. Sometimes they intensify the conversational strategies that they normally interact with successfully. The effect may be to make a bad situation worse. Investigation has shown that employers or school counselors who do not get verbal and nonverbal feedback, including eye contact, at the point in discourse where they expect it according to their culture will repeat or rephrase what they have said. They take the lack of feedback as a sign that the addressee is not understanding them. The employee or the student, feeling condescended to, will withdraw from the conversation and thus provide fewer indications that she or he is following the speaker. No one stops to think that cultural differences in gaze and head nodding behavior, along with the type and timing of a verbal response, might be working against them. Such communicative behaviors are so taken for granted, so far below our level of awareness, that we simply do not guess that they can vary from group to group (Erickson & Shultz, 1982).

In her autobiography *Singin' and Swingin' and Gettin' Merry Like Christmas*, Maya Angelou (1976) gave a hilarious example of this human tendency to do more rather than less of some behavior that is producing interactive trouble—not in talk but in music. Auditioning for a Broadway show, she realizes in mid-song that she and the accompanist are not in the same key; but instead of stopping and beginning again, she sings louder. The pianist responds by playing louder: "She would get me back on pitch or there would just be splinters left on the piano" (p. 124). The volume increases on both sides until Angelou triumphantly outdistances the piano in yelling the final note. What goes wrong here is much like what happens in conversation when speakers try vainly to get each other to play by their own cultural rules (Bateson, 1972; Tannen, 1984).

Often, speakers do not recognize that their interactive strategies are at odds, and they attribute intentions to each other erroneously. Kochman, a sociologist, noticed that the students in his university classes used a variety of different interactive strategies in discussions, as did his colleagues in faculty meetings (Kochman, 1981). When African American students and faculty members wanted to establish a point, they often did so with passion, using hyperbole, figurative language, repetition, increased volume, and a wide intonational range; but most European American students and faculty attempted to make their points dispassionately, outlining their reasoning, and speaking with controlled volume and intonation. Not only did the two groups not see that their contrasting approaches to discussion were a matter of cultural difference, they assumed malevolent intentions on the part of the other group—the kinds of intentions that they themselves would harbor if they were speaking in that way. African Americans believed that Whites were hiding their feelings about the topic and thus attempting to mislead people and camouflage the truth. Whites felt that African Americans had lost emotional control and could not reason adequately when they were out of control. The one group interpreted passion as irrationality; the other group interpreted lack of passion as deviousness.

When interaction runs into trouble as a result of culturally contrasting strategies, people can repair the problem if they recognize it. Often, however, they attribute the trouble not to misunderstanding but to the other person's ill-will or social incompetence.

Understanding Students' Language Behavior

Studies of language use in various cultures and especially studies from school settings can be very helpful in raising people's awareness of communication patterns and helping them look for cultural contrasts. Heath (1986) cautioned that descriptions of middle-class children's language do not necessarily apply to other children. Likewise her work on working-class African American and European American children's language practices in the Piedmont, mentioned in chapter 1, does not necessarily apply in all details to language behavior of other working class children of other cultural groups or from other regions (Heath, 1983). But it does raise the possibility that what teachers mean by *story* or other important classroom activities may be different from the meanings that children have acquired in their communities. It suggests that children have learned sophisticated language skills in their communities, but these may be different from those that school requires.

Heath's work, and that of other anthropologists, linguists, and educational researchers, can be very useful for opening up new possibilities. For instance, *Children of Promise* (Heath & Mangiola, 1991) outlines four programs that accommodate children's language backgrounds while involving them in stimulating literacy activities.

Profiles of cultural behavior associated with various groups have been prepared for teachers by professional organizations and school systems, but these must be used with caution because they represent generalizations that may not apply to all members of any group. Like studies of talk at school, these profiles can suggest ways in which language use can vary, but they should not be treated as predictive in any specific way or for any specific student.

Researching Classroom Interaction

Educators can learn about students' language use in their own classrooms. Suppose a teacher becomes concerned that boys as a group seem to participate more in whole-class instruction than girls as a group. In this case, gender, rather than ethnicity, may be the relevant cultural basis for language use patterns. Concerned about gender equity and girls' lower test scores in some subject areas, the teacher wants to identify the speaker selection patterns in the class. It seems that boys and girls get called on about equally, but by the end of a lesson, boys seem to be doing the talking and many of the girls seem to be uninterested.

It is quite possible to study classroom participation and quite likely that contextual explanations for the patterns will present themselves in what the teacher observes and what others have found about general tendencies of boys to engage competitively in public talk and girls to contribute more cooperatively in smaller groups (Sadker & Sadker, 1994; Tannen, 1991). Studying classroom talk requires systematic observation and analysis. Of course, doing that and teaching at the same time is nearly impossible.

Data Collection.   Two good possibilities for data collection are inviting a colleague to observe and take running notes about who is talking and what they are saying, or videotaping the class. Each method has pros and cons. Teachers who are accustomed to being observed only for evaluation may find it very stressful, and colleagues who are not accustomed to observing their peers may not know what to look for. If collegial observation is part of peer coaching, it can be extremely helpful. In the short run, without a peer observer, the teacher can experiment with videotaping by simply setting up a camera in a corner, focusing broadly on students' faces, and letting it run.

Students and teacher may be uncomfortable for a time, but once the camera becomes a classroom fixture, people will relax. No one else need see the tapes, and if the teacher never comments on them, students are likely to accept the taping as routine. In any event, videotaped data, which can be analyzed through repeated viewing, is potentially so valuable as to be worth a bit of inconvenience.

Data Analysis.   With dialect study, the investigator needs to look for instances of particular linguistic features; but in studying interaction, stretches of talk are of interest. When the teacher's question concerns interaction patterns across lessons, the whole lesson will need to be reviewed in order to find those patterns. The teacher already knows that girls and boys talk approximately equally at the beginning of the lesson, and boys talk more at the end, but what happens in the interim? How does the teacher, as the general controller of turns at lesson talk, contribute to the shift?

Basically, investigators who use videotaped data watch their tapes carefully and repeatedly, noting evidence that could be relevant to their research questions. Watching the tape for the first time, the teacher makes notes about anything interesting, jotting down the VCR index numbers to facilitate rechecking these segments. Watching it again leads to preliminary conclusions that can be checked by watching certain sections again. Videotaping another lesson or two will help to confirm, disconfirm, or, more likely, refine the original understandings.

To take another example, suppose that a teacher is concerned about David, a seventh-grade student who often seems to be disengaged. David never volunteers to participate, often mumbles something irrelevant when called on, usually turns in classwork that is only half done and mostly incorrect, and rarely does homework. The teacher is not succeeding in reaching this student, who seems to fade into the background. Are cultural differences interfering? In videotaping the class, the teacher has focused on David, hoping to gain some insight into how he manages to remain invisible.

Analysis of the tape shows David slouching down into his seat further and further. Not once does he get involved in group interaction at his table, whether or not those activities are official ones. Occasionally he talks to the student sitting next to him, however, and the teacher wants to follow up on this. The next time through the tape, the teacher notices that David acts as if he does not know what is going on. When directions are given, most students look at the teacher—but David doesn't. As activities begin, David is sometimes still daydreaming, sometimes rifling through papers on his desk, sometimes leaning on the table watching other students. When he finally does get around to the task, he leans over to his neighbor, who seems to explain the activity to him. The teacher wonders why David's significant lack of attention to the task was not more noticeable. Another viewing compares David to other students. Most do attend to teacher instructions, and when they are lost or off-task, their behaviors are eye-catching. They get involved in off-task behavior with others, or they call out to the teacher. They wave their hands and lean into the interaction, but David shrinks away from it.

This example of the analytic process involves first noticing something as simple as David's posture and then making comparisons with other students' behavior to identify how he opts out. Noticing that he is not working raises the question of whether he knows what to do, which leads the analyst to locate direction giving and focus in on David's behavior there. There is every suggestion that he is not attending to directions: He gazes into space, slouches further, taps his pencil on his desk. Having found a trouble spot, the teacher consults with a colleague who is more familiar with David's cultural background. As a result, the teacher resolves to command everyone's attention when giving directions, including David's, by using direct strategies and repeating them—to say "Look at me, everyone. Put your pencils down. Sit up straight, and listen while I tell you what to do." Although such directness may seem overbearing and even face-threatening to the teacher, direct attention getting is appropriate and expected for students from David's background.

In this case, the analyst focused on the structure of lessons (teacher direction giving, followed by student lesson activity). In another case, finer details of interaction might be important. A teacher who was concerned about a student's very poor reading found that at least some of the student's miscues seemed to be due to the teacher's turn-taking behavior. When the student paused during oral reading, the teacher immediately offered prompts that often led to outlandish responses. The teacher's culturally based turn-taking behavior demanded shorter pauses than the student expected, based again on cultural background.

When studying one's own classroom, of course, there are also opportunities for informal data gathering. One can become more observant of certain kinds of classroom happenings with or without videotapes. The teacher in the gender-based response example may start to sense the point at which girls stop volunteering or to see the more assertive body language accompanying boys' requests for a turn. The data gathering task may recede as a search for solutions starts to take over. The teacher may observe that girls are more active in cooperative learning structures, rather than when class members are competing for the one chance to respond. With this realization, the teacher can put the research task aside for the time being to try out some different social structures for learning, such as having students work in pairs on short tasks or in groups on longer ones. Research can be resumed at any time. It is wise to save the tapes and the notes, however, in case different questions come up down the road.

The analytic path may take various turns, as is typical of descriptive study. The general route is to pose a question, gather relevant data, examine it in as open-ended a manner as possible, look for recurring patterns, gather more data, and refine the pattern descriptions. Classroom research may be practically oriented, but it requires careful, thorough investigation. Practitioners must strive to view their own communicative behavior as an element of the action, rather than a fixed feature. The research questions arise in practice, and the analysis motivates change.

For work of this type to be successful, it is helpful to have a very clear objective in mind, allowing for change as understandings become enriched. The SPEAKING classification of context mentioned earlier can encourage the analyst to take into account the broad range of elements that contribute to communication. Figuring out the important aspects of the setting can be useful. It may be that students in one part of the room are more active than those in another. Repeated viewing may suggest that the teacher turns toward that side of the room more than to the other.

Practitioner research need not be a solitary enterprise. Published studies on language use in the cultural group of interest can be helpful—not because they will directly answer the research question, but because they may suggest direction. Conferring with a colleague can be stimulating and helpful. In fact, teacher research on contrasting language use patterns in a school can be a very productive professional development activity, either on its own or in concert with school renewal projects. Those who choose that work are likely to gain considerable insight into their students and their own professional practice, and they may be willing to share their knowledge and research skills with others.

LIVING WITH LANGUAGE BEHAVIOR DIFFERENCES

In the face of diverse communicative styles, schools may try to identify some basic guidelines for classroom interaction that all students need to follow. The following list, which was posted in an elementary classroom, exemplifies:

Classroom Rules

We will:

1. Enter the room quickly and quietly and take our seats.
2. Look and listen for instructions.
3. Begin work on time.
4. Work carefully and quietly.
5. Respect others.
6. Raise our hands and wait if we have a question or contribution.

These formal guidelines are different from the unconscious interactional rules of culture with which this chapter has been concerned. For one thing, these rules are prescriptive rather than descriptive of the patterns that actually underlie social interaction in most classrooms. These rules are intended to restrict student talk rather than to facilitate interaction. They predict that students will talk only when the teacher calls on them. Actually, in successful, exciting, teacher-led lessons, teachers are likely to reward spontaneous student contributions.

Certainly, there are some basic interactional guidelines for school behavior that all students have to follow, but if such guidelines aimed at repressing talk were actually enforced, they would restrict the communication that is central to learning. Many educators say or show through their interactions with students that a more effective way to diminish communication difficulties due to cultural differences is to foster trust and respect. The checklist in Box 3.3 is useful for gaining insight into how students actually do talk in the classroom.

Box 3.3

Checklist for Language Use in Classrooms

Culturally based differences in communicating may exist in many areas of language use. This list suggests some important ones. Categories overlap.

Objective: Determine whether there is a possibility for misunderstanding based on cultural contrasts in the following areas:

Classroom Speech Acts
- Explaining: giving an account
- Reporting: giving information
- Requesting: asking for actions, items, or information
- Directing: telling someone to do something
- Commenting: volunteering a remark
- Greeting: acknowledging another's presence
- Denying: contradicting
- Refusing: declining to take action
- Promising: committing to an action
- Complimenting: expressing approval
- Apologizing: regretfully acknowledging an offense
- Protesting: objecting to an offense

(continued on next page)

(Box 3.3 continued)

Participating Appropriately in Interaction

Appropriateness is defined in cultures according to social factors such as the relative age and role status of speaker and hearer, situational factors such as setting, and communication factors such as speakers' intentions and immediate linguistic environment.

Attending
- Gaze and other nonverbal behavior
- Verbal feedback ("Uh huh," "Um")
- Remaining silent

Responding
- Volunteering relevant talk
- Replying when nominated
- Requesting clarification
- Producing a speech act or other act appropriate to the preceding speech act

Turn-taking
- Talking at appropriate points in discourse
- Providing wait-time

Maintaining and changing topics
- Producing talk that is relevant
- Introducing topic change; picking up on topic change

Narrating
- Producing a story

Giving reports
- Presenting known information
- Presenting novel information

General Sociolinguistic Considerations
   Directness/indirectness
   Address terms
   Nonverbal behavior
   Paralinguistics: volume, pitch, tone, voice quality, and so forth.

(continued on next page)

(Box 3.3 continued)

Relative focus on passion versus dispassion

Appropriateness of topics

Evaluative patterns in judging communicative interactions follow the same principle as that for certain dialect structures. Members of dominant social and cultural groups typically have less experience with the interactional ways of the nondominant groups, and they may feel uncomfortable, bewildered, and dismayed in social settings where they are in the minority whereas members of nondominant groups are more likely to have facility with the cultural language use conventions of the majority.

Although culturally based interactional style differences do get in the way of understanding, it is also true that not every difference is jarring. In one multicultural first grade classroom, it became clear that two friends, an African American and a Vietnamese American, had quite different argument participation strategies but that their styles seemed not to conflict (Adger, 1986). The African American boy protested forcefully when other students offended him and continued protesting vigorously to win the argument whereas the Vietnamese American boy used language to defuse a confrontation. The fact that the boys seemed to have different conversational goals may have made it possible for each to find satisfaction in their arguments with each other. The African American boy could always get the last word because the Vietnamese American boy did not want it, and the Vietnamese American boy could defuse the argument by not seeking to win it. There was also evidence that the children gradually accommodated to these contrasts in each others' interactional style.

Recognizing the human propensity to prefer the familiar and be wary of the strange, it is no wonder that people often evaluate others' cultural styles negatively. People can increase their understanding of others' ways through formal study and informal observation, and to some extent by integrating themselves more fully into the multicultural society.

FURTHER STUDY

Heath, S. B. (1983). *Ways with words: Language, life, and work in communities and classrooms*. New York: Cambridge University Press.
An ethnographic study of two different Southern communities and how lan-

guage functions in the community and in the school. It provides important background for understanding many of the attitudes and approaches to language revealed by children from vernacular-speaking backgrounds, with significant implications for the role of educators.

Kochman, T. (1981). *Black and White styles in conflict*. Chicago: The University of Chicago Press.
An important, honest discussion of how language use differences may lead to misinterpretation and conflict. At times, the conclusions seem overstated, but there is little doubt that Kochman has captured essential language usage differences for some subcultures of Blacks and Whites in America. It is quite readable even for someone with limited or no background in language studies and has proved useful in seminars and workshops dealing with human relations as well as dialect studies.

Scollon, R., & Scollon, S. B. K. (1981). *Narrative, literacy and face in interethnic communication*. Norwood, NJ: Ablex.
Focusing on discourse involving Alaska natives, including children, the analysis shows the pervasiveness of cultural differences in conversational style. Although the discussion is technical, it is not unfriendly. The authors address educational and other institutional concerns.

Tannen, D. (1986). *That's not what I meant! How conversational style makes or breaks your relations with others*. New York: Morrow.
Using scenes from everyday life, Tannen explores the communication ups and downs that everyone experiences and traces them to desires for both closeness and distance and different groups' ways of maintaining relationships. Although she does not specifically treat language in school, her insights hold for communication there as well. Her other books for general audiences are *You just don't understand: Women and men in conversation* (1990) and *Talking from nine to five* (1994).

Trueba, H. T., Guthrie, G. P., & Au, K. H.–P. (Eds.). (1981). *Culture and the bilingual classroom: Studies in classroom ethnography*. Rowley, MA: Newbury House.
This collection of essays presents both general theoretical and methodological issues in school-community ethnography. It also has sections that focus on these issues with respect to particular ethnic groups, including Native Americans, Hawaiian Americans, Mexican Americans, Black Americans, and Puerto Rican Americans. It is an important representation of more broadly based sociolinguistic differences that impact education.

4

Language Difference Does Not Mean Language Deficit

Education reform initiatives at the close of the 20th century are creating opportunities for schools to reexamine the impact of language variation on students' school performance. As professional organizations, states, and local school systems craft standards for what students should learn, and as they translate the standards into curriculum and instruction, issues are raised concerning a key topic of this volume—the ability to produce spoken and written language in a way that meets certain expectations in society. In the process of considering expectations for spoken and written language, it is crucial to take into account the language variation that is rooted in social and regional norms.

Traditionally, responsibility for enhancing language development has been vested in English language arts. But because the language modalities—speaking, listening, reading, and writing—are central to teaching and learning across the curriculum, educators need to consider together the effects of language variation in other content areas as well. For example, in presenting content standards for math, the National Council of Teachers of Mathematics emphasizes instruction that requires students to explore ideas collaboratively and explain their thinking as they do math. More language in math class creates the need for math teachers to consider language variation in action and to examine attitudes toward students' language.

This chapter and those that follow focus on aspects of English dialects that have always been educationally relevant and that need to be revisited as schools reform. In this chapter, we examine the prevailing view of language difference as language deficit. The view that variation erodes the language—a popular, bedrock perspective—supports the illusion of a unitary English (the mistaken notion that there is one logical, correct form of English and that all other varieties are imperfect approximations). That illusion has permeated educational endeavors with serious consequences. The lack of institutional provision for different language varieties and ways of using language, for example, means that some groups do less well in the gatekeeping activities that determine program access or placement. Standardized tests assume competence in standardized English, and competence in other dialects may be defined by standardized measures to be a disability. The deficit perspective on language variation affects many aspects of schooling, several of which are examined in the following sections.

PERCEPTIONS OF STANDARDS

Language Threat Myths

There seems to be a widespread feeling that the English language is a fragile object and is constantly under siege. Like the Constitution, it needs to be protected from public use and abuse, lest it deteriorate. One guardian of the language worries about what he called "everybody's sloppiness in speech" that leads to such phenomena as "melded words" (e.g., *oughta* and *wanna*).

> Should we make an effort to resist the trend toward elision, accelerated by the spelling-out of the melded words? I think so; to some degree in speech, and to a much greater degree in the written word, we ought to … give crisp clarity a shot … because Standard English is worth preserving. (Safire, 1993, p. 81)

The notion that language is declining or vulnerable to decay is also articulated by some teachers, professors, newscasters, and television critics. These people's use of language is typically admired so they may be considered to be language experts even though they have not actually studied about language. Thus, their opinions carry weight.

Parents who are concerned that their children develop exemplary language habits may also correct what they see as their children's sloppy or improper usage learned outside the home. But opinions about language usage can be very different from an understanding of how language actually works. We can draw an analogy from the use and knowledge of technology—one can be very adept at using word processing or other software without knowing how the computer works. But one ought not to draw conclusions about the mother board based solely on the use of a particular word-processing program.

Concerns about the state of the language are not at all new and are by no means unique to the United States. Similar laments about the decline of English have been voiced in the past. Jonathan Swift, for example, observed early in the 18th century that "our language is extremely imperfect" and complained that writers, who should "polish and refine it, have chiefly multiplied abuses and absurdities ..." (cited in Shuy, 1976).

Periodically, there are outcries about the misuse of the language, part of a long and very human tradition of insecurity about language. We can be reminded of the time when only Latin was considered a worthwhile language by scholars and European society at large. The vernaculars spoken in various areas (which developed into languages such as French and Spanish) were considered to be vulgar forms of speech and certainly not fit to be written down.

Critics often decry a failure to maintain the rules of Standard English in the speech and writing of various segments of our society. Those who take this stance lack an understanding of two basic characteristics of language (all languages, not just English). First, there are a number of different dialects of the language, all of which have been shown to be equally logical and rule-governed, but they are not all standard dialects because they are not all equally valued by society. Speech and writing that do not reflect the rules of Standard English are governed by the rules of some other dialect. Language performance that reflects the rules of vernacular dialects does not signal decline in the language; rather, it signals the health of nonstandard varieties of the language.

The second characteristic of language that critics ignore is that languages are constantly changing and the evaluation of various language varieties is part of that process. Research on the history of language shows clearly that *language change is inevitable*. Just as today's English has evolved from the English of Shakespeare's time, which evolved from the English of Chaucer's time and earlier, the language is evolving right now toward some future form that will be just as different from today's version. A typical reaction to change is resistance. Speakers often feel the new alternatives being introduced are not as good as the old ones. Change, in itself, however, is neither inherently good nor bad.

Another sort of evidence that language critics frequently present concerns directness/indirectness in language use. Indirectness is really a matter of style in the use of language, rather than evidence of a decline in the language itself. When an indirect usage arises, it may exist along with another expression (as *physically challenged* and *physically disabled*) or even replace another term in people's language use (*crippled* has become highly stigmatized). In the vast majority of cases, however, the resources to say things in different ways are still available. For example, if our language limited us to saying *previously owned car* rather than *used car*, we might say that the power of the language had been lessened when new uses arise because we could no longer express some concepts directly. Far from showing decline in the language, indirectness often shows linguistic resources being used imaginatively to create effects beyond the literal meanings of words.

Relative directness is a valuable dimension of language use that enables speakers to use the language for sending metamessages about their stance toward their topics and their listeners/readers. Although direct, plain English may be desirable for IRS forms and VCR programming manuals, we need indirect communicative means for a variety of purposes such as signaling political stance. For example, the term *handicapped children* was changed to *individuals with disabilities* when special education was reauthorized in 1992. This change of terminology resulted from the efforts of disabilities rights advocates to focus on the individual first and then the disability. *Disabilities* avoided negative connotations associated with *handicapped*. Because both terms still exist in the language, using the less direct *individuals with disabilities* allows the speaker to show solidarity with those who prefer the term. Using *handicap* is also meaningful: It can show lack of familiarity with the politics of disability or distrust of politically correct language.

Language and Perceptions of Educational Decline

Education is also perceived to be declining in quality. *A Nation at Risk: The Imperative for Education Reform* (National Commission on Excellence in Education, 1983) sparked an intense school reform movement, waves of which continue in the 1990s. That publication claimed that educational standards had fallen, as evidenced by the results of the National Assessment of Educational Progress (NAEP) and other yardsticks of educational measurement. Similar calls for standards-based reform continue over a decade later.

It is important to distinguish between the conclusion that students' academic skills are inadequate in some areas and the interpretation of this inadequacy as educational deterioration. NAEP scores do not indicate a consistent longitudinal decline in literacy levels. Some writing skills, such as mechanics, seem to have stayed about the same; other skills show slight increases or decreases in achievement levels, but *no* pattern of overall decline emerges from this research base. The fact that some literacy skills levels show a decline at times does not necessarily point to an overall deterioration in reading and writing abilities. Instead there is a general condition of some inadequate literacy skills that has existed for a fairly long time in American education.

Another widely watched test, the Scholastic Aptitude Test (SAT), showed declining scores between 1960 and 1993 when the average score on the verbal test dropped 53 points out of 800 total points, from an average score of 477 in 1960 to 424 in 1993 (Bennett, 1994). In 1995, the scores were recalibrated, and since that time, scores on the verbal test have remained fairly stable (Applebome, 1997).

We must look to factors beyond a simple lowering of American educational standards for a reasonable account of students' performance in the area of literacy. A major part of the explanation for the pattern may lie in the increased participation of students from nonmainstream communities at all levels, but particularly in higher education. For example, there is a correlation between the percentage of eligible students who take the SAT and the average score: The more students taking the test, the lower the average score will be. This more expansive participation in higher education is a situation quite different from that found not too many years ago, when students who sought to extend their education beyond high school were a fairly homogeneous group. For the most part, they shared proficiency in a common variety of English and a common cultural background. In today's culturally and linguistically diverse schools, this uniformity no longer holds. Schools serve many more students from a much wider array of cultural, linguistic, and educational backgrounds and this change in the make-up of the group taking tests, in itself, could account for the figures on which conclusions about declining scores are based.

Diversity and Test Scores

Test scores are related to diversity in that the tests are not always appropriate for all the groups to which they are administered. The practice of using standardized, norm-referenced tests arose when the school population was more homogeneous than it is now and when there was more tolerance for imposing the dominant group's language and culture on other segments of society. Although test-makers have endeavored to accommodate diversity, there is still a very strong expectation of linguistic and cultural uniformity in test development, validation, and norming. Rather than measuring what they claim to measure (such as intelligence or aptitude), test items sometimes measure instead knowledge of standard forms of the language (Wolfram, 1976, 1983). This means that the standardized test may contain biases against various groups of students in the test population, resulting in somewhat lower scores for those groups. For example, a standardized test might require the student test taker to identify sentences like *Yesterday the truck come there* or *He go to work every day* as unacceptable. For speakers of a standard dialect, the correct response is obvious, based on the knowledge of language that they have acquired unconsciously. For speakers of other dialects, however, this sentence might reflect a linguistically well-formed language pattern, in that it follows a regular pattern of the test taker's dialect. In order to respond correctly to the question, these students must suppress an answer based on the knowledge of language that they acquired unconsciously and appeal to knowledge of external norms.

Do such items measure students' educational aptitude? If *educational aptitude* means ability to learn, then a test of Standard English can in no way be construed to be an appropriate measure. Students all over the world learn in many different languages and dialects. If *educational aptitude* means ability to perform in institutions whose norms call for Standard English, the test might predict future success. However, considerations of educational equity demand that test-takers' Standard English proficiency be tested separately from their ability to learn.

Language attitudes that interpret language change and dialect diversity as signs of language degradation demonstrate naive disregard for fundamental linguistic processes. Furthermore, they may preserve institutional strategies like testing that privilege speakers of standard dialects and classify speakers of other dialects as language deficient because they are outside the norm.

LANGUAGE DEVELOPMENT
IN THE EARLY YEARS OF SCHOOLING

The mismatch between standard tests and students' language may pose problems quite early in students' academic experience. Students using nonstandard grammatical forms, such as multiple negation, or nonstandard pronunciation, such as *d* for voiced *th* (pronouncing *they* as "dey") at the beginning of a word, may be at a particular disadvantage when educators are identifying children with developmental delays. Children from Standard English-speaking communities also may use some of these same forms as they are acquiring their dialect, but for them these forms indicate immature language if they persist past the age of 5, or so. In other words, identical linguistic features give different evidence about children's language development, depending on which dialect they are acquiring. Features that are developmentally inappropriate for standard dialect speakers may be developmentally appropriate for nonstandard dialect speakers. Educators of young children who do not recognize the details of language variation risk misinterpreting students' language structure.

Differences and Disorders

The key consideration in distinguishing between a language difference and a disorder is the language norm of the student's own speech community. Recall that a speech community is a group of speakers who share norms for language use. In a multicultural society, a community may actually subsume several speech communities. Individuals whose speech and language are not appropriate for the norms of their own speech communities are the ones who may be showing genuine disorders. The most effective basis for discriminating dialect difference from language disorder comes from an understanding of normal language variation and specific knowledge about local dialects.

Teachers may need not only to discriminate difference from disorder, but also to be able to react to classifications and possible misdiagnoses by others. For example, a student from an African American working-class community or a working-class European American from a rural Southern community may use the form *f* to correspond with what other speakers pronounce as a voiceless *th* sound, saying "birfday" (*birthday*), "toof" (*tooth*), and "baf" (*bath*). If this student were to be diagnosed as having a pronunciation disorder, the dialectally knowledgeable teacher could make certain observations that would clarify the situation. First of all, in the student's speech, the *f* pronunciation is used only in the middle and at the ends of words, never in the beginning (e.g., never "fick" for *thick*). Thus there is a restricted pattern to the pronunciation, not a general substitution. Secondly, other speakers from the speech community in which the student lives have a similar pronunciation pattern in their speech. Considering these facts in conjunction with other knowledge about dialect differences, the teacher could conclude that the student was using a regular rule of the community dialect and could argue against the diagnosis of disorder that had been made.

Speech and language assessment does not always take into account dialect differences (Taylor, 1986). Therefore, scores achieved on standardized tests to diagnose language disorders may be a problem. Some tests may contain items specifically designed to examine Standard English features; responses that reflect a nonstandard feature in speech are considered wrong. Thus, a speaker of a vernacular dialect might get more responses wrong than a Standard English speaker simply because of the dialect acquired, not because of any disorder (Wolfram & Adger, 1993).

Other aspects of testing may put nonmiddle-class children at a disadvantage. Some of the most innocuous-appearing procedures for getting children to produce a language sample for diagnostic purposes may be fraught with sociolinguistic values. For example, a friendly invitation by an adult to a child to "tell me everything you can about the fire engine on the table" is laden with implicit values about verbosity (the more you tell, the better), telling obvious information (describe the object even though you know the adult knows all about it), and the consequences of information sharing (what a child tells the adult will not be held against the child).

In addition to the items on tests and diagnostic tasks, bias may be introduced at the level of the norming of the test if it is standardized. When a test is normed on a Northern, middle-class population or on a population where these speakers predominate, for instance, these norms may not be at all appropriate for students from a Southern, working-class community due to language and culture differences. Some tests do provide alternative scoring guidelines to accommodate vernacular speakers. However, these norms are intended to account for speakers of the group nationwide, and not all responses are locally appropriate. Bias at both these levels is part of the reason that it is difficult to rely on standardized test results for diagnosis of oral language disorders.

Language at Home and at School

The school experience is quite different from the home experience for all students. All children have to learn new ways of interacting with language when they go to school. Typically, however, the language socialization experiences of middle-class children prepare them to ease into school language patterns. Because the gap between home and school is wider for children whose background is not middle class, their language abilities are not as relevant for schooling. The reason for this bias, as suggested earlier, is that middle-class expectations and practices generally pervade schools.

Question asking and answering behavior is one example of classroom linguistic interaction in which school may not accommodate the early language learning of nonmainstream children very well. The problem lies not so much with language form as with the function and use of certain types of questions. Mainstream children are better prepared by their home experiences to deal with questions that ask for a display of knowledge that the questioner already knows (Heath, 1982).

Consider a typical question from early childhood educational settings, "What color is this?" asked in reference to an object that is in full view of the questioner. Making an appropriate response to such questions is considered an important academic language skill: Students are frequently called on to display information that the questioner knows. But students from some backgrounds do not come to school with much practice in this form of questioning because in their communities, adults' questions more typically ask for information that is not shared (e.g., "Where did you leave your coat?") or function as something other than a request for information (e.g., "Where do you think you're going?"). Children from these communities must acquire new responding skills once they get to school. Teachers who do not share their students' backgrounds and who are unaware of community differences in interacting through language may not provide them with appropriate help. They may suspect that children have language processing problems. In schools with large populations of nonmainstream children, early referrals for language testing are common. Problems inherent in testing such as those previously mentioned make it more likely that the referring teachers' perceptions will be reinforced.

Early Literacy

Another area of school/community language use differences that present problems in the early school years relates to literacy. Many classroom activities build on literacy skills that children are assumed to have acquired at home. Middle-class children usually have many experiences with reading and writing before they come to school. For example, reading stories aloud to young children is common. However, in some communities, oral story-telling predominates. As a result of different experiences with narrative, children may have different ideas about narrative structure.

In early schooling, an important literacy activity is sharing time (or show and tell). Here students practice considering the audience, providing cohesive text, and learning other skills that figure into literacy development. Students may not all be able to profit equally from this experience. Michaels (1981) and her associates studied sharing time in urban, integrated elementary school classrooms. They found that children's story-telling styles affect their success in the sharing time activity and their chance to gain the relevant experience from it. Specifically, White, middle-class teachers expected a linear narrative style, like that used in books where events are linked sequentially. The presentation style of White children generally matched this expectation much more closely than that of working-class

African American children. As a result, the White students could receive helpful feedback for refining their narrative style whereas the Black children often experienced frustration. Their stories were likely to include several episodes rather than one, shifting scenes, and more narrative markers, such as *and then* (also). White teachers treated these episodic narratives as poorly formed and attempted to guide the students toward the literate discourse model by telling them to talk about just one thing (topic-centered discourse).

Such judgment illustrates the general problem in viewing some culturally based practices as deficient rather than different. Furthermore, misunderstanding may serve to widen the gap between home and school experiences for children from some communities. As they learn that their language skills are not valuable at school, they may learn to devalue their abilities and distance themselves from school experiences.

To test whether teacher reactions to children's stories were ethnically based, researchers played specially prepared recordings of episodic and topic-centered stories told in Standard English to students at the Harvard Graduate School of Education. As anticipated, Whites preferred the topic-centered stories and found the episodic stories hard to follow. They believed that the episodic stories were told by low-achieving students with language problems or even family or emotional problems. Black graduate students did not make this distinction. Although they appreciated the topic-centered stories, they commented that the episodic stories displayed good use of detail and description. The story that had suggested serious language problems to the White graduate students was viewed by the African American graduate students as probably produced by a highly verbal, bright child (Cazden, 1988).

Teachers encounter a wide range of language and cultural differences in early childhood and primary classrooms. Children's background experience with language and literacy remains a crucial variable in educational success, but one that may not be adequately explored in teacher education. When teachers share cultural identity with their students, they are more likely to perceive students' language use as appropriate and to support development of the academic language skills that count for success at school and in other mainstream institutions. When they are ethnically different, it becomes crucial for them to investigate the possibility that children's classroom performance is rooted in community practice. Investigation, including teacher research as outlined in chapters 2 and 3, can help educators ascertain whether students' performance is due to cultural norms with which they are unfamiliar, or whether there is a developmental delay.

DIALECT DIFFERENCES
AND CURRICULUM CONTENT

It is possible that dialect differences might affect educational skills other than those related directly to language. Thus, a book by a former high school math teacher maintains that the roots of math problems encountered by working-class African American students are found in dialect differences (Orr, 1987b). The author concludes that "the source of the problem is that certain prepositions, conjunctions, and relative pronouns—essential in English to the expression of certain quantitative ideas—are not used in Black English" (Orr, 1987a, p. 26). This view raises important questions about dialect differences and language use in science and math. Certainly, it must be recognized that some dialect differences may play a role in conveying fundamental scientific functions and operations, so that the potential for dialect interference in this processing cannot be rejected categorically.

At this point, there is little careful, controlled experimentation about language variation influences on math and science skills, so the conclusion reached in the Orr study is premature. As an initial consideration, we must keep in mind that scientific fields typically develop specialized language uses restricted to the field. All students, regardless of dialect background, must acquire the language of mathematics or the language of science, in the sense that they must learn the crucial special conventions of language use peculiar to the field. Neither standard dialect nor vernacular dialect speakers go around uttering everyday comparisons such as "one fifth as many as" or "the sum of five squared is equal to," yet such language uses must be processed and produced in learning fundamental math operations.

Language use in math and science cannot be reduced to a simplistic situation in which standard dialect speakers learn these educational skills in their native dialect and vernacular speakers learn these skills in a different one. Recognizing that all students must learn a special set of language conventions for these fields, we may also hypothesize that the differences between math language and ordinary, everyday language are probably greater for the vernacular speaker than they are for the standard speaker. But the differences are a matter of degree rather than kind, and at this point we do not know whether the extent of the dialect difference is great enough to become a significant obstacle. Only careful, matched, comparative studies of vernacular and standard dialect speakers processing the special conventions of math language can tell us the answer to this question.

We are not suggesting that language is unimportant in math, science, and other content areas. Language is crucial to learning because it is the vehicle through which so much information is processed and passed on. Without it, we would be limited to learning from experience. The National Council of Teachers of Mathematics (NCTM) recognizes the important role of communication and language in mathematics learning in their content standards (NCTM, 1989). Given the importance of language in math and science learning, some educational researchers have devised materials specifically designed to teach minority language students the conventional uses of math and science language (Crandall, Dale, Rhodes, & Spanos, 1989a, 1989b). The materials systematically introduce the language conventions used to convey operations and functions in these subject areas. Box 4.1 shows an exercise for use by student pairs. The student who takes a tutoring role helps the other student phrase algebraic expressions in common terms. Reports from using these strategies are encouraging. Such materials should prove helpful to both minority and majority language students who have to grasp these specialized language conventions.

Box 4.1

Sample Exercise on Language for Math (Crandall, Dale, Rhodes, & Spanos, 1989a, pp. 130–132.)

TUTOR: Help your partner match the algebraic expression or equation with the phrase that best translates it.

EXAMPLE: What does x • 5 represent if x stands for the number of pounds George weighs now?

A) George's weight after he gained 5 pounds.
B) George's weight before he lost 5 pounds.
C) **5 times George's weight.**

1. If h is the height of the Washington Monument, what do you supposed h/2 represents?
   A) Twice the height of the Washington Monument.
   B) The quotient of the height of the Washington Monument.
   C) One half the height of the Washington Monument.
2. What can c + .40c represent if c is the wholesale cost of a wristwatch?

(continued on next page)

(Box 4.1 continued)

A) The cost of a wristwatch after a discount of 40%.

B) The product of the wristwatch and 40% of the cost.

C) The cost of a wristwatch after a 40% markup.

3. If Harry has only dimes and nickels in the cash register, what can d(.10) + n(.05) represent?

A) The number of dimes in the cash register.

B) The number of nickels in the cash register.

C) The amount of money Harry has in the cash register.

4. If an airplane can fly coast to coast, a total of 2400 miles, in 4.5 hours, what can the equation 4.5x = 2400 be used to find?

A) The time it takes to fly coast to coast.

B) The average speed per hour the plane flies.

C) The distance traveled from coast to coast.

5. On a suit priced at $180, the sales tax is 6%. Based on this information, what can the equation $180 • 6% = x be used to find?

A) The amount of sales tax on the suit.

B) The price of the suit.

C) The sales tax rate.

From Crandall, Dale, Rhodes, and Spanos. Copyright © 1989 by Center for Applied Linguistics. Reprinted with permission.

Information about language is crucial for educators in every content area because language plays such an important role. Whether it is a focus of attention—as in English language arts—or simply the vehicle for discussion, reading, and writing in other subject areas, language is central to school curricula and the interaction through which learning is achieved.

FURTHER STUDY

Brooks, C. K. (Ed.). (1985). *Tapping potential: English and language arts for the Black learner.* Urbana, IL: National Council of Teachers of English.
A collection of articles on approaches and methods that may be appropriate for African American learners, including African American English Speakers. Subsections include articles on language, reading, writing, and literature.

Cooper, E. J. (1995). Curriculum reform and testing. In V. L. Gadsden, & D. A. Wagner (Eds.), *Literacy among African-American youth: Issues in learning, teaching, and schooling* (pp. 281–298). Cresskill, NJ: Hampton.

This chapter discusses the links between high stakes testing and curriculum, research on poor test performance by some groups of students, and instructional and testing practices that would improve education for children from minority groups.

Fair Test Examiner

National Center for Fair and Open Testing

342 Broadway

Cambridge, MA 02139

http://www.fairtest.org

The quarterly publication addresses issues in K through 12 assessment and other testing topics, emphasizing equity. The website offers fact sheets, articles from the *Fair Test Examiner*, resources, and links to other relevant sites.

Linguistics and Education. An International Research Journal.

This journal, published quarterly by Ablex Publishing Corporation, covers all aspects of language and education, including dialects. Volume 7, 1995, included two special issues on Africanized English and education.

Lucas, C., & Borders, D. G. (1994). *Language diversity and classroom discourse.* Norwood, NJ: Ablex.

A detailed, sociolinguistic investigation of dialect choice in elementary classrooms. The authors describe children's increasing understanding about the social value of standard and vernacular dialects. Chapter 5, The Bigger Picture, gives a summary and sets the work in economic and political perspective.

5

Oral Language Instruction

One of the most salient issues regarding dialects in schools concerns teaching Standard English. This chapter addresses questions about whether schools should focus on teaching Standard English as a medium of oral communication and how they might do so.

STANDARD ENGLISH AND SOCIAL REALITY

Even though we recognize the fact that all language varieties are complete and coherent linguistic systems, many people argue that the social realities of mainstream American society dictate that all students must learn Standard English and schools must teach them. If it were possible to teach Standard English quickly and successfully to members of communities where other dialects are used, doing so might provide a rather simple solution to all the language diversity problems we have mentioned. After a short time, all students would share the same advantage. Problems of language interference in test taking, writing, and reading would be eliminated. At first glance, then, the solution may seem obvious—teach students to speak Standard English if that is not their dialect. However, as might be expected, the answer is not nearly as simple as that.

For years, debate has ebbed and flowed in the education and linguistic literature, as well as in the popular press, on the topic of teaching Standard English. Just as interest in language issues seems to be waning, debate flares up again when a school system introduces a new Standard English instructional program or, as happened in 1996 and 1997, when a system—Oakland, California—drew attention to its program through an action of the School Board.

One matter to be faced relates to equity. Some observers have opposed teaching Standard English, seeing it as a discriminatory action. The only solution, they maintain, is to change society's attitudes toward various dialects, so that all varieties of English would be accepted. Because research evidence shows that dialects are inherently equal in terms of linguistic structure, there is no linguistic reason to ask people to change the way they speak. Any advantage gained by learning Standard English is social, and the educational benefits that might accrue must be weighed against the costs. In targeting Standard English, certain students would be singled out, and because the instruction would look like remediation, others would assume that these students had some sort of deficit. Proponents of teaching Standard English, on the other hand, argue that given society's attitudes, Standard English must be regarded as a necessary tool for success at school and in the workplace. Because attitudes are extremely difficult to change, schools should provide high-quality instruction in Standard English rather than waiting for attitudes to be altered.

Another issue concerns the impact of instruction. Schools have been attempting, in one form or another, to ensure that all students speak Standard English for a long time. Yet a lot of people who have gone to school continue to use nonstandard forms. We need to confront the relative lack of success that has typified both formal and informal strategies of teaching Standard English. Why isn't instruction in Standard English more successful?

As with all learning, the factor that is probably most responsible for success (or lack of it) in teaching someone to speak a standard dialect is relevance. People are motivated to learn a dialect that is relevant to their lives. With language learning, the group reference factor strongly affects relevance. The desire to belong to a group whose members use a particular language variety is a crucial motivational factor for learning success. In other words, if students from communities where vernacular dialect is the norm identify with speakers who sometimes or usually speak Standard English, the chances are better that they will learn Standard English; students who have no desire for such identification will probably resist all attempts to teach them Standard English. If identification with Standard English speakers leads to rejection of the home culture, undesirable consequences can occur as well.

Showing solidarity with one's social and/or ethnic group can be an important motivation for using a dialect. In fact, the power of language choice in conveying solidarity is so strong that people who are not fluent in a vernacular dialect may use certain highly salient terms, intonation patterns, vocal quality, or vocabulary to suggest their social loyalties. For example, middle-class people of southern origin who are living outside the South may use regional dialect vocabulary (e.g., *y'all* for the plural of *you; fixin' to*, instead of *about to*) to show affinity with other Southerners.

This students' relationships with their home communities play an important role in language learning and language resistance. Students must continue to interact and participate appropriately in the home setting and with peer groups. In order to maintain these important ties, they need to retain some aspects of the native dialect when a standard dialect is acquired.

In an effort to help educators take action with respect to dialect differences, a subdivision of The National Council of Teachers of English (NCTE), the College Composition and Communication Conference (CCCC), adopted a strong position on students' dialect rights in 1974. Part of this statement is quoted here:

> We affirm the students' right to their own patterns and varieties of the language—the dialects of their nurture or whatever dialects in which they find their own identity and style. Language scholars long ago denied that the myth of a standard American dialect has any validity. The claim that any one dialect is unacceptable amounts to an attempt of one social group to exert its dominance over another. Such a claim leads to false advice for speakers and writers, and immoral advice for humans. A nation proud of its diverse heritage and its cultural and racial variety will preserve its heritage of dialects. We affirm strongly that teachers must have the experiences and training that will enable them to respect diversity and uphold the right of the students to their own language. (*College Composition and Communication*, 1974, pp. 2–3)

Although the dialect rights position may seem overstated and unrealistic to some, it rightly points to the unequal burden placed on vernacular speakers in language accommodation. The need for linguistic adjustment is placed squarely on vernacular speakers when there should be an equally strong moral responsibility placed on the mainstream population to alter its prejudices and respect dialect differences for what they are—a natural manifestation of cultural and linguistic diversity.

The dialect rights position may be morally right, but there is still another issue to be confronted. Whether we like it or not, some type of language standardization seems inevitable. This conclusion comes not just from examining the situation in the United States or in English-speaking areas, but from surveying language situations throughout the world (Fasold, 1984). Just as language variation characterizes all languages, the drive for standardization and the tendency toward social evaluation based on language differences are ubiquitous. Thus the crux of the Standard English debate ultimately involves balancing the inevitability of dialect diversity and language standardization with the sociopolitical realities that confer the status of nonstandardness on nonmainstream, vernacular speaking groups.

NCTE did not endorse the CCCC's strong position on dialect rights, but it did prepare its own position declaring that students need to be able to write Standard English and to learn about regional and social dialects. Other language-related organizations have issued position statements regarding dialects (see Box 5.1).

Box 5.1

AAAL position statement

American Association for Applied Linguistics Resolution on Application of Dialect Knowledge to Education

WHEREAS, The American Association for Applied Linguistics recognizes the legitimacy of African American language systems, variously referred to as African-American Vernacular English, Black English, or Ebonics, and their pedagogical importance in helping students acquire standard English;

WHEREAS, Public discussion of the Oakland School Board's decision on the legitimacy of Ebonics and its usefulness in teaching Standard English demonstrates a lack of public awareness and understanding of the nature and naturalness of different varieties of language; and

WHEREAS, Students' competence in any dialect of English constitutes an important resource for learning standard English as an additional dialect;

THEREFORE BE IT RESOLVED at the general business meeting of the American Association for Applied Linguistics, convened on this 11th day of March, 1997:

1. THAT, All students and teachers should learn scientifically-based information about linguistic diversity and examine the social, political, and educational consequences of differential treatment of dialects and their speakers;

(continued on next page)

> (Box 5.1 continued)
>
> 2. THAT, Teacher education should systematically incorporate infor-
>   mation about language variation and its impact on classroom inter-
>   action and about ways of applying that knowledge to enhance the
>   education of all teachers;
> 3. THAT, Research should be undertaken to develop and test methods
>   and materials for teaching about varieties of language and for learn-
>   ing Standard English; and
> 4. THAT, Members of the American Association for Applied Lin-
>   guistics should seek ways and means to better communicate the
>   theories and principles of the field to the general public on a contin-
>   uing basis.
>
> From *AAAL Letter: The Newsletter of the American Association for Applied Linguis-
> tics, 19*(1), Spring/Summer 1997, pp. 7–8. Reprinted with permission.

When the social realities surrounding dialects are fully acknowledged,
schools face a significant challenge in managing dialect diversity respect-
fully and wisely.

STANDARD ENGLISH PROGRAM DEVELOPMENT

Some school systems have developed Standard English instructional programs that use children's implicit knowledge of another dialect to teach the
standard dialect. More often, Standard English instruction proceeds from
outdated curricula that attempt to eradicate the vernacular. This approach is
problematic for the reasons related to social identity, political power, and
pedagogical effectiveness just shown. To break this ineffectual curricular
mold, some very general recommendations can be made.

Policy Development

In the first place, explicit policy must be established with respect to teaching
Standard English, preferably at the school-system level. There is precedent
now for policy discussion because the national standards for English language arts (NCTE/IRA, 1996) and many state standards mention that students must be able to use Standard English. However, because language
variation is linked to ethnicity and social class, opening up questions of
whether or not to teach Standard English and how to treat vernacular dia-

lects may be politically difficult. Therefore, various stakeholders should be involved, including administrators, teachers, principals, parents, students, and employers. Although such discussions may be difficult, they can lead to coordinated, vibrant curriculum and engaging instruction. Whatever decision is reached about teaching Standard English, those who establish policy and set curriculum goals should be aware of the facts of their local language and culture situation and the consequences of dialect instruction. Observation of language use in classrooms will reveal actual patterns of language use. If anecdotes and stereotypes form the basis of policy decisions, there will be little point to revising curriculum.

Policy discussion about dialect curriculum should take into account the two prevailing perspectives on dialects—the **deficit position** that sees dialects other than the standard as inadequate, and the **difference position** that sees them as equal and different. The fact that language differences do not represent deficiencies is an important premise for any educational program, whether or not the choice is made to teach spoken Standard English.

Policy development should also consider curricular priorities. Because vernacular grammatical forms are perceived much more negatively than most of the distinct pronunciation features, a school district might decide that grammatical structure, not pronunciation, should be the focus for oral language instruction. Alternatively, the focus for Standard English instruction might not fall on oral language at all but on writing because the ability to speak a standard dialect may not be as crucial for later success as the ability to use standard forms in writing. The following priority list (arranged from highest to lowest) of language skills in a classroom setting takes into account the social consequences of speaking a vernacular dialect in a Standard English setting:

1. Ability to understand the spoken language of the teacher.
2. Ability to make oneself understood to the teacher.
3. Ability to read and understand conventional written English.
4. Ability to speak with standard grammar.
5. Ability to write with the conventions of standard written English.
6. Ability to speak with standard pronunciation. (Burling, 1973)

Considering where in a list of educational priorities the use of oral Standard English falls for a given school or community is an important step in deciding how, or if, it will be emphasized in the education program.

Whatever decision is made with respect to teaching Standard English, there are ramifications for all content areas. It is confusing to students and ultimately counterproductive to demand one set of language standards in one classroom and another set in others, unless the reason for doing so is established as school policy and is sensible and explicitly explained. If the decision is made to teach Standard English in English language arts, as has usually been done, it can be reinforced in other classes if all teachers share knowledge about dialects and take responsibility for implementing school policy.

Curriculum Development

Development of a program for teaching spoken Standard English should observe certain general principles:

1. *The teaching of Standard English must take into account the importance of the group reference factor.* Students will not be motivated to study a dialect that they cannot imagine themselves using; but if they see that their own group uses that dialect for certain purposes or that groups they would like to be included in use the dialect, they are more likely to regard dialect development as a sensible, natural extension of their language knowledge. Attempting to provide external sources of motivation for the students (e.g., they will need it to get a good job) is another way of dealing with this factor, but convincing students to study a dialect is a tall order when it is related to aspirations that have no immediate relevance to them. Programs of instruction in Standard English can be made optional rather than obligatory, so that some motivation may be assumed for those who enroll. However instruction is organized, the group reference factor must be accommodated.

2. *The instructional program for teaching spoken Standard English must proceed from clear curricular goals.* Two goals for Standard English programs are *bidialectalism* (adding Standard English while maintaining the native dialect) and *eradicationism* (learning Standard English to replace the native dialect). The goal of bidialectalism is preferred, but it is not easily translated into a teaching program. Such a program would emphasize the appropriateness of different dialects for different contexts—probably by including contexts where the vernacular dialect is more appropriate (e.g., talking with a

peer about a problem assignment in biology), as well as those where the standard dialect might be more acceptable (e.g., explaining a proof to the geometry class). Shifting contexts communicates in a practical way to students that standard and vernacular dialects already coexist in their lives, even in a school setting (Adger, 1998), and encourages them to note dialect shifting in contexts outside school.

3. *The teaching of Standard English should be coupled with information on the nature of dialect diversity.* Providing background information on dialect diversity will underscore the social basis for dialect evaluation and strengthen the pragmatic rationale for reinforcing students' control of a standard dialect. Furthermore, because most people find dialect diversity inherently interesting, incorporating information about a variety of dialects can enliven the program. All students in American education should, in fact, be given an opportunity to learn about dialect diversity as a general part of education in language and culture. Giving students experience in investigating various dialects, including their own, can amplify their understanding of dialect diversity and clearly demonstrate the integrity of their own dialect and those of others as full-fledged language systems. It is safe to assume that most students are still being socialized into a deficit perspective and that accurate information about dialect diversity is necessary to confront such assumptions.

4. *The teaching of Standard English should produce an understanding of the systematic differences between the standard and vernacular forms.* Although younger learners seem to profit from immersed exposure, older learners may profit from contrastive approaches that highlight some of the structural differences between the standard and vernacular varieties. Teaching materials for them should juxtapose vernacular and standard features.

5. *Instruction should begin with heavily stigmatized features.* More stigmatized features should be addressed before less stigmatized ones—both highly diagnostic features, such as "aks" for *ask* in AAVE; and general rules that affect many items, such as negation (vernacular *I can't get none* versus standard *I can't get any*). Similarly, because the deletion of the *-s* suffix on third person forms of verbs (e.g., *She goes/go*) affects almost all verbs and is highly stigmatized, it should be addressed early in the program. Less heavily

stigmatized rules, such as the "in'" pronunciation instead of "ing," could be addressed much later.

6. *The dialect of spoken Standard English that is taught should reflect the language norms of the community.* The goal of instruction should be the informal standard dialect of the local community, not some formal dialect of English that is rarely used in the area. This is particularly true for pronunciation features, where local standards tend to exist along with more general standards in grammatical features. Thus, the standard model for Eastern New England will be different from that used in Chicago, Illinois, or Raleigh, North Carolina. In Eastern New England, the standard variety may include the absence of *r* in words like "cah" for *car* and "pahty" for *party* whereas in many Southern dialect regions, the lack of contrast between words like *pin* and *pen* or *tin* and *ten* would be part of the regional standard. In chapter 2 we outline a method for investigating local dialect features.

7. *Language instruction should address interactive norms that typify mainstream speakers at the same time that it respects culturally based differences in interactive style.* Speaking a mainstream language variety includes using particular conversational strategies as well as the linguistic forms that distinguish standard from vernacular language varieties. In particular, conversational routines for specialized uses of language (such as business telephone cells and consumer service exchanges) involve behaviors that extend beyond language structures per se. In other words, using a standard language variety in a business telephone conversation is not limited to using standard grammatical and pronunciation features. It also means that a speaker knows other conventions, such as answering the phone with one's name rather than "Hello." Thus, how a person uses language to communicate particular messages must be considered as an essential part of language deportment that goes along with the use of particular standard forms. At the same time, culturally based interactive style differences must be respected.

Teaching oral Standard English should incorporate several components. Some activities should be directed at sharpening students' awareness of the nature of dialects and developing motivation for enhancing their proficiency in a second dialect. Others pertain directly to learning which structures have standard and nonstandard alternates, and practicing their use in appropriate social contexts.

Language Awareness

Any focus on oral language needs to counter the factual misinformation about language variation that often goes unchallenged in schools with a robust, scientifically based program of dialect knowledge. It becomes even more central in teaching another dialect to establish that both the native and the target dialect are full-fledged constituents of the American English family, with social and political histories and large numbers of users. To ground second-dialect teaching and learning, teachers and students need a solid understanding of the natural sociolinguistic principles that lead to the development and maintenance of language varieties. Furthermore, students, like teachers, need to understand that a dialect difference in no way represents an inherent linguistic or cognitive deficit. An outline of a language awareness program, with sample activities, appears in chapter 8.

Motivation for Learning a Standard Dialect

Often, programs assume that motivation for learning a standard dialect comes from children's desire to eventually assume Standard English speaking roles as adults. But it is hard for anyone to acquire knowledge that seems removed from one's current situation. Therefore, identifying situations in which students naturally use Standard English features can show them that Standard English is already an important medium for them. Students can be involved in identifying Standard English situations at school—probably those in which they speak with authority.

Identifying natural sites for Standard English in the classroom has several instructional implications. The teachable moment occurs in situations where students implicitly agree to use standard features but encounter difficulties. No one likes to be interrupted with edits, but the teacher can note potential problem structures and then conduct minilessons at an appropriate juncture.

Language Learning

Various strategies can be useful for learning Standard English equivalents. One that does not work is correcting vernacular features. In a study of dialect and reading, Piestrup (1973) found that vernacular speakers who were corrected when they used vernacular features actually used more, not fewer, vernacular features over time.

A more positive strategy is reinforcing and augmenting students' existing knowledge of the standard dialect. Activities include **role play** and **dramatization**—having students practice using appropriate dialect patterns as they act out a part. They may plan the scenarios in advance or they may act them out on the spur of the moment. They can assume adult roles like that of a teacher, school administrator, salesperson, doctor, newspaper reporter, or office worker where they must try to approximate the speech styles of people from different backgrounds as realistically as possible. Scenarios may come from real life or from texts the students have read. This activity gives the student the opportunity to vary verbal styles and deliberately switch to alternate dialect patterns. It also gives students practice for real-life situations outside of school where the use of Standard English forms may be crucial, such as in a job interview. (One caution is in order: In instructional settings that include students who are monodialectal in Standard English, they should not be asked to speak in a vernacular dialect. There is a likelihood that they will produce stereotyped structures that are not grammatical in that dialect.)

From a bidialectal perspective, realistic role playing might also include situations where a vernacular dialect is called for, such as in peer group and family conversations. Identifying those situations requires observational research because, again, intuitions are likely to turn up language ideals that do not match language practice. When role play uses both kinds of English, the important function of each is genuinely demonstrated, along with the fact that they coexist in the community. Students tend to be more willing to learn a standard variety when they see clearly that the solidarity functions of their vernacular variety are not necessarily threatened by the addition of a standard variety. The use of role playing and dramatization, combined with a small amount of explicit instruction in Standard English structures, is a practical approach to giving specific attention to the use of spoken Standard English.

In the past, drill techniques for practicing standard dialect structures, built on the principles and methods of foreign language teaching, dominated instruction. Focusing on the specific areas of difference between dialects, they were intended to provide concentrated practice in the new, target structures. These drills include simple **repetition** of a model and conversion of structure (such as making statements into questions), as well as a variety of exercises using realistic **dialogues** as a base.

Despite the fact that **structural drills** have been used in teaching Standard English, there is no convincing evidence that drilling supports learning. One of the major problems with drills is boredom: Information broken down into discrete bits becomes meaningless without context. The field of teaching English as a second language, which has strongly influenced the teaching of Standard English as a second dialect, has moved away from using audio-lingual drills in second-language instruction. Instead, most methods in second-language instruction now emphasize a broader-based communication approach with thematic instruction, integrated teaching, and whole language instruction. In second-language acquisition studies, an important distinction is made between *language acquisition*, which involves the tacit knowledge of language rules that accumulates through exposure to another language, and *language learning*, the explicit knowledge of language rules that derives from the overt teaching of particular structures of language (Krashen, 1981). Knowledge acquired from language learning comes into play primarily under conditions where language structures are consciously focused on, whereas knowledge from acquisition comes into play under more general conditions of communication where language structure is not a primary focus. Because structural drills typically target the forms of language rather than its communicative function, they tend to promote language learning rather than acquisition.

Given the type of knowledge highlighted in structural drills, can these drills be effective in acquiring a second dialect? After all, they are not very useful for acquiring a second language. In answering this question, we must keep in mind both the similarities and the differences between learning a second language and learning a second dialect. In acquiring a second language, communicative fluency is the primary goal, whereas in second-dialect acquisition, the consistent use of a limited set of language structures is typically the goal (because fluency is already achieved). The adjustments to be made are minor. At the same time, they involve a set of dialect items that have become thoroughly habituated for the vernacular dialect speaker. This situation is somewhat different from that of a second-language learner confronted with an entirely new set of specific language items.

It is sometimes more difficult to modify a small set of thoroughly habituated items in a pattern of overall similarity than it is to learn an entirely new pattern because modifying habituated items may involve unlearning as well as learning. If this is true for dialect differences, then there may be little alternative but to focus on some of the structural differences in the systems. If nothing else, specific attention to the structural details of dialect differences may prove useful in those situations where the conscious attention to speech is heightened, as in the direct testing of Standard English rules, in editing written communication, and for some formal social occasions that typically involve more overt attention to language forms. Thus some attention, either directly through structural drills or indirectly through some other language task, is likely to be useful in second-dialect instruction, even if it is less appropriate for second-language acquisition.

Drills may be less boring and therefore more effective when they are clearly tied to situations of authentic Standard English use, and when they are part of short minilessons intended to promote expert performance in the real situations. Consider a situation in which middle-school students are preparing presentations for back-to-school night in which they read aloud a finished piece of writing. Several students use the vernacular "Here go my essay." Whether or not anyone mentions the structure during class critique of the practice session, the opportunity arises to contrast vernacular "Here go" with standard "Here is" or "Here's." A structural drill at this point would be embedded in a naturalistic communicative event in which the standard dialect is used. Structural drills are something like swimming laps: They are not much fun, but doing them is one way to approach proficient performance.

One of the issues that comes up with respect to Standard English instruction is the broad-based influence of the home dialect. It might seem that the work in the classroom would be canceled by the way that parents, siblings, and friends in the home community talk when students leave the classroom. However, it should be noted that children in families that move from one English-speaking area to another often adapt quickly to the regional dialect spoken in the new location, even when their parents maintain the dialect of their backgrounds. Similarly, children whose home language is not English can succeed in learning English and using it in the school setting and with friends while maintaining a different language with their family.

Sometimes group reference factors do interfere, however. For example, some Hispanic students reject their home language and use English almost exclusively: Students living in larger communities where Spanish and its speakers are devalued have adopted those language attitudes. In the case of a vernacular dialect, contexts outside of school may influence dialect learning, again because of the group reference factor. Positive values attached to the native dialect may make it much more important to an individual than a standard dialect. The second dialect may not be learned as quickly because the home variety remains the predominant means of communication for most contexts.

The dialect situation in the school is another important factor. If tensions between groups of students who speak different dialects are high, then vernacular-speaking students may resist using the standard variety: African American students in an urban high school resisted speaking Standard English and other behavior that they saw as acting White (Fordham, 1998). When the vernacular dialect and the associated culture are not devalued in the school and classroom, students may not experience the disjunction between home and school in terms of language. In this case, the symbolic value of studying Standard English may not interfere with learning it.

Another factor to be considered is parents' attitudes toward Standard English instruction. Because they are likely to hold some of the entrenched and unjustified language prejudices found in the society at large, the school will need to justify a bidialectal approach. Schools may choose to make the argument directly. Teachers can help to win parent support by engaging them in community-based dialect awareness programs and asking parents to identify situations where Standard English is used in the community, other than those in which their children participate.

A final issue for developing a Standard English instructional program concerns when to introduce it. The optimum age to begin second-dialect learning has not been established. We can look to studies conducted on foreign- or second language learning for guidance, but there is no simple answer. Because of the common assumption that children can learn some aspects of a new language system more easily than adults can, many programs advocate beginning second-language instruction as early as possible. However, results of research studies have shown that this assumption is not always an appropriate guideline and a variety of cognitive, social, and educational factors must be considered. There may be some language-learning advantage in early childhood due to certain characteristics of brain development but in some situations and for some purposes, adults may actually be more efficient language learners. Care must be taken in generalizing from second-language to second-dialect learning, given the magnitude of sociocultural influences that may play a role.

Some investigators advocate postponing instruction in a second dialect until students can appreciate the social significance of different dialects of English (Burling, 1973). Language awareness instruction beginning in the primary grades can provide a good basis for Standard English instruction beginning in Grade 4 or so. In kindergarten, children can begin to pay attention to different dialects in the stories that they hear and read. They can talk about the general notion of suiting language to the situation and identify ways that language varies from situation to situation in the stories that they hear and read.

Promoting Language Development

All children need linguistically rich classrooms in all subject areas to develop expertise in literacy and in academic talk, the genre of language used in teaching and learning, and in business and professional settings. This genre contrasts with talk for interpersonal communication in that academic talk is often more decontextualized—less elliptical, less dependent on the surrounding talk and other aspects of the context. Meanings are usually made more fully explicit through words in academic talk. Language may also have different functions in academic interaction than in family and community interaction. The case of questioning discussed previously is an example. Some explicit instruction about academic language conventions may be necessary, especially in the early years and especially for children from nonmainstream communities. It will be important, of course, to teach academic language conventions as an addition to community language use, not an antidote to linguistic insufficiency, and to ground instruction in actual communicative situations.

Linguistically rich classrooms provide many opportunities for children to talk on academic topics. To make this possible, social interaction structures need to be varied. Whole class instruction is generally not a very linguistically productive format because it is dominated by teacher talk, both in terms of number of turns at talk and in terms of the amount of talk that children usually do. Moreover, certain students tend to participate more than others even when the teacher does not privilege their participation by calling on them. Pacing in whole group instruction depends on getting appropriate information into the lesson at the appropriate point. Students who are adept at doing this become more likely candidates for lesson talk with teachers. With time, other students may become less and less likely to self-nominate, and they may pay less and less attention so that when the teacher does nominate them, they have little to say. For these students, classroom communication is a listening occasion at best.

Students can be engaged in whole group instruction by varying the participation patterns. The typical classroom interchange involves some version of a basic routine—teacher elicitation/student response/teacher praise—where the teacher has two turns and one student has one turn. An alternative is Think/Pair/Share (Lyman, 1992): After the teacher poses a problem, students take 30 seconds or so to think about it, and a minute or two to consult with their partners. Then several pairs report their results to the group. The linguistic advantage to this arrangement is that because every student must engage in academic talk, each gets practice. A cognitive advantage comes from actively engaging every student in the lesson, and a social advantage from casting young people as students who construct lessons together rather than as passive listeners (Adger, Kalyanpur, Peterson, & Bridger, 1995).

Alternatives to whole group instruction, such as various cooperative learning structures, allow students to practice academic talk. No particular dialect is associated with this genre. In small group structures, vernacular speakers are likely to use vernacular features in discussing academic topics, although it can be anticipated that they will use standard features when the sociolinguistic situation calls for it.

FURTHER STUDY

Coehlo, E. (1991). *Caribbean students in Canadian schools: Book 2*. Markham, Ontario: Pippin.
The strategies for promoting the school achievement of students speaking Creole languages are relevant for teachers of vernacular speakers.

Dyson, A. H., & Genishi, C. (Eds.). (1994). *The need for story: Cultural diversity in classroom and community*. Urbana, IL: National Council of Teachers of English. This collection looks at reading, writing, and oral stories and story-telling as personal, cultural, and social practice. Chapters are organized into sections: Connections between story, self, and others: Why do we tell stories?; Ways with stories: Whose stories are told? Whose stories are heard?; and Weaving communities through story: Who are we?

Hynds, S., & Rubin, D. L. (Eds.). (1990). *Perspectives on talk and learning*. Urbana, IL: National Council of Teachers of English.
This collection includes several articles on dialects in school along with detailed discussions exploring the role that oral language plays in education.

6

Dialects and Written Language

Transforming the spoken (or signed) language system into written forms of communication is challenging for all children. For speakers of vernacular dialects, there are some additional factors to be considered, largely because the gap between the language of their speaking styles and the language of written styles is wider than it is for speakers of standard varieties. The instructional approaches related to writing that practitioners adopt need to differ from those for spoken language because these two productive language processes differ in some fundamental ways. This chapter considers a range of such issues in the teaching of writing to speakers of vernacular dialects.

ORAL AND WRITTEN LANGUAGE

The contrasts between the spoken language medium and the written language medium present several kinds of difficulty for writers. One area of difficulty stems from the need to learn features of a written language style that contrast with the spoken style. Another is a more general problem of accommodating the special communicative demands of the writing situation.

Developing written language expertise requires learning to make choices about style. One element of the stylistic contrast between spoken and written language relates to formality. School writing is generally more formal than either the spoken style that students use most often or the writing that students do in other settings. For example, the use of a phrase like "a good deal of difficulty" might be preferred in an essay or report over the more commonly spoken "a lot of trouble" that is appropriate for conversation or for a note or an e-mail message. The use of conversational features like *you know* and *well* is quite restricted in writing. In some school writing, it may not be considered appropriate to use the first person perspective: Rather than using the form *I think soccer is very popular*, a writer might say *Soccer seems to be very popular*, or *It seems that ...*, and so forth. These are just a

129

few samples of the written language style that a student must eventually learn in order to become a successful writer.

A second dimension of the difference between written language and speech is in the actual circumstances surrounding the acts of writing and speaking. The two media place differing demands on the communicator. The fact that writing is received visually means that any information that can be conveyed orally through different voice qualities (such as stress and intonation) has to be provided in another way. For example, the difference between a compound word, as in *a blackbird*, and a phrase, *a black bird*, which is a matter of stress in speaking, is converted to a spacing difference in writing. Similarly, questions that may be indicated by intonation in speech have to be marked by special punctuation in writing (e.g., *Malcolm took the train?*). Writing involves a set of conventions unique to this medium—the mechanics of writing—that determine when to capitalize, place periods, commas, and so forth. These are quite arbitrary, as indicated by the fact that writing systems vary around the world and different languages use different mechanical conventions, but learning to use them is a necessary aspect of learning to write.

The most significant difference between writing and speaking situations is in the role played by the hearer/reader. In speaking, the hearer is usually present and participating in the social interaction. The hearer is not passive: He or she provides feedback through facial expressions and body orientation, through listening behaviors like "Uh huh" and "Yeah," by commenting and questioning. The speaker and the hearer align toward each other in a kind of conversational ballet, each following the other's lead, getting and giving news about whether or not the interaction is succeeding (Tannen, 1993). If something goes wrong, they can adjust appropriately. In writing, on the other hand, the receiver of the communication is absent and the writer must take care to consider the perspective of this absent, and often unknown, reader. Immediate feedback is unavailable. Unless the reader is well known to the writer, assumptions about shared knowledge that is crucial to interpreting the message may turn out to be ill-founded. References must be made explicit so that the reader will not be confused. Taking into account the absent reader can be one of the most difficult tasks for the child who is beginning to write, as well as for the experienced writer. A young writer might report on vacation activities with *We went to visit grandma. Ginger went too ...*, without making explicit that Ginger is a dog. One of the central tasks of writing instruction is helping children develop their growing awareness of the reader.

VERNACULAR DIALECT AND WRITING

Speaking a vernacular dialect probably has less direct influence on development of writing skill than was once thought (Wolfram & Whiteman, 1971). Speakers of all dialects encounter writing difficulties like those mentioned. This does not mean, however, that the dialect of English spoken by the student can be ignored in writing instruction. In fact, vernacular speakers may have trouble in several dimensions due to differences between their language skills and those that writing requires.

Some vernacular-speaking students may seem to take longer to acquire some writing skills than others do because they are making a bigger transition. The contrast between spoken language and written styles may be wider for the vernacular dialect speaker than for the Standard English speaker in several ways. For one thing, the written style of language may not be as familiar to these students if they have had fewer experiences with written text in the community. In addition, differences in spoken dialects manifest themselves in writing. Thus, a student may write *a* as the form of the indefinite article before both a consonant and a vowel (e.g., *a teacher* and *a aunt*) if this is how the article is spoken. When faced with a great deal of correction of items that vary between vernacular and standard, students may become frustrated and hesitant to try again. Also, they may make other, different errors in an attempt to avoid certain usages from their spoken dialect, a phenomenon known as **hyper-correction**. For instance, after numerous instances of correction, a student might avoid using a structure or begin using structures like *an car* or *an city*. Such usages, which may also occur to a lesser extent in speech, represent an effort to catch potential errors.

The following paragraph, composed by a ninth grader from an African American working-class community, shows influence of vernacular dialect. It was written in response to a teacher's question on a reading passage:

> I would prefer living the way the Hunzakuts live. because they live a whole lot longer and they don't have no crime and they don't get sick and if you are the age of 60, or 80 you still can play many game like you the age of 6 or 9 and don't have to worry about Cancer or Heartattacks. Its would be a whole lot better living their way.

Given detailed knowledge about the student's spoken dialect, we can identify some instances of direct influence. For example, *they don't have no crime* is an instance of multiple negation, a common feature in vernacular dialects of English. The absence of the plural ending in *many game* is also a candidate for dialect influence, as is copula absence in *like you the age of 6 or 9*. These dialect influences can be contrasted with mechanical errors. For example, if the writer had written *your* for *you're*, as in *your the age of 6*, this would be a mechanical error. All speakers of English share the problem of writing words that sound alike but are spelled differently in various uses (*your* and *you're* are like *break* and *brake* in this respect).

This sample of student writing also shows indirect influence from spoken dialect. Hypercorrection is suggested in the construction *its would be*. A fairly common feature for speakers with backgrounds like that of the writer is the absence of the *are* and *is* forms of the verb *be* in sentences like *they nice* or *she here*. It may be that this feature had appeared in the student's writing and was corrected rather frequently, resulting in a sensitivity to the problem of leaving those verbs out. The unnecessary addition of *s* on *its* in the case of *its would be* may represent an unconscious effort to avoid the mistake of leaving *is* or *are* out, but without a full understanding of the structure in question. This example of hypercorrection illustrates that a dialect can influence production of written forms indirectly.

Indirect influence from a vernacular dialect is also evident when dialect combines with writing problems shared by all inexperienced writers. Writing samples from vernacular dialect speakers reflect only selected features from the spoken dialect; other, equally frequent characteristics of speech are seldom found in writing. Some of those that occur are apparently related to general writing development patterns. One study, which compared a large amount of spoken and written data from both standard and vernacular dialect speakers at all age levels, found that all writers, regardless of dialect background, omitted certain grammatical suffixes to some extent in early writing (Farr & Daniels, 1986). These included the verbal *-s* ending (giving *he walk*), the plural ending (as in *many game* from the sample composition), and the past ending *-ed* (*last summer she move to Texas*). For all groups in the sample, the suffixes were sometimes absent, but the frequency was much higher for the vernacular dialect speakers, who also use these features in their speech to varying extents. This pattern indicates that the absence of suffixes in writing is not solely a product of dialect influence. The influence from dialect combines with a general tendency in writing development to produce a pattern involving nonstandard structures in early writing.

TEACHING WRITING

How can teachers support the development of writing skills in their vernacular dialect-speaking students? Farr and Daniels (1986) suggested a set of key factors for writing instruction to be effective for secondary school students from vernacular dialect backgrounds that appear to be readily adaptable for students at any level:

Students should have:

1. Teachers who understand and appreciate the basic linguistic competence that students bring with them to school, and who therefore have positive expectations for students' achievements in writing.
2. Regular and substantial practice in writing, aimed at developing fluency.
3. The opportunity to write for real, personally significant purposes.
4. Experience in writing for a wide range of audiences, both inside and outside of school.
5. Rich and continuous reading experience, including both published literature of acknowledged merit and the work of peers and instructors.
6. Exposure to models of writing in process and writers at work, including both teachers and classmates.
7. Instruction in the process of writing; that is, learning to work at a given writing task in appropriate phases, including prewriting, drafting, and revising.
8. Collaborative activities for students that provide ideas for writing and guidance for revising works in progress.
9. One-to-one writing conferences with the teacher.
10. Direct instruction in specific strategies and techniques for writing.
11. Reduced instruction in grammatical terminology and related drills, with increased use of sentence combining activities.
12. Teaching of writing mechanics and grammar in the context of students' actual compositions, rather than in separate drills or exercises.
13. Moderate marking of surface structure errors, focusing on sets of patterns of related errors.
14. Flexible and cumulative evaluation of student writing that stresses revision and is sensitive to variations in subject, audience, and purpose.
15. Practicing and using writing as a tool of learning in all subjects in the curriculum, not just in English. (Farr & Daniels, 1986, pp. 45–46)

One important conclusion to be drawn from these guidelines for teaching writing is that decontextualized skills-based instruction in written Standard English ought to be avoided, just as with teaching spoken Standard English. It does not lead to able writing, and it alienates students from the pursuit of writing. The process approach to writing, which emphasizes language skills that all students can be presumed to have in rich abundance, deals with grammar and mechanics only after the writing is drafted.

We do not mean to suggest that teachers should not teach Standard English forms to students who use vernacular forms in their writing. There is fairly widespread agreement among educators and researchers that the ability to use Standard English for written work is an important skill (Smitherman, 1995). But writing instruction for speakers of vernacular dialects should not be limited to a focus on contrasting forms, and these contrasts should not be addressed out of the context of writing. Furthermore, dialect differences should not be disproportionately weighted in the evaluation of students' ability to express themselves in written form.

Areas of Vernacular Influence in Writing

Although the research base is limited in terms of the role of a student's dialect background in the writing process, some observations on dimensions of language contrast may be useful for teachers. In using a process approach to writing, teachers may find it helpful to distinguish at least three different types of problems that vernacular dialect speakers encounter in writing:

1. *Organization or progression of an argument or narrative.* Difficulties here are quite common to nearly every developing writer. Organization problems may relate to the writer's assumptions about audience that make the writing task very different from spoken language, as well as to culturally based expectations for how to tell a story or make an argument (Cazden, 1988; Gee, 1990; Michaels, 1981). Specific instruction in the organization conventions associated with literacy can occur as minilessons during the critical review phase of the writing process. They should be shaped by the teacher's clear understanding of influences from students' cultural backgrounds. These influences may reflect patterned differences in ways of achieving textual cohesion.

2. *Mechanical aspects of writing.* The conventions of capitalization, punctuation, and spelling are aspects of the system for writing Eng-

lish that all speakers of English must master, regardless of their dialect. The fact that English spelling does not signify the sounds of the language consistently in a one-to-one relation makes spelling difficult for everyone. Dialect differences, however, introduce an additional set of possibilities for spelling errors. For example, spelling the first vowel sound of *tinder* and *tender* the same way may be related to the fact that these words are pronounced the same in Southern dialects. This would be quite similar to a Standard American English speaker confusing *t* and *d* spellings a word like *therapeutic* (*therapeudic*) because the *t* and *d* are pronounced similarly in this position. This confusion would not arise for speakers of British English who pronounce *t* and *d* between vowels (as in *latter* and *ladder*) differently.

3. *Grammar.* Grammatical differences between Standard English and the student's dialect may interfere in writing. The use of nonstandard verb forms, as in *The girl knowed the answer,* may come from a spoken dialect that regularly uses these grammatical rules. Similarly, the use of expletive or existential *it* for *there* in sentences such as *It was a new student in the class yesterday* in writing may come from a vernacular speaker's normal use of this form in spoken language.

In the strictest sense, the examples given are not really errors, but rather the reflection in writing of the differences in verbal expression, pronunciation, and grammar between the students' dialect and the standard dialect against which the writing is being judged.

Teachers may want to use the classification scheme just given in classifying students' writing miscues. It might also be adopted by students as they learn the process of self-editing. Understanding precisely what kind of difficulty a writer is experiencing with respect to stylistic and dialectal contrast, students and teachers can move more surely toward achieving proficiency in appropriate written forms. Teachers and students might, for example, prioritize their difficulties and systematically focus on different kinds of writing miscues at different points in the achievement of proficient Standard English writing skills.

Another technique is to focus on a set of items rather than on every dialect error and technical mistake in each piece of writing. If possessives become a target of attention, then attending to apostrophes with singular and plural forms makes sense because these items are related. But when the class focuses on possessives, matters of verb tense, double negatives, and capitalization must be put aside for the time being, even if "we just worked on that!" The message that form is secondary to content is not convincing otherwise. There will be times to insist on perfection, but these occasions should be clearly justified by the objective for writing.

Spelling and Dialect

The problems associated with sounding out words to arrive at their spellings do not appear to be that much greater for speakers of vernacular dialects than for other speakers, although some particular items may be influenced by dialect. All speakers are faced with learning the conventions of English spelling where the sound and spelling relationship is not regular: For example, *could*, *tough*, and *though* cannot be spelled on the basis of sound. It seems likely, then, that a child who pronounces *toof* can adjust to the standard spelling *tooth* as well as another child who says *tuff* learns to spell it *tough*. Vernacular dialect speakers may make different mistakes in attempting spellings at various stages, which may draw undue attention to a spelling problem. This potential difficulty can be overcome if a teacher is well aware of the pronunciation features of the dialects spoken by the students so that the sound differences can be taken into proper account in teaching spelling. For example, a teacher in a Southern setting might have to teach the spelling of *tin* and *ten* like other homophonous words such as *two*, *to*, or *too*.

Postponing Editing

The writing process approach restricts error correction to the later phases of writing so as to encourage students to write thoughtfully and at length. Because nonstandard features such as the absence of suffixes do not signal lack of conceptual knowledge, writers can make changes during the revision phase rather easily if instances of dialect interference are pointed out to them. As a practical matter, it may be difficult for teachers who themselves learned to write in a sea of red ink to postpone editing, and students may be concerned with dialect features in their own and others' writing when they are supposed to be focusing on content. However, commitment to producing authentic, high-quality writing, rather than writing for display or remedial skill-learning purposes, suggests that editing be relegated to the back burner during the composing phase. This recommendation should not be interpreted as advice to ignore or downplay editing, but to convey to students that attention to the form of language is distinct from and secondary to conceptualizing and drafting.

Teachers are being urged to give their students frequent and varied writing activities for different purposes across the content areas. However, not all writing needs to be refined through the writing process. Jotting down ideas for a structured discussion, annotating written text, taking class notes—all of these are writing. When students are comfortable with writing, they are more likely to feel capable of producing finished written text with Standard English.

Peer Editing

Peer interaction can contribute to developing writing skills when students have been trained to critique each other's writing and to help edit out errors, when the purpose and the nature of the evaluation task is very clear, and when it is directly tied to a whole class project. From peer editing can come topics for general instruction on mechanics and standard dialect features. For example, if it becomes clear from editing sessions that many students have trouble with possessives as in writing *John hat* for *John's hat* (a problem shared to some extent by both standard and vernacular speakers at certain stages of learning to write), then this feature can become the focus of direct instruction and student attention for a time. This approach has at least two advantages: Contrasting dialect and mechanics conventions are explained in context, and students share in identifying writing problems for explicit instruction.

Dialogue Journals

One strategy to encourage writing without dwelling on form that has been found to work with both mainstream and nonmainstream children is the dialogue journal (Peyton & Reed, 1990; Staton, Shuy, Peyton, & Reed, 1988). A dialogue journal is a bound notebook in which a student and teacher communicate regularly in writing over a continuous period of time. Students can write as much as they want about topics of their choice. The teacher writes back each time the student writes—often responding to the student's topics, but also introducing new topics, making comments and offering observations and opinions, requesting and giving clarification, asking questions, and answering student questions. The teacher adopts a role as a participant *with* the student in an ongoing, written conversation, rather than an evaluator who corrects or comments on the writing. There is no overt correction of the student's writing by the teacher, although the teacher may model particular linguistic features or probe for missing information.

The advantage of this method is that students experience writing as an interactive communicative experience in a nonthreatening atmosphere. They also write about topics that are important to them and explore topics in a genre that is appropriate to their current level of proficiency in writing. Many teachers have found that this opportunity encourages students from quite different backgrounds and with quite different experiences in terms of traditional academic success to feel confident in expressing themselves in writing (Peyton, 1990). Students who feel that they have something to say in writing tend to be much more motivated to develop writing skills commensurate with academic success than those who have not overcome the initial hurdle of finding something to write about.

ASSESSMENT OF WRITING ABILITY

A further difficulty that comes from dialect influence relates to formal assessment. Although errors in writing stemming from dialect features are actually relatively minor in terms of the communicative goal of writing, they often are accorded major importance in formal evaluation. Points of mechanics and Standard English usage are often treated as measures of writing ability, putting the speakers of vernacular dialects at a disadvantage. For example, students' writing ability may be assessed formally by their ability to distinguish between the use of *good* and *well*, or the past usage of *come* (*Yesterday he come to school*) and *came*, rather than the content of their writing.

Such items privilege Standard English speakers and discriminate against speakers of vernacular dialects. In recent years the multiple choice, grammar-based tests that examine students' ability to recognize errors in Standard English usage and grammar have been balanced with writing samples. However, the grammar-based tests continue to focus precisely on those areas where there is likely to be dialect influence from a vernacular dialect. Preparation materials for the writing test in the SAT II include the following sentences as typical items. Students are to determine whether the italicized portion is correct usage:

- By the time Nick arrived at the campsite, the tents had been set up, the fire was lit, and there *wasn't hardly* anything to do except relax and enjoy the mountain air.
- Both novels deal with immigrants from Africa, who, overcoming obstacles, advance *themself* in America in spite of society's unjust treatment towards black people. (Ehrenhaft, 1994, p. 29)

Note the focus on double negatives in the first sentence and plural deletion in the second sentence, both regular vernacular features.

Bias in standardized tests of writing may come from other sources. Items written in a highly literate style, such as the following from the same SAT review manual, may be systematically more difficult to evaluate for students from some social groups:

> • Although I wish it were otherwise, by this time next week I will have had surgery on my knee, which was injured during a hockey game last winter. (Ehrenhaft, 1994, p. 32)

Those who have less experience with text may have trouble detecting that the verbs in this sentence are correct. Differing conceptions of what constitutes good style according to different cultural groups also may have an effect. For example, an item in which the correct answer requires the choice of "reach my destination" over "get there" appeals to a value on the use of a kind of superstandard English in writing. Thus, objective tests of usage and mechanics may be harder for students from vernacular dialect backgrounds because these tests tend to focus on points of dialect differences in usage. Alternatively, they may require choices based on language experiences that are not shared by all groups.

One might conclude that tests involving samples of student writing are more fair for vernacular speakers than those focusing on particular forms, but there are problems with this approach too. It may be inappropriate to judge an individual's writing ability on the basis of a limited sample of one or two short essays produced in a very short time frame. Although this limitation applies to all students, there may be an even greater effect on students who must attend to dialect choices in their writing. Writing samples present other implications for speakers from vernacular dialect backgrounds. Depending on who is scoring the writing, the writer's use of certain structures that the scorer regards as errors may lead to a lower overall score being assigned, in spite of scorer training. For example, a rater who considers a feature like suffix absence to be a very severe problem may be unable to see positive qualities in a passage when it contains such dialect influence.

There is also some possibility of cultural bias in the topics assigned by the test. F xample, a writing prompt for 13-year-olds on the NAEP asked students to describe for a friend a reproduction of a Dali painting. If students could not imagine themselves ever doing such a task, they might not be able to display their writing skills to full advantage. More holistic approaches avoid the unreasonable attention to dialect contrast, but they do not solve the dilemma of assessing writing development in a dialectally diverse population. They also do not necessarily counter the tendency of evaluators to assign lower scores in their overall assessment simply based on the occurrence of some nonstandard dialect forms in writing. Thus, the common but unjustified association of the appearance of dialect features with the inability to express oneself must be recognized and countered by those who engage in holistic assessments. The classroom teacher is probably in a much better position to assess student writing development than the scorer of a large-scale test, both because of being able to track individual progress across time and because of knowing precisely which dialect differences the student is managing. Informal classroom diagnostic assessments serve to help teachers particularize writing goals for students and plan subsequent instructional activities. Portfolio assessment, a more structured approach, has gained a wide following. Students select some of their writings for teacher evaluation and defend them in a conference with the teacher, stating why they value these writings. When this approach is used as intended, students play an active role in assessing their own work and in articulating their personal view of excellent writing.

FURTHER STUDY

Farr, M., & Daniels, H. (1986). *Language diversity and writing instruction*. Urbana, IL: National Council of Teachers of English.

This resource offers both a theoretical framework and practical suggestions to educators who wish to improve the teaching of writing to secondary-school students who speak vernacular dialects.

Hampton, S. (1995). Strategies for increasing achievement in writing. In R. W. Cole (Ed.), *Educating everybody's children: Diverse teaching strategies for diverse learners: What research and practice say about improving achievement* (pp. 99–120). Alexandria, VA: Association for Supervision and Curriculum Development.

This summary of current thinking on writing instruction does not focus on students' dialect, but it does concern teaching writing to students from outside the mainstream. It is clear and practical.

Shaughnessy, M. P. (1977). *Errors and expectations: A guide for the teacher of basic writing*. New York: Oxford University Press.

Although somewhat dated, this book provides a helpful approach to the systematic study of writing errors. It is not specifically targeted for writers from vernacular dialect backgrounds, but there are many aspects of the approach that will prove useful to teachers of these students.

7

Language Variation and Reading

A correlation between social class and reading failure seems to be indisputable. We can infer from this correlation that the likelihood of developing reading problems is increased if a person is a member of a vernacular English-speaking population. But establishing that there is a correlation does not mean that speaking a vernacular variety *causes* this failure. Actually a number of other factors correlate with low reading achievement as well, ranging from the number of books available for reading in the home to parental education (Chall & Curtis, 1991). We cannot say that any one of them is directly or solely responsible.

There are several other arguments against concluding that speaking a vernacular dialect is the primary cause of reading failure. First, there are many successful readers who come from vernacular English-speaking backgrounds. By the same token, not all Standard English speakers are proficient readers. Speaking a vernacular variety does not account for reading failure, and speaking a standard variety does not guarantee reading success. However, because a correlation has been noted between the type of dialect spoken and reading achievement, it is important to consider how dialect differences may relate to the reading process and how reading specialists, teachers, and other practitioners can take the differences into account. This chapter addresses questions about what teachers need to know and do to help vernacular dialect speakers develop reading proficiency.

WRITTEN LANGUAGE AND SPOKEN LANGUAGE

The closer a person's spoken language variety is to the language of reading materials, the easier it will be to learn to read. Because the language of most reading material is closer to Standard English varieties than to other varieties, we can predict that it is easier for the Standard English speaker to learn how to read this material. However, two points of qualification need to be

141

made. The first concerns the general relationship of spoken language and written language, and the second concerns the relationship between standard and vernacular dialects.

The language of the printed text is not as similar to the spoken language of Standard English speakers nor as different from the spoken language of vernacular English speakers as is commonly assumed. There are many differences between written and spoken language regardless of the speaker's dialect background. Certain constructions used in many early reading materials are not used by English speaking children in natural conversation. For example, adverbs are often placed at the beginning of the sentence in books for young children, both basal readers and trade books, as in *Over and over rolled the ball* or *Up the hill they ran*. Such sequences are not found in children's speech. Similarly, primers show peculiar patterns such as the repetition of noun phrases, as in *The boy has a boat. The boy likes the boat. The boat is red*. This construction is quite unlike spoken discourse, where pronouns and other anaphoric devices are used for successive references (e.g., *The boy has a boat that he likes. It's red*.) All people learning to read English actually encounter language structures that differ somewhat from their spoken language.

However, the language of reading material will differ more for the speaker of a vernacular variety than it will for the speaker of a standard variety. In addition to confronting structures that occur only in writing, the vernacular speaker will find that written language consistently uses certain structures that are spoken only occasionally in vernacular dialect. For example, a vernacular speaker who uses multiple negatives (e.g., *He didn't hit nothing*) more often that standard negatives (*He didn't hit anything*) will not find any multiple negation forms in beginning reading materials. Thus there is a contrast between spoken and written language for all readers, but the contrast is greater for the speaker of a vernacular dialect.

The second qualification concerns the vernacular English speaker's ability to understand Standard English. As mentioned in chapter 1, vernacular English speakers generally have little difficulty in comprehending spoken Standard English. Although some research has shown that dialect differences in verb tense features may cause reading difficulties for vernacular speakers (Steffensen, Reynolds, McClure, & Guthrie, 1982), in general the language of reading materials, which is more like Standard English, poses few comprehension problems for vernacular English speakers.

Thus the basic problem encountered by vernacular English speakers is not totally, or even primarily, the difference between their spoken language and the written language of the reading material. At the same time, we want to recognize that there are some aspects of dialect differences that may impact the reading process for students and the instruction process of those who teach vernacular-speaking students.

INFLUENCES OF DIALECT DIFFERENCES ON READING: WHAT TEACHERS NEED TO KNOW

For a number of reasons, detailed knowledge about dialect differences is important for anyone who teaches reading. In the first place, knowledge of these differences can affect how a teacher analyzes a student's oral rendition of a reading passage. Traditionally, oral reading has been one way of determining a student's strengths and weaknesses in handling written material, particularly in the early stages of reading development. Consider the following example of oral reading by a child who speaks a vernacular variety of English:

Text: Ruth's brother missed a game, and the coach doesn't like it.

Reader: Ruf brovuh miss' a game, and da coach don't like it.

Several items are noticeably different in the oral rendition of the passage: the pronunciations of *Ruth* and *brother*, the absence of the possessive *-s*, the absence of the *-ed*, and the form *don't* for *doesn't*. All of these contrasts are perfectly predictable in terms of the reader's spoken dialect. Furthermore, this rendition would signal appropriate decoding and accurate comprehension because none of the differences change the meaning of the text. Dialect differences do influence the oral reading of a passage, then, but they do not necessarily affect understanding of the meaning of that passage. It is important for reading teachers to know how dialect differences might be manifested in oral reading so that they can distinguish between a real reading problem (i.e., in decoding and/or comprehension) and appropriate dialect reading.

Information about dialect differences is also important for interpreting responses in student worksheets and standardized tests of reading. Consider, for example, a worksheet or a test that includes the following items:

(1) *Choose the words that sound the same*: pin/pen reef/wreath find/fine their/there here/hear

(2) *Choose the correct word to complete the sentence*:

Yesterday he *come/came* over to the house.

He *done/did* what he had to do.

In some vernacular dialects, *pen* and *pin, fine* and *find*, and *reef* and *wreath* sound the same, so all the word pairs in (1) might be chosen as identical. In some dialects, *come* and *done* are the appropriate grammatical responses for item (2). Students who make those choices may be reflecting regular patterns in their spoken language varieties. If teachers know about students' group-based pronunciation and grammatical patterns, they can see how some of these responses reflect dialect features.

Information about dialect differences is important no matter what approach is being used to teach reading. Imagine a classroom scenario from a lesson for young children using the Language Experience Approach in which students tell or retell stories for subsequent use as a reading text. When students use vernacular dialect features in presenting a story, they may be told to talk right so that the teacher can transcribe a good story. Or the grammar and vocabulary may be changed into Standard English as the student's story is written. In translating the children's stories into what the teacher considers proper English or school language, she or he communicates an attitude about the worth of the children's language. The message for students in this situation is that their language is wrong or inadequate. Teachers who are knowledgeable about dialect differences may decide to write down what students say and to use this text as one source for reading instruction.

Knowledge about dialect differences, then, affects instruction, student assessment, and attitudes about those who do not speak standard varieties of English. In fact, this conclusion has been supported by the judicial system. In a landmark court decision in Ann Arbor, Michigan in 1979, the presiding judge ruled that a school system was at fault for not taking the dialect of speakers from vernacular-speaking backgrounds into account in teaching reading. As a part of the ruling, the system was required to implement a program that would educate reading teachers about dialect differences, and to devise a reading program that would incorporate information about spoken language varieties into effective reading instruction for students from certain communities (Farr-Whiteman, 1980). This judicial decision gives legal emphasis to the importance of understanding dialect differences for those who teach reading.

What particular knowledge about dialect differences is necessary for a reading teacher to work effectively with students from a spectrum of ethnic and social class communities? Researchers who have looked at language variation and reading have suggested, either explicitly or implicitly, several types of information that reading teachers should have. First, general knowledge about the nature of language diversity is required. Without understanding the systematic and patterned nature of differences, it is difficult to appreciate dialects for what they are—natural subgroupings in a language. Second, knowledge of particular structures in the dialects spoken by their students, whether they are standard or vernacular, is also necessary. This specific information is essential to understanding why certain forms occur, where they occur, and how they should be viewed in the context of assessing reading skills. Essential to a full understanding of a reader's performance are details such as the vernacular pronunciation rule that explains why a speaker would pronounce *tint* and *tent* the same (the absence of contrast between *i* and *e* sounds before *n*) and the grammatical rule that explains why *done* may be used as a simple past tense form.

Beyond language form, information about children's cultural backgrounds can be indispensable in teaching reading. This is particularly true when there is a cultural or social class difference between the teacher and the students. Two areas of contrast are noteworthy. The first concerns the background knowledge that students bring to reading. One study showed that even highly proficient readers of English—graduate students—made glaring mistakes in comprehension when they read a text set in a different culture. After reading a passage on an agreement about gifts that the bride's family would give the groom's family, graduate students said that the passage concerned an agreement about gifts to be exchanged (Steffenson, Joag-dev, & Anderson, 1979). Students' own cultural expectations about the exchange of gifts between bride and groom certainly may have encouraged their misreading. Teachers need to examine assumptions about children's background knowledge and compare them with the experiences that students actually bring to the text.

Some teachers whose cultural backgrounds are very different from their students' have been getting first-hand knowledge of the funds of knowledge in their students' homes and communities as a way of understanding the background knowledge that students bring to reading and other school tasks (Gonzalez et al., 1993). Investigating funds of knowledge involves teacher-researchers visiting some of their students' homes to talk with parents and other family members. Their goal is to discover the knowledge and skill areas that families possess and the social networks in which they participate. Teachers engaged in this qualitative research meet in study groups to compare the findings from their visits and reflect together on the match between students' background knowledge and classroom practices.

A second domain of cultural contrast concerns the fit between reading at school and the culturally determined language and literacy patterns of the home and community. Some researchers have focused on emergent literacy—the abilities and orientation toward literacy that children develop along with other language skills before they go to school that form a basis for reading instruction. Purcell-Gates (1995) told the story of one urban Appalachian family in which the parents' lack of literacy had given the children very different experiences with reading than their schools anticipated. In this family, reading books involved inventing stories to match the pictures. As a result, the children did not understand the cuing function of print. Early reading instruction that assumed this knowledge did not meet these children's needs. Understanding the role that reading and writing play or do not play in students' homes and communities can help a teacher to make reading experiences more congruent with students' expectations and thus more meaningful.

Teachers need general knowledge about linguistic and cultural differences among the students they teach, and they need detailed knowledge about their students' dialects. Beyond that, they need to know the status of students' emergent literacy. School districts need to provide continuing professional development about linguistic issues in students' school performance.

APPROACHES TO READING
AND DIALECT DIFFERENCES

Regardless of their spoken dialect, all readers automatically, unconsciously apply their general linguistic skills to the task of reading. In order to obtain meaning from the printed page, readers must be able to recognize words and employ their tacit understandings of grammar and semantics. They figure out the grammatical relationships among the words and the meanings of sentences and longer stretches of text, drawing on both their implicit linguistic knowledge and their general background knowledge. Facility with these general language and inferencing skills is crucial regardless of the reader's dialect. Theorists do not agree about the way in which linguistic skills are applied in the reading process. Two basic models have been proposed to account for the reading process—a bottom-up model and a top-down model. A major difference between the two lies in their emphasis on the importance of word recognition in reading. In the bottom-up model, print is first translated into an inner representation of the sounds of the word.

The reader then applies the same linguistic strategies and inferencing techniques that are used in oral interaction, so that the written text is processed and understood as if it were spoken language. From this perspective, the initial critical skill in learning to read is decoding—deriving the pronunciation of the printed form from the written letter combinations provided in the text and then organizing it into larger chunks of syntax and meaning.

According to a top-down model of reading, the initial decoding into silent speech is not necessary: This bit-by-bit processing, changing print to sound, is typically bypassed by competent, mature readers in the actual reading process. Rather, the reader processes much larger chunks of information—larger syntactic and semantic units—than the bottom-up model suggests. The reader focuses on individual words to confirm expectations about the meaning of the larger chunk (Goodman, 1986; Smith, 1973).

Recently, researchers have concluded that both top-down and bottom-up processes occur in reading and that the processes are integrated (Stanovich, 1992). Word recognition is seen as a necessary first step toward comprehension for all readers. Background knowledge and expectations about meaning contribute to reading comprehension but also to word recognition, particularly for novice readers.

Models of reading that emphasize word recognition have led researchers to focus on the role of phonological processing in reading—relating print to sound. Especially for beginning readers, the ability to identify sound segments in words has been found to be very important for word recognition (Ehri, 1991). It has been recommended that early reading instruction emphasize strategies that increase students' phonemic awareness, the knowledge that print is related to sounds and sound segments that signal meaning. Beginning readers may experience that connection through activities such as moving the first phoneme (sound) of a word to the end—for example, changing *Dan* to *and*. Encouraging beginning readers to write by inventing sound/letter connections is another way of reinforcing the relationship.

In considering connections between dialects and reading, it is important to draw a distinction between *dialect influence* and *dialect interference*. *Dialect influence* refers to a dialect rendition of a piece of text that has no consequence for its meaning whereas *dialect interference* refers to renditions where dialect contrast may affect the comprehension of the passage. There is more evidence for dialect influence than there is for interference. For example, dialectal patterns of identical pronunciations for different words (e.g., *find* and *fine*; or *send* and *sinned*; or *Mary, merry, marry*) have the potential to interfere with meaning, but pronunciation differences usually result in little or no interference in reading text in context.

Generally, dialect differences in grammatical forms also reveal influence rather than interference because they do not result in meaning differences. In oral reading, changing forms such as *Sally's hat* to "Sally hat" or *five cents* to "five cent" does not show that the reader has altered the basic meaning of the text. However, some oral reading changes from the written text do not preserve the author's meaning. If a student reads *He's done trying to please everyone* as "He done tried to please everyone," the meaning of the text is not preserved. In the written sentence, the verb indicates present completed action. The text might be interpreted as *He's done trying to please everyone for the time being, but he'll resume again later.* However, in the substituted sentence, the reader seems to have comprehended a completed past action (signaled by the meaning of *done*).

As these examples show, there is a possibility of direct dialect interference, but dialect influence is more common. Naturally, students can be expected to use the pronunciations associated with their dialect group when they read aloud or when they take part in other literacy activities. From a practical standpoint, most dialect changes of the text are not important to comprehension. Teachers must have enough background knowledge about the reader's dialect to recognize when a particular variation from the text is simply a reflection of dialect influence and when a variation results in a meaning change. What can derail comprehensibility in oral reading is a teacher's interrupting reading with pronunciation corrections. Teachers who know the characteristic pronunciations of their students' dialects will expect and accommodate dialect influences on children's literacy activities.

INSTRUCTIONAL METHODS

Most researchers and educators believe that reading instruction for all students should focus on helping them to develop comprehension strategies (Garcia & Pearson, 1990). There has been considerable controversy about the best teaching methods for doing so, however, and several issues may impact reading instruction for speakers of vernacular dialects in particular.

One issue related to how teachers can help students develop reading proficiency concerns skills-based instruction and, by association, traditional basal readers. The scope and sequence approach to reading that basals support has been criticized. The problem is that anything taught out of context tends not to generalize very well. Discrete bits of knowledge about sound/letter correspondence are unlikely to help children read better when these bits are not directly connected to other aspects of the reading process. Yet vernacular dialect speakers, who belong to the groups experiencing the most trouble with reading, are more likely than standard dialect speakers to receive just this kind of instruction, for several reasons. Very often, elementary schools place students in reading groups according to their scores on the tests that accompany the basal reading series or some other standardized testing program. Problems associated with testing nonmainstream children and with the school's expectations about emergent literacy lead to these children's placement in low reading groups.

The nature of the reading experience in low reading groups may actually make it more difficult for students to learn to read. Children in low reading groups are more likely to receive skills instruction than comprehension strategy instruction and to be corrected for renditions that are attributable to dialect influence instead of decoding or comprehension difficulty (Collins, 1988). Furthermore, the teacher may be more likely to be interrupted when working with the low group because other students recognize the low social status of poor readers (Borko & Eisenhart, 1989). As a result, children in the lower groups may experience reading as fragmented and boring, and progress at a slower rate than that of children for whom reading is more interesting. Those who may have less experience with print outside of school thus may have less rich experiences with print inside school. If the home/school disjuncture is perpetuated, then these children may find themselves repeating skills lessons and basal readers, falling farther and farther behind mainstream students. Eventually they may be diagnosed as learning disabled.

The whole language approach has been seen as an alternative to skills-based basal reading programs. This approach integrates reading with writing and speaking, uses trade books, and deemphasizes skill and subskill instruction. The teacher's role is to facilitate students' experiences with literacy by providing materials and opportunities for rich, authentic encounters with written and spoken language.

The whole language approach has been criticized on several bases. Some critics claim that the antidote for decontextualized skills-based instruction should not be a disregard for reading skills, but an approach that presents reading as an authentic, interpretive experience and presents skills as secondary but still important processes (Adams, 1990; Clay, 1987). Others fault whole language for failing to teach beginning readers from nonmainstream backgrounds the sound/print correspondences that are integral to accessing print and that middle-class children may have learned outside of school (Delpit, 1988). Critics from outside of education contend that early literacy instruction encouraging children to invent spellings propels them toward a disregard for standard language conventions.

No matter what the instructional approach, teaching beginning readers to relate printed language to the sounds of oral language is vulnerable to difficulty arising from dialect variation. Two traditional methods, learning sight words (look–say) and phonics (letter/sound correspondences and sound blending), have somewhat different implications depending on students' dialects. Teaching sight words relies on the student's learning the graphic configuration of whole words. Instruction emphasizes understanding the words both individually and in the context of the sentence. Phonics instruction, on the other hand, focuses attention on the relationship of print to sounds, with the intent of helping students decode, or sound out, the combinations of letters and blend them to make words. It is one way of building phonemic awareness. As with sight-word methods, there are numerous variations to the phonics approach, but they all stress learning sounds that correspond to the letters of the alphabet.

Because the phonics approach emphasizes sounds, speakers of vernacular varieties may encounter some difficulty if a teacher is not sensitive to the pronunciation patterns in the child's language variety. If asked to sound out words, students might be confused by spelling that does not capture the sounds of their dialect, such as *tired* ("tard" in Southern dialects). In oral reading, a child who speaks AAVE may read "baf" for *bath* or "smoov" for *smooth*: These represent an appropriate sound/print relationship for that child given the rules of the dialect. Similarly, an urban or rural Appalachian child may read *yellow* as "yelr" or *fire* something like "far." These renditions represent appropriate sound/print relationships for that child because they conform to the rules for that dialect, just as pronouncing *car* as "cah" does for a child in New England. In order not to misjudge an appropriate dialect rendition as a sound/print error, the teacher needs an awareness of appropriate sound/print relationships in the child's variety of English. Disadvantages for speakers of vernacular dialects are unlikely if the sound differences are taken into proper account.

Dialect pronunciations of words are expected with the sight-word approach as well, although these may not be as problematic because the focus is on whole-word recognition rather than individual letter/sound correspondences. Nonetheless, it is important to be aware of the dialect-specific pronunciations of words that differ from Standard English. For instance, when the printed word is *then* and the student pronounces it like "den" or "din," or when the student who speaks AAVE pronounces *stream* as *skream*, it should not be assumed that the item has been misidentified.

It is unlikely that vocabulary differences between dialects would affect students' performance in word identification exercises in the sight-word approach; that would be more likely to occur in reading extended text. For example, if a student's native dialect uses *sack* as the word referring to what the text calls a *bag*, this difference may occur in the student's oral reading. In the phonics approach, such a difference is not as likely to occur as in the sight-word approach because of the emphasis on breaking down the word into its individual letter/sound correspondences. The need for understanding vocabulary differences between dialects is especially important in teaching sight words.

Beyond issues of teaching children to convert print to sound, there remain questions about how to facilitate students' ability to comprehend the printed word. A consensus model for teaching students who are placed at risk for school failure, developed from research, incorporates features from several reading instruction models (Garcia & Pearson, 1990). First, the consensus model emphasizes teacher modeling: Teachers describe their own practices in comprehending a piece of text by reading and thinking aloud about their inferential processes. Teachers of vernacular speakers could express their knowledge of predictable dialect influence on the reading process. For example, teachers might analyze the sentence considered earlier, *He's done trying to please everyone*, anticipating possible dialect interference. This sort of demonstration has the effect of demystifying the reading process for children who may have had less exposure to reading or different experiences with it before coming to school.

Another dimension of the consensus model is the use of authentic texts: trade books, content area texts, class members' and other children's writing. This is writing intended to communicate, to engage, to delight readers rather than to drill them in reading skills. It stands in contrast to texts or text fragments contrived for teaching reading. Teaching comprehension strategies occurs in the context of children's efforts to comprehend an interesting text, rather than as a decontextualized exercise with a lesson on finding the main idea, for instance. Including work by authors who share the students' cultural background and who incorporate vernacular dialect in their writing can entice children who might otherwise experience literacy as focusing exclusively on other people's cultures and other people's language. The model's third element concerns managing the complexity of the reading task. Instruction that decomposes reading into separate tasks (e.g., decoding skills and decontextualized comprehension strategy instruction) has resulted in stultifying reading experiences that have not been very successful. The consensus model highlights scaffolding—supporting students' efforts to get meaning as they read. The scaffolding principle would encourage teachers to ignore dialect pronunciations that do not interfere with meaning.

Actual dialect interference could be handled in minilessons that are explicitly linked to the text but do not interrupt the reading process.

Work at the Kamehameha Early Education Program in Hawaii incorporated a kind of scaffolding based in children's home culture (Au & Jordon, 1981). In an attempt to address the problem of poor reading by Hawaiian students, educators made reading lessons more like important language events in Hawaiian culture, called talk story and storytelling. Rather than taking turns at talk during teacher-led discussion, children jump in to extend each other's ideas in talking about the text. Children volunteer their responses, rather than waiting for the teacher to call on them. The program also incorporated forms of classroom organization that led to informal learning situations for the students. Students worked together in small groups at learning centers. By responding to narrative and social conventions of the students' background, this approach helped to narrow the gap between home and school learning.

Finally, the consensus model has students participate in planning reading and writing activities and in evaluating their own performance. Teachers maintain control of instruction but students share responsibility for their own literacy development. This principle may be particularly important for vernacular-speaking students, whose literacy performance sometimes strikes teachers as being impoverished and in need of discipline. When teachers see students taking responsibility for learning, they are more likely to view them as competent.

Other approaches to literacy development that integrate strategies have been quite successful with student populations that include vernacular dialect speakers. Success for All is one example. This program balances basic skills instruction with reading for comprehension and pleasure and emphasizes expert tutoring for students having trouble with reading. Originated at Johns Hopkins University, Success for All aims to help students develop strong literacy and math skills by the third grade (Slavin, Madden, Dolan, & Wasik, 1996).

A number of specific strategies could be mentioned as appropriate for these same student populations. One is Reciprocal Teaching (Palincsar & Brown, 1987), a strategy that groups children with diverse abilities and achievement levels for reading and writing tasks. Teachers work with the groups, helping children talk and write about what they have read and how they understood the text. This process engages students in talk about literacy and literature in order to scaffold reading development. It invites vernacular dialect speakers to use their oral language abilities in literacy activities.

Expert teachers have a repertoire of instructional strategies that is continually refreshed through professional development experiences. When teachers understand and value students' language abilities and previous literacy learning, when they acknowledge and accommodate low literacy, they are able to continually adapt reading instruction to their students' needs. In their classrooms, students engage with text in ways that build reading abilities throughout the school years.

READING MATERIALS AND DIALECT DIFFERENCES

One of the issues that has been raised by linguists and educators with respect to dialects is the nature of the reading materials used in schools. Are the same reading materials appropriate for students from middle-class, standard-speaking communities and for vernacular-speaking students from non-middle-class communities? For schools that do use basal reading programs, should anything be done about the language in reading materials in light of the different dialect backgrounds that students bring to the reading task?

Two basic positions have been taken regarding the language found in the reading materials that are written especially for beginning readers—texts with controlled vocabulary and sentence structure. Some investigators advocate changing the language in the text because it is inappropriate for speakers of vernacular dialects; others maintain that Standard English language texts can be used for everyone because speakers of other dialects can make the necessary adjustments to the text. Both positions arise from a concern about the mismatch between the oral language of the students and the language typically found in Standard English reading materials, but they differ in the strategies they propose for dealing with this issue. The alternatives also seem to be based on different assumptions about the significance of the mismatch, which we have discussed.

Matching Materials and Dialects

Those who advocate changing the materials focus on reducing the mismatch between reader and materials by making the language of the materials more closely resemble the student's language. This change can be accomplished in several ways. One strategy is to remove (or avoid) certain constructions that are sensitive to dialect differences. For example, in standard varieties, an indirect question can be formed as *He asked if he could come*; other dialects might use *He asked could he come*. In dialect-neutral materials, this structure would be avoided. A structure common to all dialects of English could be used instead (in this case, a direct question such as *Can he come?*). Such grammatical changes in the texts are intended to make the materials as neutral as possible with respect to dialect differences.

Dialect Readers

Another way of changing the text advocated by some investigators involves actually incorporating vernacular English constructions. Thus, an indirect question formed as *He asked could he come* would be used instead of *He asked if he could come*. Similarly, multiple negatives (e.g., *He didn't do nothing*), vernacular subject–verb agreement patterns (e.g., *We was here*), and alternate tense markings (e.g., *In those days, we went to the fiesta and we have a good time*) would be used in the texts designed for communities where these patterns are the norm. Such texts are used to build on the existing language skills of beginning readers, not to replace other reading materials.

In the dialect-reader approach illustrated next, a child who speaks a variety such as AAVE could use a reading text that is written in the dialect (as in Version 2) rather than a text that is written in Standard English (as in Version 1). The AAVE passage, taken from one of the early experiments in dialect readers (Fasold & Wolfram, 1969), represents a deliberate attempt to incorporate the grammatical and vocabulary features of this dialect. Changes in spelling to capture pronunciation contrasts are generally considered nonessential.

Version 1: *Standard English*

> "Look down here," said Suzy.
>
> "I can see a girl in here.
>
> The girl looks like me.
>
> Come here and look, David.
>
> Can you see that girl?"

Version 2: *Vernacular Black English*

> Susan say, "Hey you-all, look down here!"
>
> "I can see a girl in here.
>
> The girl, she look like me.
>
> Come here and look, David!
>
> Could you see the girl?"

                                        (Fasold & Wolfram, 1969, p. 52)

Once word recognition skill is well established, the reader would begin a transition to reading Standard English texts with vernacular and standard dialect versions placed side by side. Later texts would gradually eliminate vernacular constructions, and the materials would eventually conform to the patterns of Standard English. Even though the original intent was that dialect readers would be written for all vernacular English dialects, the only materials that have ever been prepared are in AAVE.

The use of dialect readers has always met with very mixed reactions. Many people, including traditional educators and community leaders, view anything that is written for children in a dialect other than Standard English as educationally unsound. They consider dialect readers to be patronizing and unnecessary educational accommodations (Labov, 1995).

Despite strong opposition, a small group of people enthusiastically advocated the use of dialect readers. Some research was conducted on the effectiveness of these materials as compared to traditional reading materials. Field-testing of *Bridge: A Cross-cultural Reading Program* (Simpkins, Holt, & Simpkins, 1977) with secondary students receiving remedial reading instruction found that the gains of these students in the Iowa Test of Basic Skills exceeded those of the students who were given regular reading materials (6.2 months of gain for a 4-month period versus 1.2 month gain for those using the regular reading materials). Nonetheless, research on the effectiveness of dialect readers has been very limited, probably because of public criticism. Negative reactions from a wide range of people virtually eliminated dialect readers from consideration as a serious alternative to more traditional basal reading texts for a long time.

Recently, linguist John Rickford and educator Angela E. Rickford contended that it was a mistake to discard dialect readers and that experimental research on their effectiveness should be resumed (Rickford & Rickford, 1995). They recommended experimenting also with new ways of introducing and using dialect readers that would allay people's wariness. Because dialect readers are so different from basal readers and because they use language that is unexpected and even sometimes proscribed at school, stakeholders would need to be informed about the rationale for their use. Parents and other community members would need to be told that dialect readers represent a transition to reading Standard English, and that teachers share with parents the goal of supporting children's Standard English development. The Rickfords and their students have conducted research on a small scale with dialect readers that include both vernacular and standard versions of the text. Their work, which is still quite preliminary, suggests that vernacular dialect readers may be most effective with middle school boys.

Language Experience

Dialect readers attempt to be true to the general language patterns of a particular group of speakers. Language Experience texts reflect the language patterns of an individual speaker. The rationale for this approach is that the greatest asset of beginning readers is their existing ability to use and understand language. Building on this assumption, the teacher guides students in creating their own texts—stories that the children initially present orally and the teacher writes down. As a result, these texts reflect individual children's linguistic systems and interests.

In using a language experience approach with vernacular dialect speakers, transcribing can become problematic, as we noted. If teachers edit the stories into Standard English, the written version is not a fully accurate rendition of what the child actually said. But even with some editing, the language of the written text is still closer to the child's own language experience than that found in either traditional basal reading texts or reading materials for vernacular dialect speakers. Moreover, the content reflects familiar contexts and activities.

Materials that match students' dialects fall on a continuum. At one end are language experience materials, which in their unedited form represent the closest written rendition of any given reader's language system. At the other end are dialect readers. When accurately written, they are certainly a closer representation of the oral language patterns of dialect speakers than are Standard English texts, but they are still only an approximation of an individual reader's speech.

Despite the differences between them, dialect readers and student-created texts that incorporate dialect differences may be lumped together when people react negatively to their use with dialect speakers. At the heart of most people's objections is the use of nonstandard linguistic patterns in print.

Vernacular Dialect for Rhetorical Purpose

People seem willing to suspend their objections to printed vernacular dialect in literature where it is used to evoke cultural identity. The audience for the text in this case is all students rather than only those who are vernacular speakers, and the works are selected for their literary value rather than their language form. Reading work by established writers such as Mark Twain, Richard Wright, and Nora Zeale Hurston can present the opportunity for high school students to extend their knowledge about language in society, and for teachers to introduce language study into the study of literature.

Discussion might focus on the authors' purposes for using vernacular features in writing, where readers are more accustomed to seeing standard dialect. Students could consider whether the features seem to be an accurate rendition of speech or a general means of conveying a character's social identity. They might investigate whether the language of the text matches dialects in their own area. They might compare vernacular dialect in fiction with that in poetry, and recent works with older ones. How does Alice Walker's use of vernacular in the novel *The Color Purple* compare to Paul Laurence Dunbar's in the poem "When Malindy Sings"? Is dialect used similarly in Richard Wright's *Native Son* and Toni Morrison's *Beloved*, novels written 50 years apart? How does Lee Smith, who often uses versions of Appalachian English in novels such as *Oral History*, represent the dialect of some of her mountain personalities? Studying the dialect of written text can be a valuable route to enhancing students' knowledge about their own dialects as well as those of others.

READING AND THE ACQUISITION
OF STANDARD ENGLISH

Sometimes, educators have suggested that it is easier for a young vernacular-dialect speaker to learn to read if Standard English is taught first. If this strategy were used successfully, then the question of dialect mismatch and reading would be a moot point. There are several reasons why making Standard English a prerequisite for reading instruction is unadvisable, however. In the first place, mismatch between the oral dialect and the written text cannot be eliminated completely: All speakers of English are confronted with differences between written and spoken language, regardless of their dialect. Furthermore, many speakers of vernacular dialects show little difficulty in overcoming this mismatch. There is no clear-cut evidence that learning Standard English will, in itself, increase the ease of learning to read. On top of that, there is little evidence that spoken Standard English is being taught successfully to young children. Even if Standard English could be taught successfully, postponing reading instruction until children achieve Standard English fluency might cause delays in other academic areas that are dependent on reading skills.

Another approach is teaching Standard English simultaneously with teaching phonics by correcting a student's vernacular English response to a Standard English response during phonics instruction (Piestrup, 1973). This approach has some serious pedagogical flaws. It is very confusing to mix teaching Standard English with teaching reading because the two goals are not necessarily linked. If an AAVE speaker reads *find* as *fin'*, or a rural Appalachian dialect speaker reads *cliff* as *clifft*, or a Southwestern Latino or Native American student reads *sing* as *sin*, there is no reason to suspect a letter/sound correspondence problem. Such a problem would be indicated, however, if the same students read *cup* as *sup* or *big* as *dig*. The first set of examples involves accurate reflections of sound/letter correspondences in particular dialects, whereas the second set does not reflect the patterns of any of the dialects. To correct both types of productions as if they were the same phenomenon can only lead to confusion on the part of the learner because readers depend on their tacit knowledge of language to guide their approach to the printed page. A New England child might similarly be confused if told that the only correct way to read *car* is with an *r* at the end, or that *caught* and *cot* must contain different vowel sounds to be read accurately. The acquisition of a spoken Standard English dialect requires different skills from those involved in the acquisition of word recognition skills. If the two activities are combined in the same instructional task, student confusion can be expected. If comprehension is the aim of reading, then teaching Standard English is a quite irrelevant task.

BEYOND DIALECT IN MISMATCH

The mismatch in language form is not always the central factor in accounting for reading difficulty among some speakers of vernacular dialects. It has been pointed out that there are situations in the world where the mismatch between reading materials and oral language is much greater than that experienced by vernacular dialect speakers in the United States, yet there do not appear to be significant numbers of problem readers in these countries. In Switzerland, the texts are written in standard German and much of the northern population speaks Swiss–German, which is quite different from standard German, yet significant reading problems are not encountered (Fishman, 1969).

A further consideration about materials for teaching reading to vernacular dialect speakers concerns their content. Those that assume background knowledge from mainstream culture can be problematic for readers from other backgrounds. For example, a student having little direct experience with mountain biking or mowing lawns might find passages that presume knowledge about these topics somewhat difficult, based solely on written materials.

Researchers investigating the role of background knowledge in reading comprehension asked urban African American children and rural White children to read a passage about a sounding episode—an African American speech event involving ritual insults (Reynolds, Taylor, Steffensen, Shirey, & Anderson, 1982). Clearly the reading was culturally biased in favor of the African American readers: As anticipated, the African Americans scored considerably higher in comprehension than the rural students, a fact suggesting that some of the problems of African American readers are due to differences in background knowledge. (As the researchers discussed the experiment with the African American readers, they explained that some of the rural students might not understand the story. An African American student exclaimed, "What's the matter? Can't they read?")

Teachers can accommodate students' background knowledge in a number of ways when they recognize what their students' funds of knowledge consist of. There are any number of excellent trade books from which teachers may select those that closely match students' cultural background. Other books will entice readers to return to them repeatedly for deepening comprehension. Thematic approaches to reading can build up background knowledge in such a way that children have the resources that they need to become interested in a text. Integrated approaches such as whole language in all of its guises extend background knowledge as children write and talk about the content of texts that may be distant from their experience. Prereading experiences for students of any age can help them activate relevant knowledge. After reading, students may do response-to-literature tasks that lead them into the text again from a different approach. For example, they may rewrite a part of the story or enact a sequel to it. Older readers might try their hand at writing a new passage, emulating the author's style.

Cultural and social values about the role of reading in community life play an enormous role in learning to read and in developing reading proficiency. In fact, the cultural and social value assigned to reading may be one of the most essential factors correlating with reading success (Purcell-Gates, 1995). Perceptions about reading as an essential skill for social and occupational ability can be quite class- and culture-specific. Expert teachers of children from nonmainstream backgrounds often organize instruction in ways that create a literacy-valuing classroom culture—with frequent, informal writing tied to reading; regular journal writing; literacy events across the curriculum; silent reading; oral story reading; and story performance: in short, a highly participatory, highly literate environment. One study showed the value of such classrooms for children from vernacular dialect speaking backgrounds who came to school with very limited literacy experiences. By the end of first grade, they were able to catch up in reading with children who had been read to at home. They also scored higher than children from similar backgrounds in skill-based curricula (Purcell-Gates, McIntyre, & Freppon, 1995).

Thus, reading problems and reading failure for different dialect speakers and cultural groups have a complex explanation. The kinds of materials that are read play a role. Language structure, content, and readers' background knowledge all may influence reading success. The nature of the interaction between reading materials and different groups of vernacular English speakers is still being investigated.

READING TESTS AND DIALECT DIFFERENCES

A final issue regarding the correlation of low reading scores and vernacular-speaking populations concerns reading assessment. There has been debate for some time as to whether standardized tests, especially standardized reading tests, reflect the linguistic and cultural realities of vernacular English speakers. Some test takers who score low on these tests do, in fact, have genuine reading problems of one type or another, and this diagnosis holds up through multiple measures of reading ability. Concern about the quality, form, and context of the tests is not meant to deny the seriousness of the reading problems that do exist for some individuals. The question is whether the tests accurately reflect the nature or existence of reading problems for all students.

In some cases, serious misclassification may occur on the basis of test scores; some students may be classified as overall poor readers even if they are not, due to the kinds of language and cultural items included in the test. In other cases, particular reading problems may be indicated by scores that are really a function of language differences. Certain speakers may be penalized because their native dialect is different from that used by the norming sample on standardized tests. For example, a deficiency in word recognition skills might be diagnosed from the results of a test when, in fact, the test taker has simply applied the pronunciation rules of the native dialect in responding to the test items. The possibility of language bias in standardized reading tests along with other factors that have been identified must be taken into account in order to make an accurate assessment of reading skills.

There are several ways in which dialect differences may affect scores on standardized reading tests. First, some reading tests may contain sections that depend on Standard English pronunciations. The decoding exercise mentioned earlier that relies on the ability to distinguish *pen* from *pin* and *death* from *deaf* clearly indicates a bias against speakers of Southern-based dialects in which these pairs of items are pronounced the same. In responding to the test items, the child sounds the words out according to the dialect's pronunciation rules and does not note a difference. Because the norms for the test reflect the Standard English pronunciation distinction, the child's responses are marked as incorrect, even though they accurately follow precise rules of the native language variety.

In some elementary level tests, students may be required to choose the correct word to complete a sentence. For example, the child must choose between *them* and *those* in a sentence such as *I have read (them, those) books* or between *no* and *any* in a sentence such as *I didn't hear (no, any) noise*. According to the Standard English norm, one correct form is predicted (*those* and *any*) in these sentences, but the grammatical rules of the test taker's home dialect may predict another choice (*them* and *no*). It should be noted, in fact, that responses produced in accordance with native dialect rules show accurate word recognition and thus demonstrate reading skill. But systematic grammatical differences may lead to faulty assessment of reading ability.

In another testing task, students are asked to match words to pictures, demonstrating their word recognition skills. For example, students are given a drawing that shows trees with falling leaves and are asked to select the word that appropriately labels the picture. The options in the test are *aunt, autumn, summer,* and *town*. This test item holds several potential difficulties. First, the term *autumn*, which the test developers consider correct for this scene, may not be thoroughly familiar to some children because it is associated more with written language contexts than spoken language. Children with less written language experience may expect the word *fall*. Another difficulty with this item concerns students' cultural experiences with seasons. Elementary schools typically emphasize seasons as a school topic, thus establishing the relationship between leaves and fall as background knowledge that is relevant to school tasks. For children in Northern rural and suburban locations in much of the United States, this emphasis is congruent with out-of-school experience. But for children living in the inner city, wearing jackets may be a more salient indicator of fall than is falling leaves. In areas that do not have deciduous trees, such as South Florida and Southern California, or where seasons are marked in a different way, such as rainy and dry seasons in the U.S. Virgin Islands, the test item makes a different semantic demand than it does for children in the East and Midwest.

A test may assume that vocabulary items have the same meaning associations for all readers when that is not the case. It can inaccurately assess the reader from a region, social class, or cultural group that uses a vocabulary form different from the response required by the test. The vocabulary test in

Box 7.1 is intended to demonstrate what can happen when a reader's skill is assessed using unfamiliar test items. In this instance, the vocabulary is from a historically isolated island dialect spoken on the Outer Banks. It includes items discussed in chapter 2.

Box 7.1

An Ocracoke Vocabulary Test (or How to Tell a Dingbatter from an O'cocker)

1. *dingbatter*
   a. baseball player in a small boat
   b. a husband
   c. a wife
   d. an outsider

2. *up the beach*
   a. by the sea
   b. north of the island
   c. the national parkland area
   d. Oyster Creek

3. *meehonkey*
   a. a call used in hide-and-seek
   b. a call made to attract ducks
   c. the call of an angry person
   d. an island marsh plant

4. *quamish*
   a. an upset stomach
   b. a fearful feeling
   c. a bad headache
   d. an excited feeling

5. *pizer*
   a. a small boat
   b. a deck
   c. a porch
   d. a small Italian pie with cheese

(continued on next page)

(Box 7.1 continued)

6. *mommuck* (also spelled *mammock*)

   a. to imitate someone

   b. to bother someone

   c. to make fun of someone

   d. to become close friends with someone

7. She's *to* the restaurant.

   a. She ate at the restaurant twice.

   b. She's been to the restaurant.

   c. She's at the restaurant.

   d. She's going to the restaurant.

8. *fladget*

   a. gas in the alimentary canal

   b. an island men's game

   c. a small island bird

   d. a small piece of something

9. *puck*

   a. a small disk used in island hockey games

   b. a sweetheart

   c. a kiss on the cheek

   d. a mischievous person

10. *O'cocker*

    a. a derogatory term for an Ocracoker

    b. an outsider's mispronunciation of the term Ocracoker

    c. an island term for a native Ocracocker

    d. an island term for bluefish

11. *token of death*

    a. a coin needed for admission to Hades

    b. a sickness leading to death

    c. a fatal epidemic

    d. an unusual event that forecasts a death

12. *louard*

    a. lowering an anchor

(continued on next page)

(Box 7.1 continued)

   b. an exaggerated exclamation, as in "louard have mercy"

   c. moving away from the wind

   d. a fatty substance

13. *Russian rat*

   a. a unique island rodent

   b. an island gossip

   c. a vodka-drinking narc

   d. a mink

14. *Hatterasser*

   a. a storm that blows in from Hatteras

   b. a ferry ride from Ocracoke to Hatteras

   c. a person from Hatteras

   d. a fishing trip in Hatteras Inlet

15. *skiff*

   a. a large boat

   b. a small boat

   c. a strong wind

   d. a light wind

16. *scud*

   a. a dirty person

   b. a tire mark in the sand

   c. a ride in a car or boat

   d. a missile

17. *dost*

   a. sick, especially with the flu

   b. a square dance step

   c. a small crab

   d. toast, especially wheat bread

18. *fatback*

   a. bacon

   b. an overweight Hatterasser

   c. an island pig

(continued on next page)

(Box 7.1 continued)

    d. menhaden, a type of oily fish

19. *goaty*

    a. a small beard on the chin

    b. smelling foul, like a goat

    c. having the appearance of a goat

    d. silly

20. *slick cam*

    a. a well-oiled engine part

    b. greased down hair

    c. a glossy picture

    d. very still water

Ocracoke Vocabulary Score

    0-5=a complete dingbatter

    6-10=an educable dingbatter

    11-15=an average O'cocker

    16-20=an island genius

Answers:

1. d	11. d
2. b	12. c
3. a	13. a
4. a	14. c
5. c	15. b
6. b	16. c
7. c	17. a
8. d	18. d
9. b	19. b
10. c	20. d

Group-based differences in language are not limited to pronunciation, grammar, and vocabulary, even though these are the ones most commonly referred to in discussions of dialects. Tests of comprehension entail language processes beyond the literal meaning of a passage. Comprehension tests assess the child's ability to make inferences—the ability to connect explicitly stated information with other information believed to follow naturally from it.

Background knowledge is among the factors that contribute in an essential way to inferring meanings from text. We have pointed out that what constitutes a person's background knowledge is constrained to an enormous extent by considerations of culture and ethnicity, social class, gender, race, age, geographical location, and other factors. Consider the following description of redwood trees in terms of the background information that a child from New York City and a resident of Northern California near the Redwood Forests might bring to the test:

> They are so big that roads are built through their trunks. By counting the rings inside the tree trunk, one can tell the age of the tree. (from the Metropolitan Reading Test for third graders, cited in Meier, 1973, p. 17)

If an urban child is less familiar with the use of the terms *rings* and *trunk* in connection with trees, this passage might conjure up a fairy tale image. On the other hand, a child raised in proximity to the forest might find such a description almost trivial by the third grade. Background knowledge is an essential consideration in reading comprehension.

Consider another account, also taken from a disclosed version of the Metropolitan Reading Test:

> "Good afternoon, little girl," said the policeman. "May I help you?"
>
> "I want to go to the park. I cannot find my way," said Nancy. "Please help me."

> Given this part of the reading passage, the child is supposed to select the one right ending for the story:

> The policeman said,
>
> a. Call your mother to take you.
>
> b. I am in a hurry.
>
> c. I will take you to the park. (from Meier, 1973, p. 22)

Quite obviously, cultural values about the role of the police play an important part in selecting the answer: Readers with different value orientations might select different answers.

Background knowledge, cultural presuppositions, and vocabulary, along with grammatical constructions, may be subject to group-based constraints. Standardized tests have no way of accommodating these regular differences between social, regional, and ethnic groups.

It is important, then, to consider various kinds of systematic characteristics of social and ethnic groups in scoring test responses. Test responses may be analyzed in terms of the systematic differences between dialects. If a working-class African American child marked *mile* and *mild* as sounding the same because of the regular pronunciation rule that can eliminate the *d* in *mild* or a Southern rural child noted that *tire* and *tar* sounded the same, this response would be interpreted as a legitimate reflection of a dialect difference, and not a reading error. Similarly, if a native Philadelphian marked items such as *ran* and *man* as not rhyming because of the distinct vowels in these items (the *a* in *ran* as *a*, and the *a* in *man* something like *e-u*), this, too, would be interpreted as a legitimate reflection of the Philadelphia pronunciation system, and not as a reading error. An interpretation of responses that takes into account dialect differences can help the evaluator see what effect dialect may be having by identifying responses that are legitimate in terms of the language system of the test taker but not in terms of the standardized norms of the test. In order to make such an interpretation, the evaluator must be familiar with the systematic differences between the various dialects of test takers, whether they be rural Southern, urban African American, or Southwestern Chicano. Naturally this need holds for informal assessment as well—understanding why certain forms might occur in the oral reading of passages in contrast to the actual forms written in the passage. It is crucial, however, to determine the test-taker's dialect and not to assume it, based on race or ethnicity.

But other factors bear on fairness in testing as well. Certain aspects of the testing situation favor social and behavioral traits typically associated with middle-class children. For example, values about early acquisition of reading and writing skills, displaying abilities through paper and pencil tasks or performing for unfamiliar adults, working quickly, concentrating on the test topic, among others, can be quite culture-specific.

The techniques used to obtain information in many standardized reading tests also presume particular kinds of skill-training that may be culture-specific. For example, phonics skills are often measured through tasks that focus on rhyming words, words sounding the same, or parts of a word rather than the whole word. Reading vocabulary may be measured by tasks that call for identifying word association types: same meanings (synonyms such as *proprietor* and *owner*), opposite meanings (antonyms such as *tall* and *short*), specific and general category relationships (e.g., *python* and *snake*), or descriptive, dictionary-like definitions (e.g., a *linguist* is a person who studies the patterning and organization of language). These assessment tasks for getting at meaning are, of course, different from real life language use where meaning is derived from words in context. A specialized set of skills may be needed to succeed in tests of various facets of reading; the test-taker's failure to interpret the tasks in the intended way can lead to a diagnosis of reading failure where, in fact, it may not exist.

Equity in assessment is a very complex issue, and no simple approach emerges as best. Schools often use multiple methods of assessing reading achievement so that scores from standardized reading tests are not the exclusive measure of reading skills. Informal assessments and criterion referenced tests are being recommended. Performance-based assessments in which test-takers are required to produce a product or a process based on their understanding of a text are being used for state-wide assessment in several states.

Asking students why they chose particular answers is also useful. Getting a glimpse of the reasoning behind the child's answer can be quite enlightening. In the comprehension test item about the police officer just mentioned, a child could supply a very appropriate rationale for selecting the alternative, "I am in a hurry," instead of "I will take you to the park." Background knowledge from the child's culture might indicate that police officers are doing their job when they are hurrying from one place to another taking care of troublesome situations. Investigation may determine that there are very different cultural perceptions regarding officers' responsibilities. Certain answers that are wrong according to the norms of a test might be very reasonable indications that the child is, in fact, reading with considerable understanding, even if it involves a perspective different from that assumed by the author or test constructor. For educators who are concerned with a genuine understanding of students' reading skills, specific information of this type may be considerably more useful for placement and instruction than objective scores.

This chapter argues, as do other chapters, that educators need to have broad understanding about variation in language. Beyond that, they need to know the details about their students' dialects and cultural backgrounds. It is not enough to have a general respect for group-based differences. Specific understanding of students' dialects makes it possible for teachers to support their students' reading development in concrete, informed ways as they engage students from diverse communities and language varieties.

FURTHER STUDY

Gadsden, V. L., & Wagner, D. A. (Eds.). (1995). *Literacy among African-American youth: Issues in learning, teaching, and schooling.* Cresskill, NJ: Hampton Press.
Well-known researchers and educators discuss issues of historical and contemporary access to literacy, literacy in home and school contexts, school policy and classroom practice concerning literacy, and curriculum and testing.

Purcell-Gates, V. (1995). *Other people's words: The cycle of low literacy.* Cambridge, MA: Harvard University Press.
This case study tells the compelling story of the author's work with a nonliterate mother and her young son who are urban Appalachians. The title comes from the mother's assessment of her difficulty in learning to read books written in language that was not her own. The writer shows how she took into account the home literacy traditions and dialect difference in supporting the mother's and son's literacy development.

Rickford, J., & Rickford, A. (1995). Dialect readers revisited. *Linguistics and Education, 7,* 107–128.
This article discusses a recent attempt to experiment with dialect readers. It also reviews some previous experimentation with dialect readers and concludes that the abandonment of dialect readers was premature and empirically unwarranted.

Simpkins, G., Holt, G., & Simpkins, C. (1977). *Bridge: A cross-culture reading program.* Boston: Houghton Mifflin.
One of the few programs in which vernacular dialect is incorporated into reading material at an incipient stage in the reading process, this is a primary example of a highly controversial approach.

8

Dialect Awareness for Students

Dialects are often treated exclusively as problems that must be accommodated at school. If different communities use different patterns of speaking, then educators must guard against bias in testing, for example, or they must consider dialects when confronting writing problems. In point of fact, language variation can also be a fascinating area of study for students that invites them to learn how languages are structured and how they are used. Many educators and linguists are now encouraging the active study of dialects—including vernacular ones—as a regular part of the curriculum for all students. For example, the standards for the English language arts developed jointly by the International Reading Association and the National Council of Teachers of English include, "Students develop an understanding of and respect for diversity in language use, patterns, and dialects across cultures, ethnic groups, geographic regions, and social roles" (NCTE/IRA, 1996, p. 3). Many of the standards developed by states have a similar focus. The study of dialect diversity in the language arts curriculum can benefit standard and vernacular dialect speakers alike by giving them information and skills for language investigation to counter the simplistic, erroneous language stereotypes that are ubiquitous in our society.

Investigating the structure of vernacular dialects and their role in speech communities has additional advantages for students from vernacular-speaking backgrounds. When the language of indigenous communities becomes an object of serious study for students, rather than a problem or a taboo topic, the gap between home and school that vernacular-speaking children frequently encounter is diminished. Students at all grade levels can conduct ethnographic and linguistic research in their own communities, gathering information, testing hypotheses, and writing reports (Heath, 1994). Dialect patterns in the community form a natural topic for this kind of activity.

170

This chapter suggests what inclusion of dialect diversity as a topic in the school curriculum—in English, language arts, social studies, and elsewhere—might entail. It presents excerpts from dialect awareness curricula that have been used successfully in several locations, including a Northern metropolitan area and several areas in the rural South. This curriculum exemplifies the sort of information about dialects that students need to know and that they enjoy learning. Awareness about dialects and knowledge about dialect diversity form the basis for student inquiry into dialects in their communities.

RESOURCES FOR LEARNING ABOUT DIALECTS

Traditionally, language arts materials for both primary and secondary levels have neglected dialect diversity. If they treat it at all, materials focus on regional differences in vocabulary and do not address systematic pronunciation differences in any detail. Matters of social dialect contrasts have usually been taken up from a deficit perspective, particularly with regard to grammar. Nevertheless, such materials have some utility. Teachers may find them useful for presenting dialect vocabulary differences from different parts of the country. Rather than merely noting that regional differences exist, however, students might make use of this information for a cross-disciplinary project in which they plan a hypothetical month-long trip around the United States. Their projects could incorporate attention to vocabulary (and other dialect) differences that the travelers are likely to encounter, in addition to other information considered relevant, such as topography and population density. Better yet, students can go out into the community and interview residents of different ages or people who have moved in from different areas to get a living picture of dialect differences in their community.

Dialects can be approached more comprehensively as an active object of study for the students and as a key to insights about the nature of language that would be almost impossible to get from secondary reference sources. Every school has nearby communities that are linguistically interesting both in their own right and in how they compare with other communities. They can be valuable sources of data for the students, giving them an opportunity for first-hand observation of dialect diversity. Observation of diversity can, of course, often be accomplished in the school, but going out into the community will seem more like research, at least at first. Consider, for example, a student in New York City. For the most part, New Yorkers are aware of dialect differences in the city and between speakers from their region and other regions of the United States. Unfortunately, such diversity is often seen in terms of unwarranted stereotypes rather than as a valid object of study (consider the topic of so-called Brooklynese). Carefully collected data from some of the New York communities can provide a base from which an accurate understanding of the systematic nature of dialects can be developed (consider the availability of ethnic groups—Jewish, Italian, and Puerto Rican, for example—and social class varieties that may be in proximity to the school). In a locale that is not ethnically diverse, students may have to travel to find dialect diversity, but even in such a setting there will be diversity according to age and status. There are also likely to be some residents who have moved from other areas and retained certain contrasting linguistic features. Both individual introspection on the part of the students about their own speech and collection of samples of speech from other residents in the area may serve as a database.

WORKING WITH DATA

Data from speech communities around the school can help students understand concepts like the nature of language and the nature of language variation that are mentioned in state standards and local curricula aligned with them. Specific activities can be designed dealing with particular features of a dialect along the lines of the dialect study procedures outlined in chapter 2. For example, a class of students might consider the use of structures like *He come here yesterday*. In collecting similar instances from the speech they hear around them, some students may notice that *have came* also occurs. When they find instances like *knowed, I seen it*, or *have went*, they may begin to notice that some verbs seem to take different forms from those used by their teachers and from the writing in their standard school materials. They may also notice patterns in the degree to which different people tend to use forms like these.

From an investigation of past tense verb forms, students can be led to make many valuable observations. First they will have to consider the notion of standard usage as they use it as a basis for comparison. Then they will need to consider the system of irregular verbs in English, so they can identify those that do not take the regular past tense ending *-ed* (like *knew* or *came*). At this point the class might delve into the history of English in order to find out where these irregular verbs come from. They could look into the older patterns where there were more extensive endings used on verbs and see that today's irregular verbs are the descendants of the strong verbs of earlier periods in the development of English. They could also see that at one point, there were many more irregular verbs than there are today (Millward, 1989; Pyles & Algeo, 1982). This inquiry would allow them to see firsthand the shifting nature of what is considered standard and what is considered nonstandard usage.

In looking at the different forms used by different speakers, they also can discover some principles about the nature of language. For instance, several of the patterns that emerge in nonstandard use of irregular verbs involve processes of regularization. Speakers in some groups may use *knowed* or *growed*, with the regular *-ed* ending on the verb, rather than an irregular form. This pattern of use shows how living languages treat irregularity. Students may discover controversy over verbs like *dive* or *sneak*, where some members of the class and individuals in the community prefer the regular form, and some prefer the irregular version (*dived/dove, sneaked/snuck*). This is a case where no single standard form is accepted. There are numerous other lines of inquiry that can open up from the initial investigation of how speakers actually use a feature like irregular verb usage—as opposed to how they think they use it. With some planning, students working through a unit like this could learn a great deal about their language and their community.

Further value comes from the opportunity for students to engage in a kind of scientific investigation. Examining how speakers in their community use language provides a natural laboratory for the students to make generalizations based on an array of data. Their own knowledge of the language can form the basis for hypothesizing rules that govern the use of particular linguistic items. These hypotheses, formulated on the basis of initial observation, can then be checked against additional data that they can also provide or obtain from other speakers. In a sense, then, the process of hypothesis construction and testing that is fundamental to scientific inquiry can be practiced in the unique laboratory of language in use. This training gives such a program value beyond what can be learned about the language. It also suggests links to other content areas.

It is possible to develop specific lessons relating dialect study to science and history. The true value of broad-based approaches to dialect study is realized by allowing groups of students to examine complementary topics in the content areas and share their investigations with other class members. There are a number of ways in which students can examine how language and culture go hand in hand.

Student investigation of dialects serves other functions. It can be recommended as a way to get at the attitudes about language held by all students, to enhance self-awareness, and to gain insight into the nature of culturally based behavior. Using language as a subject, attitudes toward differences between people can be explored and the integrity of all cultural and language systems can be emphasized. At issue is how students feel about other students and themselves. Students who speak socially favored varieties may view their dialectally different peers as linguistically deficient. Worse yet, speakers of socially disfavored varieties may come to accept this viewpoint about their own variety of language. Students need to understand the natural sociolinguistic principles that lead to the development and maintenance of language varieties apart from their relative social status. Furthermore, students need to understand that a dialect difference is not an inherent linguistic or cognitive deficit. Only when this kind of information is widespread will we start seeing some change in the current practice of discrimination on the basis of dialect. If the whole class has been introduced to such a perspective on standard and vernacular forms of language, an environment has been created in which the vernacular dialect speakers can maintain their native forms of speech while acquiring standard forms where needed.

The use of the community as a language resource can have other advantages as well. Sending students into the community as researchers can contribute to preserving the region's cultural and oral traditions as well as providing an authentic, active learning experience. An early model for this approach is the successful *Foxfire* project that began with the idea of having students put together a magazine simply as a way of making language arts more interesting (Wigginton, 1981). The bulk of the magazine was composed of stories about traditions from the Southern Appalachia area—folk tales, superstitions, and reports on events in the community's history. The magazine not only succeeded in terms of the language arts experience but also preserved local traditions and enhanced students' educational experiences. Students writing about local lore gathered in their ethnographic inquiry tend to be more motivated to write using the conventions associated with text. Another way to use the community as a resource is to have members of the community visit the classroom for specific purposes—including being interviewed by students—and then have students write up what they have learned.

The concept of using dialect diversity and the cultural diversity that accompanies it as a resource in the language arts curriculum presents a viewpoint that is very different from traditional approaches. Instead of seeing differences as barriers to be overcome, proponents of this approach have found that the differences provide fascinating topics for study.

DIALECT AWARENESS

This section presents some sample lessons from a dialect curriculum developed and tested successfully in different locations in North Carolina (e.g., Wolfram & Creech, 1996; Wolfram, Dannenberg, Anderson, & Messner, 1996; Wolfram, Schilling-Estes, & Hazen, 1997;) and also to a limited extent in Baltimore, Maryland (Wolfram, Adger, & Detwyler, 1992). The lessons suggest the kind of language exercises that students can do and that they enjoy. In keeping with the range of concerns that might be addressed in a comprehensive dialect awareness program, there are materials related to affective, cognitive, and social parameters. A brief introduction to each lesson is given, indicating the rationale for the lesson and, in some cases, observations about its effectiveness.

Introduction to Language Diversity

One essential component of any program on dialect awareness is a unit that considers the naturalness of dialect variation in American English. Students need to confront popular stereotypes and misconceptions about dialects. This is probably best done inductively. An easy method involves having students listen to representative speech samples of regional, class, and ethnic varieties. Students need to hear how native Standard English speakers in diverse regions such as New England, the rural South, and urban North compare to appreciate the reality of spoken regional standards, just as they need to recognize the difference between standard and vernacular varieties in these regions. And students in the Midwest need to consider some of the dialect traits of their own variety as it compares with others in order to understand that everyone really does speak a dialect.

Although most tape-recorded collections of dialect samples are personal ones that are not commercially available, the video production *American Tongues* (Alvarez & Kolker, 1987) is an especially effective tool for having students confront the affective parameters related to dialect diversity. It offers an entertaining introduction to dialects while exposing basic prejudices and myths about language differences. Box 8.1 illustrates a sample introductory unit for students from Ocracoke in North Carolina's Outer Banks, from Wolfram, Schilling-Estes, and Hazen (1997). It explores the naturalness of dialects and the attitudes often associated with this diversity.

Box 8.1
Sample Introductory Lesson on Dialect Diversity and Attitudes

INTRODUCTION

In this unit, we are going to study about language and dialects. We will look at how dialects work in general and how the dialect of Ocracoke works in particular. We will figure out some of the dialect patterns found on the island and see how these patterns have developed. As you work with this unit you should pay close attention to the dialects spoken by people around you. Dialects are a fascinating window into culture and history, and we will see how the dialect of Ocracoke reflects the history and culture of the island.

At the end of this workbook is a section for you to write down some of your thoughts and observations about language. Each day you should write at least a couple of sentences that capture your thoughts about what you are learning. Feel free to write about things you are observing about dialect outside the classroom.

A VIDEO EXERCISE

You will watch segments from the video called *American Tongues*, which shows different dialects of English and shows some people's attitudes about dialects. After you watch the video, you will be asked to discuss these questions in small groups and share your reactions.

1. What is a dialect?
2. What do people think about dialects?
3. Are people's feelings about dialects fair? Why or why not?
4. What do you think about dialects?
5. Can you give one example of a dialect difference from the video and one that is not on the video?
6. Give two examples of pronunciation and vocabulary differences from Ocracoke that haven't been presented so far.

LANGUAGE JOURNAL

Write several impressions in your language journal. How do you feel about other dialects that you heard on the video? How do you feel about the Ocracoke dialect? Are there any questions you have about the Ocracoke dialect?

Levels of Dialect

As we have pointed out in chapters 2 and 3, language is simultaneously organized on several different levels, including phonology, grammar, semantics, and language use. Understanding of the simultaneous organization of language on these various levels is essential for those who examine dialect diversity. It is important in understanding the ways in which language can vary, and how this variation may be interpreted. Many different types of activities can be offered to engage students in recognizing these levels of language organization.

Box 8.2 includes three examples of exercises on levels of dialect difference. The first is a written task; the second involves listening to a local dialect speaker; and the third is based on listening to a commercially available audio tape of an Appalachian story teller, Adrienne Belcher. Thus, students have an opportunity to identify levels of dialect differences for local and nonlocal dialects. There are a number of commercially available storytelling tapes that may be used, as well as tapes from the archival collections of the *Dictionary of American Regional English* and the Center for Applied Linguistics Collection of *American English Speech Recordings* (Christian, 1986), available at the Library of Congress along with other dialect and oral history recordings.

Box 8.2
Sample Exercises on Levels of Dialect
(from Wolfram, Schilling-Estes, & Hazen, 1997)

In this unit, we will be looking at the components that make up a dialect, or *dialect levels*. In doing this, we will listen to some examples of dialect from Ocracoke and Appalachia. We will also take a closer look at some of the vocabulary items found on Ocracoke and see how these words are different from, and similar to, other English dialects.

(continued on next page)

(Box 8.2 continued)

LEVELS OF DIALECT

Language is organized on several different levels. One level of organization is *pronunciation*, which concerns how sounds are used in a language. Different dialects may use sounds in quite different ways. Sometimes this is referred to simply as **accent**. For example, some people from New England pronounce the words *car* and *far* without the *r*. Also, some people from the South may say *greasy* with a *z* sound in the middle of the word, so that they pronounce it *greazy*. In Ocracoke, the way some people say *hoi toiders* or *sound* are examples of differences in pronunciation.

Another level of language organization is *grammar*. Grammar concerns the particular ways in which speakers **arrange sentences** and **words**. Different dialects may arrange words and sentences in different ways. For instance, in some parts of Western Pennsylvania, speakers may say *The car needs washed* where other speakers say *The car needs washing*. Also, some people from the Appalachian mountains or from the Outer Banks may say *The man went a-hunting* when other people say *The man went hunting*. When a person from Ocracoke says *It weren't me*, as opposed to *It wasn't me*, we have an example of **dialect grammar**.

A third level of language involves how different words are used, called the *vocabulary* or *lexicon* of the language. Speakers of different dialects use **different words to mean the same thing**. Thus, some people in Philadelphia, Pennsylvania, use the word *hoagie* in reference to the same kind of sandwich that other people call a *sub*—or a *grinder, torpedo, hero, poor boy*, and so forth. People living in Ocracoke use the term *buck* to mean *a good friend*, but the term commonly refers to a *male deer* or *one dollar* in other regions. Also, a **common word might be used with different meanings** across dialects. Thus, in some areas, *soda* is used for a carbonated drink with ice cream whereas in other areas, *soda* is used just to refer to a carbonated drink without anything added to it. In Ocracoke, the use of the term *mommuck* for 'hassle', *quamish* for 'sick stomach', or *scud* for 'ride' are examples of vocabulary differences.

(continued on next page)

(Box 8.2 continued)

WHAT KIND OF DIFFERENCE IS IT?

In the sentences given below, decide whether the difference in each pair is at the pronunciation, vocabulary, or grammar level. Place a *P* for **pronunciation**, a *V* for **vocabulary**, and a *G* for **grammar** level difference in the blank provided beside each pair.

1. _____ That *feller* sure was tall.
   That *fellow* sure was tall.

2. _____ She needed a *rubberband*.
   She needed a *gumband*.

3. _____ They usually *be doing* their homework.
   They usually *do* their homework.

4. _____ I *weren't* there yesterday.
   I *wasn't* there yesterday.

5. _____ She drank a *milkshake*.
   She drank a *cabinet*.

6. _____ I asked him *if he was going over the beach*.
   I asked him *is he going to the beach*?

7. _____ The *skeeters* are bad in August.
   The *mosquitoes* are bad in August

8. _____ That meal was *good-some*.
   That meal was *good*.

9. _____ They caught two hundred *pound* of flounder.
   They caught two hundred *pounds* of flounder.

10. _____ They went *hunting and fishing*.
    They went *a-hunting and a-fishing*.

(continued on next page)

(Box 8.2 continued)

SOME EXAMPLES FROM OCRACOKE

The excerpt below is from a taped interview with a middle-aged islander. As you listen to the tape, read through the passage, but do not make any marks on the paper. As you listen to the tape a second time, determine whether the bold face words are on the grammar, pronunciation, or vocabulary level of the dialect. In the blanks following the bold face words, place a **G** for grammar, **P** for pronunciation, or a **V** for vocabulary.

[The remarks of the person conducting the interview are not included]

Well we, like, say we started on that end and started runnin' 'em back this way, and then they used to come on to the — you know—see there **weren't**___1 all this—this was swamp here, we used to hunt. On every one of these **houses**___2 ; all these houses from where we turned at the **fire**___3 station up this way **has**___4 been built here since the sixties. There was only one house was up here in the sixties. All this subdivision, Jackson Dunes, Oyster Creek. And then the ponies would come around, you know, you'd pen 'em up and they'd come right on the shore, out here. And then we had beaches, you know, before everybody started building, you had a little beach all the way around on the sound **side**___5, just like you do on the ocean. But now you don't. And everybody's **breakwatered**___6 and filled in, built. And then in June, we had a cattle **penning**___7.

—(Thanks to James Barrie Gaskill for allowing us to use this portion of an interview conducted with him in February, 1993)

(continued on next page)

(Box 8.2 continued)

AN EXAMPLE OF APPALACHIAN ENGLISH:
AUDIO EXERCISE

The following excerpt is a recorded version of an Appalachian tale, *The Story of Ashley Lou*, a version of the traditional folktale, *Cinderella*. As the tape plays, listen closely to the story, paying close attention to the dialect. After you listen to the story, the instructor will play or read each excerpt below and you will be asked to identify the level of dialect in the space provided. Place a **G** for grammar, **P** for pronunciation, and **V** for vocabulary.

1. _____ but they had a good **life**
2. _____ and they had a whole woods full of timber to burn in the **gratefire**
3. _____ they **was** happy
4. _____ until one winter, Luella's mommy **took sick** and died
5. _____ but her Daddy **plumb** fell all to pieces
6. _____ there was this big **sweet gum tree**
7. _____ when she **growed** up
8. _____ couldn't sleep the night before for hearing the wind **a-whistling**
9. _____ For **of the nighttime**, see, he'd go a-coonhunting and **of the daytime**, he'd go down to town to watch them build that new road.
10. _____ and all the **washing** and **ironing**

Local vocabularies are a rich source for engaging students in examining dialect differences. The activity illustrated in Box 8.3, again taken from the Ocracoke dialect curriculum, is offered as a prototype for student involvement in gathering data. Students can take an active role in constructing local adaptations of this exercise. From these types of activities, students should become aware of the culturally specific, relative nature of vocabulary.

Box 8.3
Examples of Dialect Vocabulary Exercises

VOCABULARY IN OCRACOKE

There are lots of vocabulary differences that can be described for Ocracoke. Each of the words has a unique history. Some words we can trace back in the English language over a thousand years and some go back just a few years. For example, words like *token* (in *token of death*), *mommuck*, and *quamish* were used centuries ago in ways similar to how they are used in Ocracoke today. Other terms such as *dingbatter*, *scud*, and *up the beach* are relatively recent uses. We can trace certain vocabulary forms confidently, but can make only educated guesses about the origins of other words. For example, a unique Ocracoke use of the phrase *call the mail over* may be traced to the custom of distributing mail by calling aloud the names of those who received letters at the dock when the mail boat arrived. We're not exactly sure how *meehonkey* came into use, but we guess that it had something to do with the attempt to imitate the call of a goose.

Of course, most of the dialect words found in Ocracoke are found in other dialects as well, but a few are found only in Ocracoke. And the use of vocabulary in Ocracoke differs according to age and background. Following is a sample of some of the dialect words that have been collected. As you examine these words, think of the following questions:

1. Which of these words do you use?
2. Which of these words do you know? If you don't know the word, who do you think would?
3. Do you think people from other areas use these words? Where do you think they might use the words?

(continued on next page)

(Box 8.3 continued)

A SAMPLE OF SOME DIALECT VOCABULARY
IN OCRACOKE

Following are a few words that have been described as a part of the Ocracoke dialect. Use these examples in order to do the exercise that follows.

buck n.   A friend, usually a male friend.
He's a real buck.

call the mail over Distribute the mail. Comes originally from the custom of distributing mail by calling aloud the names of those who received letters at the dock when the mail boat arrived. Now used for more general reference to the distribution of mail in the boxes at the post office. *Is the mail called over yet?*

catawampus adj. In a diagonal position, crooked, not square. *The box was sitting there catawampus.* Also **cattywampus**.

dingbatter n.   A non-native of Ocracoke or the Outer Banks. Sometimes it is used somewhat negatively to refer to someone who is ignorant of island life. *The dingbatter kept getting his fishing line tangled with mine.*

fladget n.   A piece of something. This term seems to be used mostly in reference to food or wounds. *He cut a fladget of skin off his finger.*

guano, also
goana, goanner n. Fertilizer, often from fowl such as chickens or coastal birds. By extension, it can refer to any

(continued on next page)

(Box 8.3 continued)

	type of fertilizer, including commercial fertilizer. Comes from the Spanish term *guano* (from Peru) where it was used to refer to dung from coastal birds. *Did Owen put lots of goanner on his garden?*
gutful n.	A full stomach, typically from eating. *Rex had a gutful of food last night.*
haint n.	A ghost. *Some people think they've seen haints on the island.*
miserable 'n the wind adj.	Agitated, feeling very uneasy or unsettled. Very bad. A shortened version of the phrase *miserabler than the wind. Rudy is miserable 'n the wind when he's on his week off from the ferry. The day was miserable 'n the wind.*
mommuck Also *mammock, mommick* v.	To harass or bother. In Shakespeare's day, this term had a slightly different meaning: to break, cut, or tear into fragments or shreds. The sentence, *Young'uns, haint I been mommucked this day?*, is a classic island phrase that focuses on some traditionally recognized dialect traits, including the verb *mommuck.*
pizer n.	Porch. From Italian *piazza. We sat on the pizer and watched the young'uns.*
quamish adj.	Sick to the stomach. This term comes from *qualmish*—that is, prone to qualms or spells of sickness—and is found in Shakespeare and even earlier writings. *I felt quamished on the ferry.*

(continued on next page)

(Box 8.3 continued)

slick cam adj	A very calm water, typically used with reference to the sound. *It was a slick cam out there today.*
to prep.	At, located at, used generally where *at* is used in other dialects. *Lydia is over to the restaurant.*
up the beach adv.	North of Ocracoke, for example, Hatteras, Nags Head, or Norfolk. *Dave is going up the beach this weekend.*
wampus cat n.	A fictitious cat, used to refer to a rascally person. May refer to a person who is abnormal in some respect. It may have developed from a creative reversal of *cattywampus*. *He's a classic example of an off-island wampus cat.*
young 'uns n.	Young children. *The young 'uns don't like the same games we played in our day.*

(continued on next page)

(Box 8.3 continued)

AN EXERCISE WITH OCRACOKE
DIALECT VOCABULARY

Following are some words that are part of the Ocracoke dialect vocabulary. For each of the words, do the following:

- Figure out what the word means, if you don't already know. You can usually do this by asking some different island residents of different ages about the words.
- Use the word in a sentence and try to figure out what part of speech it is.
- Ask people of different ages about these words. Do older people use them? Do younger people use them? Do they know all of them? Identify the type of people who know the word and who use it: Is it used by older people, younger people, by non-islanders?
- Which of the words do you think are used ONLY in Ocracoke or in the Outer Banks? How did you come to your conclusion?

- Write your answers down here.

down below

puck

across the beach

up the beach

meehonkey

nor'easter

scuttle

scud

(continued on next page)

(Box 8.3 continued)

token of death

yaupon

OCRACOKE DIALECT VOCABULARY GAME: HOW TO TELL AN O'COCKER FROM A DINGBATTER

Fill in the blanks in the sentences below, choosing your answer from the list provided. You only have five minutes to complete the worksheet, and you **may not** look at the lexicon or share answers. At the end of five minutes, you will swap your book with a neighbor to check each other's work. For each correct answer, you will receive 1 point and for each question missed, you will receive **no** points. Good luck.

WORD LIST: across the beach, buck, call the mail over, dingbatter, doast, goaty, good-some, meehonkey, miserable 'n the wind, mommuck, O'cocker, pizer, quamish, Russian rat, say a word, scud, smidget, slick cam, to, up the beach, yaupon, young 'uns

1. They went _____ to Hatteras to do some shopping.

2. That _____ is from New Jersey.

3. That place sure was smelling _____.

4. Elizabeth is _____ the restaurant right now.

5. I put a _____ of salt on my apple.

6. We took a _____ around the island in the car.

7. They're always together because he's his _____.

(continued on next page)

(Box 8.3 continued)

8. At night we used to play _____.

9. The ocean was so rough today I felt _____ in the boat.

10. Last night she came down with a _____.

11. I saw a big _____ in the road.

12. They sat on the _____ in the evening.

13. When Rex and James Barrie get together they sure can _____.

14. You can't be an _____ unless you were born on the island.

15. The sea was real rough today; it was _____ out there.

16. When they _____ I hope I get my letter.

17. She used to _____ him when he was a child.

18. There was no wind at all today and it was a _____ out there on the sound.

19. There was a big, dead shark that they found _____.

20. _____ don't act like they used to back then.

Put a **1** by all the correct answers and an **X** by all the incorrect answers. Add up all of the correct answers and place the answer in the blank. Hand the workbook back to its owner.

(continued on next page)

(Box 8.3 continued)

number of correct answers _____

Check your number of correct answers against the continuum below. Place an **X** where you would fall on this continuum.

O'cocker 20----------15----------10----------5---------- Dingbatter

The Patterning of Dialect

Language is a unique form of knowledge in that speakers know a language simply by virtue of the fact that they speak it. Much of this knowledge is not on a conscious level, but it is still open to systematic investigation. The study of dialects affords us a fascinating window through which we can see how language works: The inner workings of language are just as readily observed in examining dialect patterning as through the exclusive study of a single standard variety.

Making generalizations drawn from carefully described sets of data, we can hypothesize about the patterning of language features and then check our hypotheses on the basis of actual usage patterns. Such a strategy is quite within the grasp even of younger students. In fact, we have led classes of students in the upper elementary grades through the steps of hypothesis formation and testing by using exercises involving dialect features, like those in Boxes 8.4 and 8.5. These exercises include several types of language patterning. The exercises in Box 8.4 illustrate patterning in pronunciation, and those in 8.5, the patterning of grammatical differences. It is helpful to do pronunciation exercises like those in 8.4 with supportive audio recordings of the actual pronunciation. These exercises represent both regional and social dimensions of dialects, ranging from Southern regional speech to New England speech, as well as Appalachian and African American Vernacular English. They allow students to experience inductively how patterned all varieties of language are regardless of their social valuation.

Box 8.4
Illustrative Exercises in Pronunciation Patterning

HOW DIALECTS PATTERN

In this unit, we are going to see how dialects are constructed. All languages and each dialect of a language follow definite patterns in the way they are organized. When we say that the dialects of a language follow a pattern, or have rules, we mean that the various language forms are arranged in **regular** and **predictable** ways. For example, in English, adjectives are placed before a noun, as in *blue car, nice person*, or *sad dog*. In other languages like Spanish, the adjective is placed after the noun so that people would say *car blue (carro azul)*. So we can say that the placement of adjectives before nouns, as in English, or after nouns, as in Spanish, is a regular pattern that simply differs in English and Spanish.

We learn language patterns or rules unconsciously when we learn our language as children. Without even thinking about it, we will learn to place adjectives before nouns so that it becomes an automatic habit when we speak. For example, if we hear a new word to describe a color somewhere between blue and purple called *blurple*, we would automatically say *the blurple car*, not *the car blurple*. This pattern for adjective placement is therefore regular and predictable. Sometimes these patterns can be very complicated and difficult to figure out, but the human mind has the capacity to learn all of these intricate patterns without even thinking about them. This ability is one of the most amazing and impressive traits of the human mind.

We will see that the same principles of patterning apply to dialect grammar and pronunciation. And we will try to figure out some dialect patterns as we think about language like a linguist. A **linguist** is a person who studies language as a scientist in order to figure out the specific patterns of language arrangement. Linguists do not create language patterns, just as scientists do not create laws of nature. The patterns already exist in the minds of the speakers of language. The linguist simply tries to state the regular, predictable design that guides the use of language.

We will try to figure out some patterns for different dialect forms, including some that have been used in Ocracoke. The challenge is to

(continued on next page)

(Box 8.4 continued)

come up with a rule that accurately describes all the examples. If the rule is correct, it should predict how new forms will be treated.

How Pronunciation Differences Work: Dropping *r* in English Dialects

In some dialects of English, the *r* sound of words like *car* or *poor* can be dropped. In these words, the *r* is not pronounced, so that these words sound like "*cah*" and "*po*." However, not all *r* sounds can be dropped. In some places in a word, the *r* sound may be dropped and in other places it may NOT be dropped. By comparing lists of words where the *r* may be dropped with lists of words where it may NOT be dropped, we can figure out a pattern for *r* dropping.

List A gives words where the *r* may be DROPPED.

LIST A: Words that Can Drop *r*

1. ca*r*
2. fathe*r*
3. ca*r*d
4. bigge*r*
5. ca*r*dboa*r*d
6. bee*r*
7. cou*r*t

List B gives words where the *r* sound may NOT be dropped. In other words, speakers who drop their *r*'s in List A, pronounce the *r* in the words in List B.

LIST B: Words that CANNOT Drop *r*

1. *r*un
2. b*r*ing
3. p*r*incipal
4. st*r*ing
5. ok*r*a
6. app*r*oach
7. Ap*r*il

To find a pattern for dropping the *r*, look at the type of sound that comes before the *r* in List A and in List B. Does a vowel or a consonant

(continued on next page)

(Box 8.4 continued)

come before the *r* in **List A**? What comes before the *r* in **List B**? How can you predict where an *r* may or may not be dropped?

In **List C**, pick those words that may drop their *r* and those that may not drop their *r*. Use your knowledge of the *r* dropping pattern that you learned by comparing **Lists A** and **B**. Put *Y* for "Yes" if the word can drop the *r* and *N* for "No" if it cannot drop the *r*.

LIST C: Applying the Rule for *r* Dropping

1. bea*r*
2. p*r*og*r*am
3. fea*r*ful
4. *r*ight
5. compute*r*
6. pa*r*ty
7. fou*r*teen

Think of two new words that may drop an *r* and two new words that may NOT drop an *r*.

More about r Dropping Patterns

In the last exercise we saw that *r* dropping only takes place when the *r* comes after a vowel. Now we are going to look at the kinds of sounds that may come **AFTER** the *r* in some dialects of English. This pattern goes along with the one you already learned. Let's see if we can figure out the pattern.

Here are some words where the *r* may **NOT** be dropped even when it comes after a vowel.

List A: Words that Do NOT Drop r

1. bea*r* in the field
2. ca*r* ove*r* at the house
3. ga*r*age
4. ca*r*ing
5. take fou*r* apples

(continued on next page)

(Box 8.4 continued)

6. pear on the tree

7. far enough

What kinds of sounds come after the *r* in **List A**? Are they vowels or consonants?

In **List B** the *r* MAY be dropped. What kind of sounds come after the *r* in this list?

List B: Words that Drop r

1. bear by the woods

2. car parked by the house

3. parking the bus

4. fearful

5. take four peaches

6. pear by the house

7. far behind

What does the sound that comes after *r* do to *r* dropping?

Use what you know about the pattern for *r* dropping to pick the *r*'s in List C that can be dropped. Say why the *r* can or cannot be dropped. Write *Y* for "Yes" if the *r* can be dropped, and *N* for "No" if it cannot be dropped. Remember that the *r* must come after a vowel to be dropped, but it cannot have a vowel after it.

List C: Words that May or May Not Drop r

1. pear on the table

2. pear by the table

3. park in the mall

4. program in the mall

5. car behind the house

Practicing the r Drop Pattern

Try to pronounce the two sentences given here according to the *r* drop pattern that you learned.

1. **The teacher picked on three students for an answer.**

(continued on next page)

(Box 8.4 continued)

2. **Fou*r* ca*r*s pa*r*ked fa*r* away f*r*om the fai*r*.**

A Southern Vowel Pronunciation

In some Southern dialects of English, words like *pin* and *pen* are pronounced the same. Usually, both words are pronounced as *pin*. This pattern of pronunciation is also found in other words. **List A** has words where the *i* and *e* are pronounced the **SAME** in these dialects.

LIST A: I and E Pronounced the Same

1. *tin* and *ten*
2. *kin* and *Ken*
3. *Lin* and *Len*
4. *windy* and *Wendy*
5. *sinned* and *send*

Although *i* and *e* in **List A** are pronounced the **SAME**, there are other words where *i* and *e* are pronounced differently. **List B** has word pairs where the vowels are pronounced **DIFFERENTLY**.

LIST B: I and E Pronounced Differently

1. *lit* and *let*
2. *pick* and *peck*
3. *pig* and *peg*
4. *rip* and *rep*
5. *litter* and *letter*

Is there a pattern that can explain why the words in **List A** are pronounced the **SAME** and why the words in **List B** are pronounced **DIFFERENTLY**? To answer this question, you have to look at the sounds that are next to the vowels. Look at the sounds that come after the vowel. What sound is found next to the vowel in all of the examples given in **List A**?

(continued on next page)

(Box 8.4 continued)

Use what you know about the pronunciation pattern to pick the word pairs in **List C** that are pronounced the **SAME** and those that are pronounced **DIFFERENTLY** in this Southern dialect. Mark the word pairs that are pronounced the same with *S* and the word pairs that are pronounced differently with *D*.

LIST C: Same or Different?

1. *bit* and *bet*
2. *pit* and *pet*
3. *bin* and *Ben*
4. *Nick* and *neck*
5. *din* and *den*

How can you predict where *i* and *e* will be pronounced the same and where they will be pronounced differently?

Exercises on grammatical patterning as indicated in Box 8.5 can go a long way toward dispelling the notion that dialects are simply imperfect renditions of the standard variety. Working with them sets the stage for generating a nonpatronizing respect for the complexity of systematic differences among dialects. The advantage of the *a-* prefixing exercise in particular is that it involves a form whose patterning is intuitive to both those who use the form in their vernacular dialect and those who do not (Wolfram, 1982). This fact makes the exercise appropriate for students regardless of their native dialect. Working through exercises of this type is an effective way of confronting the myth that dialects have no rules of their own; at the same time, such exercises effectively demonstrate the underlying cognitive patterning of language. The second exercise in Box 8.5 on habitual *be* has been used along with a video of AAVE speakers who systematically make the correct choices because they have unconsciously learned the pattern for the use of the verb. It demonstrates that dialect patterning can be unique to a particular dialect and that we cannot make assumptions about other dialects based on our own.

Box 8.5
Illustrative Exercises of Grammatical Patterning

The Use of a- prefix

In some traditional rural dialects of the South, some words that end in
-*ing* can take an *a-*, pronounced as *uh*, in front of the word. We call this
a- prefix because it attaches to the front of the -*ing* word. The language
pattern or rule for this form allows the *a-* to attach to some words but
not to others. We will try to figure out this fairly complicated rule by
looking at the kinds of -*ing* words *a-* can and cannot attach to. We will
do this using our inner feelings about language. These inner feelings,
called **intuitions**, tell us where we **CAN** and **CANNOT** use certain
forms. Our job as linguists trying to describe this dialect is to figure
out the reason for these inner feelings and to state the exact pattern.

Look at the sentence pairs in **LIST A** and decide which sentence in
each pair sounds better for attaching the *a-*. For example, in the first
sentence pair, does it sound better to say, *A-building is hard work* or
He was a-building a house? For each sentence pair, just choose one
sentence that sounds better with the *a-*.

LIST A: Sentence Pairs for A- Prefixing

1. a.___Building is hard work.
   b.___She was building a house.

2. a.___He likes hunting.
   b.___He went hunting.

3. a.___The child was charming the adults.
   b.___The child was very charming.

4. a.___He kept running to the store.
   b.___The store was shocking.

5. a.___They thought fishing was easy.
   b.___They were fishing this morning.

6. a.___The fishing is still good here.
   b.___They go fishing less now.

(continued on next page)

(Box 8.5 continued)

Examine each of the sentence pairs in terms of the choices for the *a*-prefix and answer the following questions.

- Do you think there is some pattern that guided your choice of an answer? You can tell if there is a definite pattern by checking with other people who did the same exercise on their own.
- Do you think that the pattern might be related to parts of speech? To answer this, see if there are any parts of speech where you CANNOT use the *a*- prefix. Look at *-ing* forms that function as verbs and compare those with *-ing* forms that operate as nouns or adjectives. For example, look at the use of *charming* as a verb and adjective in sentence 3.

The first step in figuring out the pattern for *a*- prefix is related to the part of speech of the *-ing* word. Now let's look at another difference related to prepositions such as *from* and *by*. Based on the sentence pairs in **LIST B**, say whether or not the *a*- form can be used after a preposition. Use the same technique you used for **LIST A**. Select the sentence that sounds better for each sentence pair and say whether it is the sentence with or without the preposition.

LIST B: A Further Detail for A- Patterning

1. a.___They make money by building houses.
   b.___They make money building houses

2. a.___People can't make enough money fishing.
   b.___People can't make enough money from fishing.

3. a.___People destroy the beauty of the island through littering.
   b.___People destroy the beauty of the island littering.

Now we have another detail for figuring the pattern for the *a*- prefix use related to prepositions. But there is still another part to the pattern for *a*- prefix use. This time, however, it is related to pronunciation. For the following *-ing* words, try to figure out what it is about the pronunciation that makes one sentence sound better than the other. To help you figure out the pronunciation trait that is critical for this pattern, the

(continued on next page)

(Box 8.5 continued)

stressed or accented syllable of each word is marked with the symbol
′. Follow the same procedure that you did in choosing the sentence in
each sentence pair that sounds better.

LIST C: Figuring out a Pronunciation Pattern for A- Prefix

1. a.___She was discóvering a trail.
   b.___She was fóllowing a trail.

2. a.___She was repéating the chant.
   b.___She was hóllering the chant.

3. a.___They were fíguring the change.
   b.___They were forgétting the change.

4. a.___The baby was récognizing the mother.
   b.___The baby was wrécking everything.

5. a.___The were décorating the room.
   b.___They were demánding more time off.

Say exactly how the pattern for attaching the *a-* prefix works. Be sure
to include the three different details from your examination of the examples in **LISTS A, B**, and **C**.

In **LIST D,** say which of the sentences may attach an *a-* prefix. Use
your understanding of the rule to explain why the *-ing* form may or
may not take the *a-* prefix.

LIST D: Applying the A- Prefix Rule

1. She kept handing me more work.

2. The team was remémbering the game.

3. The team won by playing great defense.

4. The team was playing real hard.

5. The coach was charming.

(continued on next page)

(Box 8.5 continued)

BE IN AFRICAN AMERICAN ENGLISH

Now we are going to look at a form that is used in a dialect that is sometimes used by young African American speakers in large cities. The form *be* is used where other dialects use *am*, *is*, or *are*, except that it has a special meaning. People who use this dialect can tell where it may be used and where it may not be, just like you did for the *a-* prefix. In the sentences given here, choose one of the sentences in each pair where *be* fits better. Choose only one sentence for each pair. If you're not sure of the answer, simply make your best guess. Put a check next to the answer you think is right. *Do this work by yourself.*

1. __ a. They usually be tired when they come home.
   __ b. They be tired right now.

2. __ a. When we play basketball, she be on my team.
   __ b. The girl in the picture be my sister.

3. __ a. James be coming to school right now.
   __ b. James always be coming to school.

4. __ a. Wanda don't usually be in school.
   __ b. Wanda don't be in school today.

5. __ a. My ankle be broken from the fall.
   __ b. Sometimes my ears be itching.

Now that you have given your answers, you will see a video of some speakers of this dialect doing the same exercise. How well did you do on the exercise compared to these students in the video who regularly use the *be* form?

Following the Patterns for *be* Use

Now that you know how the form *be* is used, predict which of the sentences below follow the rule for *be* use in the African American English dialect and which do NOT. Write (**Y**)es if the sentence follows the dialect pattern and (**N**)o if it doesn't.

1. __ The students always be talking in class.

(continued on next page)

(Box 8.5 continued)

2. ___ The students don't be talking right now.

3. ___ Sometimes the teacher be early for class.

4. ___ At the moment the teacher be in the lounge.

5. ___ Linguists always be asking silly questions about language.

In addition to showing students how linguists collect and organize data to formulate rules, such exercises provide students with a model for analyzing data that they might collect from their own community. In the best case scenario, students should record language data, extract particular examples from the recordings, and formulate linguistic rules themselves. In this way, they can learn firsthand to examine language in a scientific way.

Language Change

It is important for students and instructors to understand how inevitable and natural language change is. An understanding of the processes of change should provide a basis for understanding the orderly cognitive and behavioral processes that bring about change. For example, languages tend to level irregular patterns over time: Regularization is a normal and natural change that takes place in language. When students from vernacular-speaking backgrounds regularize the past tense of irregular verbs such as *knowed* for *knew* and *growed* for *grew*, they are simply following a time-honored and natural tradition of leveling irregular verb forms—the same processes that gave Standard English *worked* (once *wrought*) and *help* (once *holp*). Many of the regular verbs we accept as part of present-day Standard English were, in fact, once irregular forms. Thus, current changes in progress simply follow the principles that have guided language change in the past.

Second, an understanding of the dynamic nature of language change should foster an appreciation for the flexible nature of language. Language is not set once and for all, and language change may affect all levels of language in significant ways. All of the changes of English, including drastic changes in grammatical paradigms and word order, are part of a continuously changing language; no one language state is superior. An appreciation for how radically the English language has changed over time should promote more tolerance for the small types of changes it is currently undergoing.

Finally, an understanding of language change should broaden the viewpoint on language standards. History belies the myth that standards are firm and consistent, a point that we have emphasized throughout this book. The lessons of language history should teach students that language is much more flexible than it is made out to be.

Box 8.6 is a simple comparative activity that shows how dramatically language can change over the centuries. By examining a familiar passage, in this case the Lord's Prayer, students can see how radically a language can change at every level—the sounds, the words, and the orderly arrangement of words in sentences.

Box 8.6
An Illustrative Exercise in Language Change

THE CHANGING OF THE ENGLISH LANGUAGE

English has changed quite dramatically over the centuries. In fact, if we go back far enough, we can barely recognize the language as English. Compare the versions of English at various stages in its history, as found in the first verse of the Lord's Prayer.

Old English (about 950 A.D.)
Fader urer ðu bist in heofnas, sie gehalgad noma ðin

Middle English (about 1350 A.D.)
Oure fadir þat art in heuenes, halwid be þi name

Early Modern English (about 1550 A.D.)
O oure father which arte in heven, hallowed be thy name

Modern English (about 1985 A.D.)
Our father, who is in heaven, may your name be sacred

or

Our father, who art in heaven, hallowed be your name

1. Try pronouncing the different versions of English. In the older versions (Old and Middle English), silent letters do not exist, so you will need to pronounce all the letters. The symbol ð is pronounced something like the *th* of *this*, and the þ is pronounced like the *th* or *think*. (continued on next page)

> (Box 8.6 continued)
>
> **2.** Try to identify some of the older versions of modern words. For example, trace the words that became the current words *father*, *heaven*, *name*, *is*, and *our*. What modern English word, besides sacred, did hallow become?
>
> **3.** What does this comparison tell you about the way the English language has changed over the centuries?

One of the greatest advantages of a curriculum on dialects is its potential for tapping the language resources of students' indigenous communities. In addition to classroom lessons, students can learn by going into the community to collect live dialect data. In most cases, the language characteristics of the local community should make dialects come alive in a way that is unmatched by textbook presentations. Educational models that treat the local community as a resource to be tapped rather than a liability to be overcome have been shown to be quite effective in other areas of language arts education, and there is no reason why this model cannot be applied in an analogous fashion to the study of community dialects. A model that builds on community strengths in language, even when the language is different from the norm of the mainstream educational system, seems to hold much greater potential for success than one that focuses exclusively on language conflicts between the community and school. In fact, the community dialect may just turn out to be the spark that ignites students' interest in the study of language arts. The study of dialects can, indeed, become a vibrant, relevant topic of study for all students.

Author's Note: Some lesson meaterials in this chapter were taken from Wolfram, Schilling-Estes, and Hazen (1997). Copyright © 1997 by W. Wolfram. Reprinted with permission. Other lesson materials were taken from Wolfram, Dannenberg, Anderson, and Messner (1996). Copyright © 1996 by W. Wolfram. Reprinted with permission.

Appendix:
A Selective Inventory
of Vernacular Structures

The following inventory summarizes many of the vernacular dialect structures of English mentioned in the text; it also introduces other structures not covered in the preceding chapters. It is limited to pronunciation and grammatical structures. For each of the structures, a brief general comment is given about the linguistic patterning of the structure, as well as a statement about its dialect distribution. We try to avoid phonetic symbols as much as possible, but there are a few cases in which we include them along with conventional spelling to indicate the sound of a form.

PHONOLOGICAL STRUCTURES

Consonants

Final Cluster Reduction

Word-final consonant clusters ending in a stop can be reduced when both members of the cluster are either voiced (e.g., *find, cold*) or voiceless (*act, test*). This process affects both clusters that are a part of the base word (e.g., *find, act*) and those clusters formed through the addition of an *-ed* suffix (e.g., *guessed, liked*). In Standard English, this rule may operate when the following word begins with a consonant (e.g., *best kind*), but in vernacular dialects it is extended to include following words beginning in a vowel as well (e.g., *best apple*). This pattern is quite prominent in AAVE and in dialects of English that retain influence from other languages, such as Hispanic English and Vietnamese English. It is not particularly noticeable in other American English dialects.

Plurals Following Clusters

Words ending in *-sp* (e.g., *wasp*), *-sk* (e.g., desk), and *-st* (e.g., *test*) may take an *-es* (phonetically [Iz]) plural in many vernacular varieties, following the reduction of their final clusters to *-s*. Thus, items such as "tes'" for *test* and "des'" for *desk* will be pluralized as "tesses" and "desses," respectively, much as words ending in *s* or other *s*-like sounds in Standard English (e.g., *bus*, *buzz*) are pluralized with an *-es* ending (*busses*, *buzzes*).

In some historically isolated varieties of English such as Appalachian and Southeastern coastal varieties, the *-es* plural may occur even without the reduction of the final cluster to *-s*, yielding plural forms such as "postes" and "deskes." Such forms are considerably rarer in AAVE.

Intrusive t

A small set of items, usually ending in *s* and *f* in the standard variety, may be produced with a final *t*. This results in a final consonant cluster. Typical items affected by this process are "oncet," "twicet," "clifft," and "acrosst." Intrusive *t* is primarily found in Appalachian varieties and other rural varieties characterized by the retention of older, or relic, forms.

A quite different kind of intrusive *t* involves the doubling of an *-ed* form. In this instance, speakers add an *-ed* ending (phonetically [Id]) to verbs that are already marked with an *-ed* ending pronounced *t* (e.g., [lUkt] *looked*). This process yields forms such as "lookted" for *looked* and "attackted" for *attacked*.

th Sounds

There are a number of different processes that affect *th* sounds. The phonetic production of *th* is sensitive to the position of *th* in the word and the sounds adjacent to it. At the beginning of the word, *th* tends to be produced as a corresponding stop, as in "dey" for *they* and "ting" for *thing*. These pronunciations are fairly typical of a wide range of vernaculars, although there are some differences in the distribution of different *th* sounds. The use of *t* in *thing* (voiceless *th*) tends to be most characteristic of selected Anglo and second-language-influenced varieties, whereas the use of *d* in *they* (voiced *th*) is spread across the full spectrum of vernacular varieties.

Before nasal sounds like *m*, *n*, and *ng*, *th*, along with *s* and *v*, may become a stop sound like *t* or *d*, resulting in forms such as "aritmetic" for *arithmetic* or "headn" for *heathen*, as well as "wadn't" for *wasn't*, "idn't" for *isn't*, and "sebm" for *seven*. This pattern is typically found in Southern-based vernacular varieties, including Southern Anglo and African American vernacular varieties.

In word-final position and between vowels in a word, *th* may be produced as *f* or *v*, as in "efer" for *ether*, "toof" for *tooth*, "brover" for *brother*, and "smoov" for *smooth*. This production is typical of AAVE, with the *v* for voiced *th* of *brother* more typical of Eastern varieties of the vernacular. Some Southern-based Anglo dialects, as well as some varieties influenced by other languages in the recent past, also have the *f* production in *tooth*.

Some restricted Anglo varieties use a stop *d* for voiced *th* as in "oder" for *other* or "broder" for *brother*, but this pattern is much less common than the use of a stop for *th* in word-initial position.

r and l

R and *l* may be lost or reduced to a vowel-like quality in a number of different positions in words. After a vowel, as in *sister* or *steal*, the *r* and *l* may be reduced or lost. This feature is regionally diagnostic and is quite typical of traditional Southern speech and Eastern New England speech.

Between vowels, *r* also may be lost, as in "Ca'ol" for *Carol* or "sto'y" for *story*. The loss of *r* between vowels is more socially stigmatized than its loss after a vowel and is found in rural, Southern-based vernaculars.

Following a consonant, the *r* may be lost if it precedes a rounded vowel such as *u* or *o*, resulting in pronunciations such as "thu" for *through* and "tho" for *throw*. The loss of *r* may also take place if *r* occurs in an unstressed syllable, as in "p'ofessor" for *professor* or "sec'etary" for *secretary*. This type of *r*-lessness is found primarily in Southern-based varieties. Before a labial sound such as *f* or *p*, *l* may be lost completely, giving "woof" for *wolf* or "hep" for *help*. Again, this is characteristic only of Southern-based varieties.

Sometimes, the loss of *r* causes one lexical item to converge with another. Thus, the use of *they* for *their* as in *theyself* or *they book* apparently derives from the loss of *r* on *their*, even though speakers who currently use *they* in such constructions no longer associate it with *r*-less *their*.

There are also occasional instances in which an intrusive *r* may occur, so that items such as *wash* may be pronounced as "warsh" and *idea* as "idear." Certain instances of intrusive *r* are the result of a generalized pronunciation process, whereby *r* can be added onto the ends of vowel-final words (e.g., "idear"), particularly when these words precede vowel-initial words ("the idea**r of** it"). Other cases (e.g., "warsh") seem to be restricted to particular lexical items and are very regionally restricted as well.

Initial w Reduction

A word-initial *w* may be lost in items such as *was* and *one* when it occurs in an unstressed syllable. This results in items such as "She's here yesterday" for *She was here yesterday* and "young 'uns" for *young ones*. This process is found in Southern-based vernaculars.

Unstressed Initial Syllable Loss

The general process of eliminating unstressed initial syllables in informal speech styles of standard English (e.g., *because* → "'cause"; *around* → "'round") is extended in vernacular varieties so that a wider range of word classes (e.g., verbs such as "'member" for *remember* or nouns such as "'taters" for *potatoes*) and a wider range of initial syllable types (e.g., *re-* as in "'member" for *remember*, *su-* as in "'spect" for *suspect*) are affected by this process.

Initial h Retention

The retention of *h* on the pronoun *it* ("hit") and *ain't* ("hain't") is still found in vernacular varieties retaining some older English forms, such as Appalachian English, the Outer Banks, and other rural parts of the South. The pronunciation is fading out among younger speakers.

Nasals

There are a number of processes that affect nasal sounds like *n*, *m*, and *ng*; there are also items that are influenced by the presence of nasals in the surrounding linguistic environment.

One widespread process in vernacular varieties is so-called g-dropping, in which the nasal sound represented as *ng* pronounced as *n*. This process takes place when the *ng* occurs in an unstressed syllable, as in "swimmin'" for *swimming* or "buyin'" for *buying*.

A less-widespread phenomenon affecting nasals is the deletion of the word-final nasal segment in items such as *man*, *beam*, and *ring*, particularly when the item is in a relatively unstressed position in the sentence. Even though the nasal is deleted, the words still retain their final nasal in a way similar to the nasalized vowel sounds of French. Thus, *man, beam*, and *ring* may be pronounced as "ma'," "bea'," and "ri'," respectively, with the vowel carrying a nasal quality. Most frequently, this process affects the segment *n*, although all final nasal segments may be affected to some extent. This process is typical of AAVE.

The phonetic quality of vowels may be affected before nasal consonants, as in the well-known merger of the contrast between the vowels of *pen* and *pin*. Some Southern dialects restrict this merger to a following *n*, whereas others extend it to following *m* (e.g., *Kim* and *chem*) and *ng* well.

Other Consonants

There are a number of other consonantal patterns that affect limited sets of items or single words. For example, speakers have used "aks" for *ask* for over 1,000 years and still continue to use it in several vernacular varieties, including AAVE. The form "chimley" or "chimbley" for *chimney* is also found in a number of Southern-based vernaculars. The use of *k* in initial *(s)tr* clusters as in "skreet" for *street* or "skring" for *string* is found in AAVE, particularly rural Southern varieties. Such items are quite socially obtrusive but occur with such limited sets of words that they are best considered on an item-by-item basis.

Vowels

There are many vowel patterns that differentiate the dialects of English, but the majority of these are more regionally than socially significant. The back vowel *ô* [ɔ] of *bought* or *coffee* and the front vowel *a* [æ] of *cat* and *ran* are particularly sensitive to regional variation, as are vowels before *r* (e.g., compare pronunciations of *merry, marry, Mary, Murray*) and *l* (compare *wheel, will, well, whale*, etc.). Although it is not possible here to indicate all the nuances of phonetic difference reflected in the vowels of American English, several major patterns of pronunciation may be identified.

Vowel Mergers

There are a number of vowel mergers in which distinct vowel sounds are produced the same or nearly the same when vowels occur before certain kinds of consonants. The following mergers may occur before *r*, *l*, and the nasal segments.

- the ē [i] and *i* [I], as in *field* and *filled* and *peel* and *pill* (Texas and the South, Pittsburgh)
- the ā [e] and e [ɛ] before /l/, as in *sale* and *sell* and *whale* and *well* (Texas and the South)
- the ōō [u] and oo [U], as in *pool* and *pull* (Texas and the South, Pittsburgh) and *fool* and *full*
- the *i* [I] and *e* [ɛ] before nasals, as in *pin* and *pen* and *windy* and *Wendy* (South)
- the ô [ɔ] and *o* [a] of *caught* and *cot* or *dawn* and *Don*

Other dialects may indicate vowel shifts in which a vowel moves so close to another vowel that speakers from other dialect areas may think the two sounds have merged. In reality, a subtle distinction between the two sounds is maintained. For example, the backed and raised vowel of the Outer Banks of North Carolina in words like *tide* may seem quite similar to *oi* (as in *boy*), but it is maintained as distinct. Similarly, the *i* vowel as in *bit* may be moved so that it sounds almost like ē of *beet*, particularly before sounds like *sh* and *tch* so that people may hear "feesh" for *fish* and "reach" for *rich*. Isolated varieties may also retain a lower vowel production of *a* before *r* so that *there* may sound like "thar" and *bear* like "bar".

Ungliding of ī

The glide part of the vowel in words such as *time*, *tide*, and *tight* may be reduced, yielding pronunciations such as [tam] for *time* and [tad] for *tide*. This ungliding is characteristic of practically all Southern-based vernaculars. The absence of the glide is more frequent when the following segment is a voiced sound, as in *side* or *time*, than when it is voiceless one, as in *sight* or *rice*.

Final Unstressed ow

In word-final position, standard English *ow*, as in *hollow* or *yellow*, may become *r*, giving "holler" or "yeller," respectively. This intrusive *r* also occurs when suffixes are attached, as in "fellers" for *fellows* or "narrers" for *narrows*. This production is characteristic of Upper Southern varieties such as those found in Appalachia or the Ozarks, although it is found to some extent in Southern rural varieties as well.

Final Unstressed ə Raising

Final unstressed *a* (phonetically [ə], as in *soda* or *extra*, may be raised to a high vowel ē, giving pronunciations such as "sody" for *soda* and "extry" for *extra*. Again, this production is found in rural vernaculars of the Upper and Lower South.

ire/our Collapse

The sequence often spelled *ire* as in *fire* and *tire* is usually pronounced in Standard English as a two-syllable sequence which includes ī and *u*. In Southern-based vernacular dialects, the sequence can be collapsed into a one-syllable sequence so that *tire* sounds like *tar* and *fire* like *far*. It affects not only root words like *fire* but also sequences formed by the addition of an *-er* suffix, as in *buyer* as "bar" and *retired* as "ritard." A similar process affects *-our/ower* sequences that consist of a two-syllable sequence in *flower* or *hour*. These sequences may be reduced to a single syllable, so that *flower* sounds like "fla'r" and *hour* like "a'r."

GRAMMATICAL STRUCTURES

The Verb Phrase

Many of the socially significant grammatical structures in American English involve aspects of the verb phrase. Some of this variation is due to natural principles of language change, but there are also some items that have their roots in the historical origins of different dialect varieties.

Irregular Verbs

There are five ways in which irregular verbs pattern differently in standard and vernacular dialects of English. For the most part, these different patterns are the result of analogy, but there are also some retentions of patterns that have become obsolete in standard varieties. These differences are as follows:

I. past as participle form
    I *had went* down there.
    He may *have took* the wagon.

2. participle as past form

   He *seen* something out there.

   She *done* her work.

3. bare root as past form

   She *come* to my house yesterday.

   She *give* him a nice present last year.

4. regularization

   Everybody *knowed* he was late.

   They *throwed* out the old food.

5. different irregular form

   I *hearn* something shut the church house door.

   Something just *riz* up right in front of me.

Different dialects may differ according to which of these patterns are found in the variety. The majority of vernaculars in the North and South indicate patterns 1, 2, and 3. Some rural vernaculars in the South may exhibit pattern 5 in addition to the first three. Varieties subject to the influence of second-language-learning strategies (e.g., Vietnamese English) will often reveal a higher incidence of regularization pattern 4 than other varieties.

Co-occurrence Relations and Meaning Changes

There are a number of different types of constructions that can vary from dialect to dialect based on the types of structures that can co-occur with certain verbs or meaning changes that affect particular verbs. These constructions include the following types:

1. shifts in the transitive status of verbs (i.e., whether or not the verb is required to take an object)

   If we *beat*, we'll be champs.

2. types of structures co-occurring with particular verbs

   The kitchen *needs remodeled*.

   The students *started to messing* around.

   I'll *have* him *to do* it.

   The dog *wanted out*.

   Walt *called himself dancing*.

3. verb plus verb particle formations

   He *happened in* on the party.

   The coach *blessed out* his players.

4. verbs derived from other parts of speech (e.g., verbs derived from nouns)

Our dog *treed* a coon.

We *doctored* the sickness ourselves.

5. Broadened, narrowed, or shifted semantic reference for particular verb forms

He *carried* her to the movies.

My kids *took* the chicken pox when they were young.

I been *aimin'* to go there.

For the most part, differences related to meaning changes and co-occurence relations between verbs and other sentence elements have to be dealt with on an item-by-item basis. All vernaculars, and many regional varieties, indicate meaning shifts and co-occurrence relations not found in standard English to some extent.

Special Helping Verb Forms

There are a number of special uses of helping or auxiliary verb forms that set apart vernacular dialects of English from their standard counterparts. Many of these indicate subtle but significant meanings related to the duration or type of activity indicated by verbs, or verb aspect.

Completive done

The form *done* may mark a completed action or event in a way somewhat different from a simple past tense form, as in a sentence such as *There was one in there that **done** rotted away* or *I **done** forgot what you wanted*. In this use, the emphasis is on the completive aspect or the fact that the action has been fully completed. The *done* form may also add intensification to the activity, as in *I **done** told you not to mess up*. This form is typically found in Southern Anglo- and African-American vernaculars.

Habitual be

The form *be* in sentences such as *Sometimes my ears **be** itching* or *She usually **be** home in the evening* may signify an event or activity distributed intermittently over time or space. The predominant construction for habitual *be* involves a form of *be* + verb *-ing*, as in *My ears **be** itching*. The unique aspectual meaning of *be* is typically associated with AAVE although isolated and restricted constructions with habitual *be* have been found in some rural Anglo varieties.

Be + s

In some restricted parts of the South (e.g., areas of the Carolinas where the historic influence of Highland Scots and Scots Irish is evident), *be* may occur with an *-s* third-person suffix as in *Sometimes it **bes** like that* or *I hope it **bes** a girl*. However, *bes* is not restricted to contexts of habitual activity and thus is different from habitual *be* in AAVE. *Bes* is also distinguished from *be* in contemporary AAVE by the inflectional *-s*; further, *bes* is obviously a receding form whereas *be* in AAVE is quite robust.

Remote Time béen

When stressed, *béen* can serve to mark a special aspectual function indicating that the event or activity took place in the distant past. In structures such as *I **béen** had it there for about three years* or *I **béen** known her*, the reference is to an event that took place, literally or figuratively, in some distant time frame. This use, which is associated with AAVE, is dying out in some varieties of the vernacular, but is still prominent in those varieties more closely aligned with the apparent creole predecessor of AAVE, in which the form most likely was used much more extensively.

Fixin' to

The use of *fixin' to* (also produced as "fixta," "fista," "finsta," and "finna") may occur with a verb with the meaning of about to or plan to. Thus, in a sentence such as *It's **fixin' to** rain*, the occurrence of rain is imminent. In a construction such as *I was **fixin' to** come but I got held up*, the speaker is indicating that he or she had intended to come. This special use of *fixin' to* is found only in the South, particularly in the South Atlantic and Gulf states.

A- Prefixing

An *a-* prefix may occur on *-ing* forms functioning as verbs or adverbs, as in *She was a-comin' home* or *He starts a-laughin' at you*. This form cannot occur on *-ing* forms that function as nouns or adjectives. Thus, it cannot occur in sentences such as *He likes a-sailin'* or *The movie was a-charmin'*. The *a-* is also restricted phonologically, in that it occurs only on forms whose first syllable is accented; thus, it may occur on *a-fóllowin'* but not *a-discóverin'*. The *a-* prefix is also preferred on items beginning with a consonant (e.g., *Kim was a-drinkin'*) over those beginning with a vowel (e.g., *Kim was a-eatin'*). As currently used by some speakers, the *a-* prefix may be used to indicate intensity, but it does not appear to have any unique aspectual marking analogous to habitual *be* or completive *done*. It is quite characteristic of vernacular Appalachian English but is found in other rural varieties as well.

Double Modals

Double modals are combinations of two modal verbs, or verbs expressing certain moods such as certainty, possibility, obligation, or permission. Possible combinations include *might could, useta could, might should, might oughta*, and so forth. Sentences such as *I **might could** go there* or *You **might oughta** take it* are typically Southern vernacular structures; in Northern varieties, modal clustering occurs only with *useta*, as in *He **useta couldn't** do it*. Double modals tend to lessen the force of the attitude or obligation conveyed by single modals, so that *She **might could** do it* is less forceful than either *She **might** do it* or *She **could** do it*. In some Southern states, double modals are quite widespread and not particularly stigmatized.

liketa and supposta

The forms *liketa* and *(su)poseta* may be used as special verb modifiers to mark speakers' perceptions of significant events that were on the verge of happening. *Liketa* is a counterfactual, in that it is used in a nonliteral way to indicate that an impending event did not occur. In a sentence such as *It was so cold, I **liketa** froze to death, liketa* conveys the meaning not only that the speaker did not freeze to death but also that the speaker was never in any real danger of freezing. *Supposeta*, in sentences such as *You **(su)poseta** went there*, parallels the standard English construction *supposed to have*.

Absence of be Forms

Where contracted forms of *is* or *are* may occur in standard English, these same forms may be deleted in some vernacular varieties. Thus, we get structures such as *You ugly* or *She taking the dog out* corresponding to the Standard English structures *You're ugly* and *She's taking the dog out*, respectively. It is important to note that this absence only takes place on contractible forms; thus, it does not affect *they are* in a construction such as *That's where **they are*** because *they are* cannot be contracted to *they're* in this instance. Furthermore, the absence of *be* does not usually apply to the *am* form, so that sentences such as *I ugly* do not occur. The deletion of *are* is typical of both Southern Anglo and AAVE varieties, although the absence of *is* is not very extensive in most Anglo varieties. A more general version of *be* absence that includes *am* is sometimes found in varieties developed in the process of learning English as a second language (e.g., Vietnamese English).

Subject–Verb Agreement

There are a number of different subject–verb agreement patterns that enter into the social and regional differentiation of dialects. These include the following:

1. agreement with expletive *there*
   There was five people there.
   There's two women in the lobby.
2. leveling to *was* for past tense forms of *be*
   The cars was out on the street.
   Most of the kids was younger up there.
3. leveling to *were* with negative past tense *be*
   It weren't me that was there last night.
   She weren't at the creek.
4. leveling to *is* for present tense forms of *be*
   The dogs is in the house.
   We is doing it right now.
5. agreement with the form *don't*
   She don't like the cat in the house.
   It don't seem like a holiday.
6. agreement with *have*
   My nerves has been on edge.
   My children hasn't been there much.
7. -*s* suffix on verbs occurring with third person plural noun phrase subjects
   Some people likes to talk a lot.
   Me and my brother gets in fights.
8. -*s* absence on third person singular forms
   The dog stay outside in the afternoon.
   She usually like the evening news.

Different vernacular varieties exhibit different combinations of the above patterns. Virtually all vernacular varieties show patterns 1, 2, and 5 (in fact, standard varieties are moving toward the pattern found in 1), but in different degrees. The patterns illustrated in 6 and 7 are most characteristic of rural varieties in the Upper and Lower South, and those found in 8 are most typical of AAVE. The leveling of past *be* to *weren't* in 3 appears to be regionally restricted to some coastal dialect areas of the Southeast and a few historically isolated Southern dialect areas.

Past Tense Absence

Many cases of past-tense *-ed* absence on verbs (e.g., *Yesterday he **mess** up*) can be accounted for by the pronunciation process of consonant cluster reduction found in the discussion of phonology. However, there are some instances in which the use of unmarked past-tense forms represents a genuine grammatical difference. Such cases are particularly likely to be found in varieties influenced by other languages in their recent past. Thus, structures such as *He **bring** the food yesterday* or *He **play** a new song last night* may be the result of a grammar-based process rather than a pronunciation-based one. Grammatically based tense unmarking tends to be more frequent on regular verbs than irregular ones, so that a structure such as *Yesterday he **play** a new song* is more likely than *Yesterday he **is** in a new store*, although both may occur. In some cases, both pronunciation and grammatical processes operate in a convergent way.

Tense unmarking has been found to be prominent in varieties such as Vietnamese English and Native American English in the Southwest. In the latter case, unmarking is favored in habitual contexts (e.g., *In those days, we **play** a different kind of game*) as opposed to simple past time (e.g., *Yesterday, we **play** at a friend's house*).

Historical Present

In the dramatic recounting of past time events, speakers may use present tense verb forms rather than past tense forms, as in *I **go** down there and this guy **comes** up to me ....* In some cases, an *-s* suffix may be added to non-third person forms, particularly with the first person form of *say* (e.g., *so I **says** to him ...*). This structure is more prominent in Anglo vernaculars than in AAVE.

Perfective be

Some historically isolated varieties of American English may use forms of *be* rather than *have* in present perfect constructions, as in *I'm been there before* for *I've been there before* or *You're taken the best medicine* for *You have taken the best medicine.* This construction occurs most frequently in first person singular contexts (e.g., *I'm forgot*) but can also occur in the first person plural and in second person contexts as well (e.g., *We're forgot, You're been there*). Occasionally, the perfect tense can even be formed with invariant *be*, as in *We be come here for nothing* or *I'll be went to the post office.* Perfective *be* derives from the historic formation of the perfect with *be* rather than *have* for certain verbs (e.g., earlier, *He is risen*; currently, *He has risen*) and is restricted to historically isolated dialect areas.

Adverbs

There are several different patterns that distinguish adverb usage among vernacular varieties. These involve differences in the placement of adverbs in the sentence, differences in the formation of adverbs, and differences in the use or meaning of particular adverbial forms.

Adverb Placement

There are several differences in terms of the position of the adverb in the sentence, including the placement of certain time adverbs in the verb phrase, as in *We were **all the time** talking* or *We watched **all the time** the news on TV.* These cases do not hold great social significance and are not particularly socially stigmatized. More socially marked is the change in order with various forms of *ever*, as in *everwhat, everwho,* or *everwhich* (e.g., ***Everwho** wanted to go could go*). These older English forms are generally found only in vernaculars retaining relic forms of English, but even in these contexts they are currently dying out.

Comparatives and Superlatives

Most vernacular varieties of English indicate some comparative and superlative adjective and adverb forms that are not found in standard varieties. Some forms involve the regularization of irregular forms, as in *badder* or *mostest* whereas others involve the use of *-er* and *-est* on adjectives of two or more syllables (e.g., *beautifulest, awfulest*), where the standard variety uses *more* and *most*. In some instances, comparatives and superlatives are doubly marked, as in *most awfulest* or *more nicer*.

-ly Absence

In present-day American English, some adverbs that used to be formed by adding an *-ly* suffix no longer take *-ly*. Thus, in informal contexts, most Standard English speakers say *They answered wrong* instead of *They answered wrongly*. The range of items affected by *-ly* absence can be extended to various degrees in different vernacular dialects. These items may be relatively unobtrusive (e.g., *She enjoyed life **awful** well*) or quite obtrusive (e.g., *I come from Virginia **original***). The more obtrusive forms seem to be more prominent in Southern-based vernacular varieties than Northern dialects, particularly Upper Southern varieties such as Appalachian and Ozark English.

Intensifying Adverbs

In some Southern-based vernaculars, certain adverbs can be used to intensify particular attributes or activities. In Standard English, the adverb *right* is currently limited to contexts involving location or time (e.g., *He is **right** around the corner*). However, in Southern-based vernaculars, *right* may be used to intensify the degree of other types of attributes, as in *She is **right** nice*. Other adverbs, such as *plumb*, serve to intensify attributes in totality, as in *The students fell **plumb** asleep*. Additional intensifying adverbs found in these varieties include items such as *big old*, *little old*, *right smart*, and *right much*, among others.

Other Adverbial Forms

There are a number of other cases in which the adverbial forms of vernacular varieties differ from their standard counterparts. Some of these involve word class changes, as in the use of *but* as an adverb meaning *only*, as in *He ain't **but** thirteen years old*, or the item *all* in *The corn got **all***. In many midland dialects of American English, *anymore* may be used in positive constructions with a meaning of *nowadays*, as in *She watches a lot of videos **anymore***.

Some vernacular dialects contain adverbial lexical items not found at all in standard varieties (e.g., *yonder*, as in *It's up **yonder***) whereas other adverbial differences come from the phonological fusion of items, as in *t'all* from *at all* (e.g., *It's not coming up **t'all***), *pert' near* (e.g., *She's **pert' near** sev-*

enty), or *druther* (e.g., ***Druther*** *than lose the farm, he fought*). Again, such differences must be considered on an item-by-item basis.

Negation

The two major vernacular negation features of American English are the use of so-called double negatives, or the marking of negative meaning at more than one point in a sentence, and the use of the lexical item *ain't*. Other forms, resulting directly from the acquisition of English as a second language (e.g., *He no like the man*) are found in the speech of people learning English as a second language but do not seem to be perpetuated as a continuing part of the vernacular English variety of such speakers once they have completed the transition to English. An exception may be the negative tag *no* as found in some Hispanic English varieties as in *They're going to the store, **no**?*.

Multiple Negation

There are four different patterns of multiple negative marking found in the vernacular varieties of English:

1. marking of the negative on the auxiliary verb and the indefinite(s) following the verb
   The man *wasn't* saying *nothing*.
   He *didn't* say *nothing* about *no* people bothering him
       or *nothing* like that.
2. negative marking of an indefinite before the verb phrase and of the auxiliary verb
   Nobody didn't like the mess.
   Nothing can't stop him from failing the course.
3. inversion of the negativized auxiliary verb and the preverbal indefinite
   Didn't nobody like the mess.
   Can't nothing stop him from failing the course.
4. multiple negative marking across different clauses
   There *wasn't* much that I *couldn't do*
       (meaning "There wasn't much I could do").
   I *wasn't* sure that *nothing wasn't* going to come up
       (meaning "I wasn't sure that anything was going to come up").

Virtually all vernacular varieties of English participate in multiple negation of type 1 in the inventory, restricted Northern and most Southern vernaculars participate in 2, most Southern vernaculars participate in 3 and
restricted Southern and AAVE varieties participate in 4.

ain't

The item *ain't* may be used as an alternate for certain standard English
forms, including the following:

1. forms of *be* + *not*
    She *ain't* here now.
    I *ain't* gonna do it.
2. forms of *have* + *not*
    I *ain't* seen her in a long time.
    She *ain't* gone to the movies in a long time.
3. *did* + *not*
    He *ain't* tell him he was sorry.
    I *ain't* go to school yesterday.

The first two types are found in most vernacular varieties, but the third
type, in which *ain't* corresponds with standard *didn't*, has only been found in
AAVE.

Nouns and Pronouns

Constructions involving nouns and pronouns are often subject to socially
significant dialect variation. The major types of differences involve the at-
tachment of various suffixes and the use of particular case markings, or
markings that indicate the role that nouns and pronouns play in the particular sentences in which they occur.

Plurals

There are several different ways in which plurals may be formed that differentiate them from plurals found in standard varieties of English. These
include the following:

1. general absence of plural suffix
    Lots of *boy* go to the school.
    All the girl liked the movie.

2. restricted absence of plural suffix with measurement nouns
   The station is four *mile_* down the road.
   They hauled in a lotta *bushel_* of corn.
3. regularization of various irregular plural noun forms.
   They saw the *deers* running across the field.
   The *firemans* liked the convention.

Plural absence of type 1 is found only among varieties where another language was spoken in the recent past and, to a limited degree, in AAVE. In category 2, plural suffix absence is limited to nouns of weights (e.g., *four pound, three ton*) and measures (e.g., *two foot, twenty mile*), including some temporal nouns (e.g., *two year, five month*); this pattern is found in Southern-based vernaculars, particularly in historically isolated areas. Category 3 includes regularization of plurals that are not marked overtly in Standard English (e.g., *deers, sheeps*), forms marked with irregular suffixes in the standard (e.g., *oxes*), and forms marked by nonsuffix plurals (e.g., *firemans, snowmans*). In the last case, plurals may be marked with both plural forms, as in *mens* or *childrens*. Some kinds of plurals in category 3 are quite widespread among the vernacular varieties of English (e.g., regularizing nonmarked plurals such as *deers*), whereas others (e.g., the double marking in *mens*) are more limited.

Possessives

There are several patterns involving possessive nouns and pronouns, including the following:

1. the absence of the possessive suffix
   The *man_ hat* is on the chair.
   John_ coat is here.
2. regularization of the possessive pronoun *mines*, on the basis of analogy with *yours, his, hers,* and so forth.
   Mines is here.
   It's *mines*.
3. the use of possessive forms ending in *-n,* as in *hisn* or *yourn*. Such forms can only be found in phrase- or sentence-final position as in *It is **hisn*** or *It was **yourn** that I was talking about*; *-n* forms do not usually occur in structures such as *It is **hern** book*.
   Is it yourn?
   I think it's *hisn*.

The first two types of possessives are typical of AAVE, and the third type is found in vernacular Appalachian English and other rural varieties characterized by the retention of older forms, although it is now restricted to older speakers in these varieties.

Pronouns

Pronoun differences typically involve regularization by analogy and rule extension. The categories of difference include the following:

1. regularization of reflexive forms by analogy with other possessive pronouns
   He hit *hisself* on the head.
   They shaved *theirselves* with the new razor.
2. extension of object forms to coordinate subjects
   Me and him will do it.
   John and them will be home soon.
3. adoption of a second person plural form to fill out the person-number paradigm
   a. *Y'all* won the game.
      I'm going to leave *y'all* now.
   b. *Youse* won the game.
      I'm going to leave *youse* now.
   c. *You'uns* won the game.
      I'm going to leave *you'uns* now.
4. extension of object forms to demonstratives
   Them books are on the shelf.
   She didn't like *them* there boys.
5. a special personal dative use of the object pronoun form
   I got *me* a new car.
   We had *us* a little old dog.

The first four types of pronominal difference are well represented in most vernacular dialects of English. The particular form used for the third person plural pronoun (type 3) varies by region; 3a, of course, is the Southern form and 3b the Northern form, with some specific regions (e.g., Western Pennsylvania, Southern Appalachia) using 3c. The so-called personal dative illustrated in 5 is a Southern feature, but it is not particularly stigmatized in the South.

Other pronoun forms, such as the use of an object form with a noncoordinate subject (e.g., *Her in the house*) and the use of subject or object forms in possessive structures (e.g., *It is she book*; *It is he book*) are quite rare in most current vernaculars, except for those still closely related to a prior creole state. The use of possessive *me* as in *It's me cap* is occasionally found in historically isolated varieties that have some Scots-Irish influence.

Relative Pronouns

Differences affecting relative pronouns (e.g., *who* in *She's the one who gave me the present*) include the use of certain relative pronoun forms in contexts where they would not be used in standard varieties and the absence of relative pronouns under certain conditions. Differences in relative pronoun forms may range from the relatively socially insignificant use of *that* for human subjects (e.g., *The person that I was telling you about is here*) to the quite stigmatized use of *what*, as in *The person what I was telling you about is here*. One form that is becoming more common and spreading into informal varieties of Standard English is the use of the relative pronoun *which* as a coordinating conjunction (i.e., *and*), as in *They gave me this cigar, which they know I don't smoke cigars*.

In Standard English, relative pronouns may be deleted if they are the object in the relative clause, so that *That's the dog that I bought* can alternately be rendered as *That's the dog I bought*. In most cases where the relative pronoun is the subject, however, the pronoun must be retained, as in *That's the dog that bit me*. However, a number of Southern-based varieties may sometimes delete relative pronouns in subject position, as in *That's the dog bit me* or *The man come in here is my father*. The absence of the relative pronoun is more common in existential constructions such as *There's a dog bit me* than in other constructions.

Existential It/They

As used in sentences such as *There are four people in school* and *There's a picture on T.V.*, the standard English form *there* is called an existential because it indicates the mere existence of something rather than specific location (as in *Put the book over there*). Vernacular varieties may use *it* or *they* for *there* in existential constructions, as in *It's a dog in the yard* or *They's a good show on TV. They* for *there* seems to be found only in Southern-based vernaculars; *it* is more general, and appears to be spreading.

Other Grammatical Structures

There are a number of additional structures that we have not included in this overview of vernacular grammatical constructions. Some of the forms we have not included are those that were once thought to be confined to vernacular varieties but have been shown, through empirical sociolinguistic study, to actually be quite common in informal standard varieties. For example, we did not include the structure known as pronominal apposition, in which a pronoun is used in addition to a noun in subject position, as in *My father, he made my breakfast,* because this feature is found in practically all social groups of American speakers, even though it is often considered to be a vernacular dialect feature. Furthermore, it is not particularly obtrusive in spoken language. It has also been found that the use of inverted word order in indirect questions, as in *She asked could she go to the movies* is becoming just as much a part of informal spoken standard English as indirect questions without inverted word order, as in *She asked if she could go to the movies.* Other differences, such as those affecting prepositions, have to be treated on an item-by-item basis and really qualify as lexical rather than grammatical differences. Thus, forms such as *of a evening/of the evening* (in the evening), *upside the head* (on the side of the head) *leave out of there* (leave there), *the matter of him* (the matter with him), *to* for *at* (e.g., *She's to the store right now*), and so forth have to be treated individually. In most cases, their social significance is also secondary to their regional significance, so that we have not treated them in detail. Traditional regional surveys such as the *Dictionary of American Regional English* give much more adequate detail about these forms than could be given in this overview.

Author's Note: Material in this Appendix was taken from Wolfram and Schilling-Estes (1998). Copyright © 1998 by Basil Blackwell. Reprinted with permission.

References

Adams, M. J. (1990). *Beginning to read: Thinking and learning about print.* Cambridge, MA: MIT Press.

Adger, C. T. (1986). When difference does not conflict: Successful arguments between Black and Vietnamese classmates. *Text, 6,* 223–237.

Adger, C. T. (1998). Register shifting with dialect resources in instructional discourse. In S. Hoyle & C. T. Adger (Eds.), *Kids talk: Strategic language use in later childhood* (pp. 151–169). New York: Oxford University Press.

Adger, C. T., & Detwyler, J. (1992, April). *Empowering talk: African American teachers and classroom discourse.* Paper presented at the annual meeting of the American Educational Research Association, Atlanta.

Adger, C. T., Kalyanpur, M., Peterson, D. B., & Bridger, T. L. (1995). *Engaging students: Thinking, talking, cooperating.* Thousand Oaks, CA: Corwin.

Adger, C. T., & Wolfram, W. (in press). Demythologizing the home/school dichotomy: Sociolinguistic reality and instructional practice. In P. Griffin, J. Peyton, W. Wolfram, & R.W. Fasold (Eds.), *Language in action: New studies of language in society.* Cresskill, NJ: Hampton Press.

Alvarez, L., & Kolker, A. (Producers). (1987). *American tongues.* New York: Center for New American Media.

American speech. A publication of the American Dialect Society. Tuscaloosa: the University of Alabama Press.

Angelou, M. (1976). *Singin' and swingin' and gettin' merry like Christmas.* New York: Bantam.

Applebome, P. (1997, September 3). Students' test scores show slow but steady gains at nation's schools. *The New York Times,* p. A4.

Au, K., & Jordan, C. (1981). Teaching reading to Hawaiian children: Finding a culturally appropriate solution. In H. Trueba, G. P. Guthrie, & K. H. Au (Eds.), *Culture and the bilingual classroom: Studies in classroom ethnography* (pp. 139–152). Rowley, MA: Newbury.

Bateson, G. (1972). *Steps to an ecology of mind.* New York: Ballantine.

Bauer, L., & Trudgill, P. (Eds.). (1998). *Language myths.* New York: Penguin.

Baugh, J. (1991). The politicization of changing terms of self-reference among American slave descendants. *American Speech, 66*(2), 133–146.

Bennett, W. T. (1994). *The index of leading cultural indicators: Facts and figures on the state of American society.* New York: Touchstone.

Bereiter, C. (1965). Academic instruction and preschool children. In R. Corbin & M. Crosby (Eds.), *Language programs for the disadvantaged* (pp. 195–203). Champaign, IL: National Council of Teachers of English.

Bernstein, C, Nunnally T., & Sabino, R. (1997). *Language variety in the South revisited.* Tuscaloosa: The University of Alabama Press.

Borko, H., & Eisenhart, M. (1989). Reading ability groups as literacy communities. In D. Bloome (Ed.), *Classrooms and literacy* (pp. 107–133). Norwood, NJ: Ablex.

225

Brend, R. M. (1975). Male–female intonation patterns in American English. In B. Thorne & N. Henley (Eds), *Language and sex: Difference and dominance* (pp. 84–107). Rowley, MA: Newbury.

Brooks, C. K. (Ed.). (1985). *Tapping potential: English and language arts for the Black learner.* Urbana, IL: National Council of Teachers of English.

Brown, P., & Levinson, S. (1987). *Politeness: Some universals in language usage.* New York: Cambridge University Press.

Burling, R. (1973). *English in Black and White.* New York: Holt, Rinehart and Winston.

Carver, C. (1987). *American regional dialects: A word geography.* Ann Arbor: University of Michigan Press.

Cassidy, F. G. (1985). *Dictionary of American regional English* (Vol. I, A–C). Cambridge, MA: Belknap Press of Harvard University Press.

Cassidy, F. G., & Hall, J. H. (1991). *Dictionary of American regional English* (Vol. II, D–H). Cambridge, MA: Belknap Press of Harvard University Press.

Cassidy, F. G., & Hall, J. H. (1996). *Dictionary of American regional English* (Vol. III, I–O). Cambridge, MA: Belknap Press of Harvard University Press.

Cazden, C. (1988). *Classroom discourse: The language of teaching and learning.* Portsmouth, NH: Heinemann.

Chall, J. S., & Curtis, M. E. (1991). Responding to individual differences among language learners: Children at risk. In J. Flood, J. M. Jensen, D. Lapp, & J. R. Squire (Eds.), *Handbook of research on teaching the English language arts* (pp. 349–355). New York: Macmillan.

Christian, D. (1986). *American English speech recordings.* Washington, DC: Center for Applied Linguistics.

Christian, D. (in press). Reflections of language heritage: Choice and chance in vernacular English dialects. In P. Griffin, J. Peyton, W. Wolfram, & R. W. Fasold (Eds.), *Language in action: New studies of language in society.* Cresskill, NJ: Hampton Press.

Christian, D., Wolfram, W., & Dube, N. (1988). *Variation and change in geographically isolated speech communities.* Publication of the American Dialect Society No. 74. Tuscaloosa: University of Alabama Press.

Clay, M. (1987). *The early detection of reading difficulties* (3rd ed.). Auckland, New Zealand and Portsmouth, NH: Heinemann.

Coehlo, E. (1991). *Caribbean students in Canadian schools: Book 2.* Markham, Ontario: Pippen.

College Composition and Communication Conference. (1974). *Students' rights to their own dialects.* Urbana, IL: Author.

Collins, J. (1988). Language and class in minority education. *Anthropology and Education Quarterly, 19,* 299–326.

Cooper, E. J. (1995). Curriculum reform and testing. In V. L. Gadsden & D. A. Wagner (Eds.), *Literacy among African-American Youth* (pp. 281–298). Cresskill, NJ: Hampton.

Crandall, J., Dale, T., Rhodes, N., & Spanos, G. (1989a). *English skills for algebra.* Englewood Cliffs, NJ: Prentice-Hall & Washington, DC: Center for Applied Linguistics.

Crandall, J., Dale, T., Rhodes, N., & Spanos, G. (1989b). *English skills for algebra: Tutor book and resource materials.* Englewood Cliffs, NJ: Prentice Hall Regents & Washington, DC: Center for Applied Linguistics.

Delpit, L. (1988). The silenced dialogue: Power and pedagogy in educating other people's children. *Harvard Educational Review, 58,* 280–298.

Delpit, L. (1995). *Other people's children: Cultural conflict in the classroom.* New York: The New Press.

Dumas, B., & Lighter, J. (1976). Is slang a word for linguists? *American Speech, 51,* 5–17.

Dyson, A. H., & Genishi, C. (Eds.). (1994). *The need for story: Cultural diversity in classroom and community.* Urbana, IL: National Council of Teachers of English.

Eble, C. (1996). *Slang and sociability: In-group language among college students.* Chapel Hill: The University of North Carolina Press.

Edwards, J., & Doviak, E. (1975, December). *Linguistic constraints on variation in Chicano English.* Paper presented at the meeting of the Linguistic Society of America San Francisco.

Ehrenhaft, G. (1994). *How to prepare for SAT II: Writing*. New York: Barrons.

Ehri, L. C. (1991). Development of the ability to read words. In R. Barr & P. D. Pearson (Eds.), *Handbook of reading research* (Vol. 1, pp. 383–417). New York: Longman.

Erickson, F., & Mohatt, G. (1982). Cultural organization of participation structures in two classrooms of Indian students. In G. D. Spindler (Ed.), *Doing the ethnography of schooling* (pp. 132–174). New York: Holt, Rinehart and Winston.

Erickson, F., & Shultz, J. (1982). *The counsellor as gatekeeper: Social interaction in interviews*. New York: Academic Press.

Farr–Whiteman, M. (Ed.). (1980). *Reactions to Ann Arbor: Vernacular Black English and education*. (ED 197 624). Washington, DC: Center for Applied Linguistics.

Farr, M., & Daniels, H. (1986). *Language diversity and writing instruction*. New York: ERIC Clearinghouse on Urban Education, and Urbana, IL: ERIC Clearinghouse on Reading and Communication Skills.

Fasold, R. (1972). *Tense marking in Black English: A linguistic and social analysis*. Arlington, VA: Center for Applied Linguistic.

Fasold, R. (1984). *The sociolinguistics of society*. Oxford, England: Basil Blackwell.

Fasold, R. (Ed.). (1987). Are Black and White vernacular dialects diverging: Papers from the NWAVE XIV panel discussion. *American Speech, 62(1)* 3–5.

Fasold, R., & Wolfram, W. (1969). Toward reading materials for speakers of Black English: Three linguistically appropriate passages. In J.C. Baratz & R.W. Shuy (Eds.), *Teaching Black children to read* (pp. 41–86). Washington, DC: Center for Applied Linguistics.

Ferguson, C., & Heath, S. B. (Eds.). (1981). *Language in the USA*. Cambridge, England: Cambridge University Press.

Fishman, J. A. (1969). Literacy and the language barrier [Review of the books *Intelligence and cultural environment* and *Teaching Black children to read*]. *Science, 165,* 1108–09.

Fordham, S. (1998). Speaking standard English from nine to three: Language as guerrilla warfare at Capital High. In S. Hoyle & C. T. Adger (Eds.), *Kids talk: Strategic language use in later childhood* (pp. 205–216). New York: Oxford University Press.

Foster, M. (1989). "It's cookin' now": A performance analysis of the speech events of a Black teacher in an urban community college. *Language in Society, 18,* 1–29.

Fulghum, J. S., Jr. (1993, June). Letter to the editor. *The Alumni Magazine of North Carolina State University,* p. 43.

Gadsden, V. L., & Wagner, D. A. (Eds.). (1995). *Literacy among African-American youth: Issues in learning, teaching, and schooling*. Cresskill, NJ: Hampton Press.

Garcia, G., & Pearson, P. D. (1990). Modifying reading instruction to maximize its effectiveness for "disadvantaged" students. In M. S. Knapp & P. M. Shields (Eds.), *Better schooling for the children of poverty: Alternatives to conventional wisdom* (pp. II-1–II-23). Washington, DC: U.S. Department of Education, Office of Planning, Budget & Evaluation.

Gee, J. P. (1990). *Social linguistics and literacies*. New York: Falmer Press.

Gonzalez, N., Moll, L., Floyd–Tenery, M., Rivera A., Rendon, P., Gonzales, R., & Amanti, C. (1993). *Teacher research on funds of knowledge: Learning from households*. Santa Cruz: National Center for Research on Cultural Diversity and Second Language Learning, University of California, Santa Cruz.

Goodman, K. (1986). *What's whole in whole language*. Portsmouth, NH: Heinemann.

Goodwin, M. (1990). *He-said-she-said: Talk as social organization among Black children*. Bloomington: Indiana University Press.

Grice, H. P. (1975). Logic and conversation. In P. Cole & J. L. Morgan (Eds.), *Speech acts* (pp. 41–58). New York: Academic Press.

Hampton, S. (1995). Strategies for increasing achievement in writing. In R. W. Cole (Ed.), *Educating everybody's children: Diverse teaching strategies for diverse learners: What research and practice say about improving achievement* (pp. 99–120). Alexandria, VA: Association for Supervision and Curriculum Development.

Hazen, K. A. (1996). Dialect affinity and subject–verb concord: The Appalachian-Outer Banks connection. *SECOL Review, 20,* 25–53.

Heath, S. B. (1982). Questioning at home and at school: A comparative study. In G. Spindler (Ed.), *Doing the ethnography of schooling: Educational anthropology in action* (pp. 102–131). New York: Holt, Rinehart & Winston.

Heath, S. B. (1983). *Ways with words*. Cambridge, England: Cambridge University Press.

Heath, S. B. (1986). Sociocultural contexts of language development. In Bilingual Education Office (Ed.), *Beyond language: Social and cultural factors in schooling language minority students* (pp. 144–186). Los Angeles: Bilingual Education Office, California State Department of Education.

Heath, S. B. (1994). Stories as ways of acting together. In A. H. Dyson & C. Genishi (Eds.), *The need for story: Cultural diversity in classroom and community* (pp. 206–220). Urbana, IL: National Council of Teachers of English.

Heath, S. B., & Mangiola, L. (1991). *Children of promise: Literate activity in linguistically and culturally diverse classrooms*. Washington, DC: National Education Association.

Herrnstein, R. J., & Murray, C. (1994). *The bell curve*. New York: The Free Press.

Hoover, M. (1978). Community attitudes toward Black English. *Language in Society, 7,* 65–87.

Hymes, D. (1974). *Foundations in sociolinguistics: An ethnographic approach*. Philadelphia: University of Pennsylvania Press.

Hynds, S., & Rubin, D. L. (1990). *Perspectives on talk and learning*. Urbana, IL: National Council of Teachers of English.

Kochman, T. (1981). *Black and White styles in conflict*. Chicago: The University of Chicago Press.

Krashen, S. (1981). *Second language acquisition and second language learning*. Oxford: Pergamon.

Kurath, H. (1949). *Handbook of the linguistic geography of New England*. Ann Arbor: University of Michigan Press.

Labov, W. (1963). The social motivation of sound change. *Word, 19,* 273–307.

Labov, W. (1966). *The social stratification of English in New York City*. Washington, DC: Center for Applied Linguistics.

Labov, W. (1969). The logic of nonstandard English. In J. Alatis (Ed.), *Georgetown monograph series on languages and linguistics, 22,* 1–44.

Labov, W. (1972). *Language in the inner city: Studies in the Black English Vernacular*. Philadelphia: The University of Pennsylvania Press.

Labov, W. (1987). Are Black and White vernaculars diverging? *Papers from the NWAVE XIV panel discussion. American Speech, 62,* 5–12.

Labov, W. (1995). Can reading failure be reversed: A linguistic approach to the question. In V. L. Gadsden & D. A. Wagner (Eds.), *Literacy among African-American youth* (pp. 39–68). Cresskill, NJ: Hampton, Press.

Labov, W., Ash, S., & Boberg, C. (1997). *A national map of the regional dialects of American English*. Unpublished manuscript, University of Pennsylvania.

Leap, W. (1993). *American Indian English*. Salt Lake City: University of Utah Press.

Lippi-Green, R. (1997). *English with an accent: Language, ideology, and discrimination in the United States*. New York: Routledge.

Lucas, C., & Borders, D. G. (1994). *Language diversity and classroom discourse*. Norwood, NJ: Ablex.

Lyman, F. (1992). Think-pair-share, thinktrix, thinklinks, and weird facts: An interactive system for cooperative thinking. In N. Davidson & T. Worsham (Eds.), *Enhancing thinking through cooperative learning* (pp. 169–181). New York: Teachers College Press.

McKay, S. L., & Hornberger, N. H. (Eds.). (1996). *Sociolinguistics and language teaching*. Cambridge, England: Cambridge University Press.

Meier, D. (1973). *Reading failure and the tests* (Occasional Paper). New York: Workshop for Open Education.

Michaels, S. (1981). "Sharing time": Children's narrative styles and differential access to literacy. *Language in Society, 10,* 423–442.

Miller-Cleary, L., & Linn, M. D. (Eds.). (1986). *Linguistics for teachers*. New York: McGraw-Hill.

Millward, C. M. (1989). *A biography of the English language*. Orlando: Harcourt, Brace, Jovanovich.

Mohatt, G., & Erickson, F. (1981). In H. Trueba, G. Guthrie, & K. Au (Eds.), *Culture and the bilingual classroom: Studies in classroom ethnography* (pp. 105–119). Rowley, MA: Newbury House.

Mufwene, S. S. (1996). The development of American Englishes: Some questions from a creole genesis hypothesis. In E. W. Schneider (Ed.), *Focus on the USA* (pp. 231–264). Philadelphia: John Benjamins.

Mufwene, S., Rickford, J., Bailey, G., & Baugh, J. (Eds.). (1998). *African American Vernacular English*. New York: Routledge.

Myhill, J. 1988. Postvocalic /r/ as an index of integration into the BEV speech community. *American Speech, 63,* 203–213.

National Commission on Excellence in Education. (1983). *A nation at risk*. Washington, DC: Author.

National Council of Teachers of English/International Reading Association. (1996). *Standards for the English language arts*. Newark, DE: IRA/NCTE.

National Council of Teachers of Mathematics. (1989). *Curriculum and evaluation standards for school mathematics*. Reston, VA: NCTM.

National Public Radio, Prairie Home Companion, July, 1986.

North Carolina Professional Practices Commission. (Sept., 1992). *A time for understanding and action.* Raleigh, NC: North Carolina Department of Education.

Orr, E. W. (1987a November 1). Does Black English hinder learning mathematics? *Washington Post Education Review*, pp. 1, 26–27.

Orr, E. W. (1987b). *Twice as less: Black English and the performance of Black students in mathematics and science*. New York: Norton.

Palincsar, A. S., & Brown, A. L. (1987). Instruction for self-regulated reading. In L. B. Resnick & L. E. Klopfer (Eds.), *Toward the thinking curriculum: Current cognitive research* (pp. 19–39). Alexandria, VA: Association for Supervision and Curriculum Development.

Peñalosa, Fernando. (1980). *Chicano sociolinguistics*. Rowley, MA: Newbury House.

Peyton, J. K. (Ed.). (1990). *Students and teachers writing together: Perspectives on journal writing*. Alexandria, VA: Teachers of English to Speakers of Other Languages.

Peyton, J. K., & Reed, L. (1990). *Dialogue journal writing with nonnative English speakers: A handbook for teachers*. Alexandria, VA: Teachers of English to Speakers of Other Languages.

Philips, S. U. (1993). *The invisible culture: Communication in classroom and community on the Warm Springs Indian Reservation* (2nd ed.). Prospect Heights, IL: Waveland Press.

Piestrup, A. M. (1973). *Black dialect interference and accommodations of reading instruction in first grade*. (University of California, Berkeley, Language and Behavior Research Lab, Monograph 4, ED 119 113).

Preston, D. R. (Ed.). (1993). *American dialect research*. Philadelphia: John Benjamins.

Preston, D. R. (1996). Whaddayaknow? The modes of folk linguistic awareness. *Language Awareness, 5*(1), 40–77.

Purcell-Gates, V. (1995). *Other people's words: The cycle of low literacy*. Cambridge, MA: Harvard University Press.

Purcell-Gates, V., McIntyre, E., & Freppon, P. A. (1995). Learning written storybook language in school: A comparison of low-SES children in skills-based and whole language classrooms. *American Educational Research Journal, 32,* 659–685.

Pyles, T., & Algeo, J. (1982). *The origins and development of the English language*. New York: Harcourt Brace Jovanovich.

Resolution on application of dialect knowledge to education (1997, Spring/Summer). *The Newsletter of the American Association for Applied Linguistics, 19*(1), 7–8.

Reynolds, R. E., Taylor, M., Steffensen, M. S., Shirey, L., & Anderson, R. C. (1982). Cultural schemata and reading comprehension. *Reading Research Quarterly, 17,* 357–66.

Rickford, J., & Green, L. (1998). *African American vernacular English*. New York: Cambridge University Press.

Rickford, J., & Rickford, A. (1995). Dialect readers revisited. *Linguistics and Education, 7*, 107–128.

Rosenthal, M. S. (1977). *The magic boxes and Black English*. Washington, DC: ERIC Clearinghouse.

Rosenthal, R., & Jacobson, L. (1968). *Pygmalion in the classroom: Teacher expectations and pupils' intellectual achievement*. New York: Holt, Rinehart & Winston.

Sadker, M., & Sadker, D. (1994). *Failing at fairness: How America's schools cheat girls*. New York: Touchstone.

Safire, W. (1993). *Quoth the maven*. New York: Random House.

Schiffrin, D. (1994). *Approaches to discourse*. Oxford, England: Blackwell.

Schneider, E. W. (1989). *American earlier Black English: Morphological and syntactic variables*. Tuscaloosa: University of Alabama Press.

Schneider, E. W. (Ed.). (1996). *Varieties of English around the world: Focus on the USA*. Philadelphia: John Benjamins.

Scollon, R., & Scollon, S. B. K. (1981). *Narrative, literacy and face in interethnic communication*. Norwood, NJ: Ablex.

Shaughnessy, M. P. (1977). *Errors and expectations: A guide for the teacher of basic writing*. New York: Oxford University Press.

Shuy, R. W. (1976). *Confronting the literacy crises*. Unpublished manuscript, Georgetown University.

Shuy, R. W., & Fasold, R. W. (Eds.). (1973). *Language attitudes: Current trends and prospects*. Washington, DC: Georgetown University Press.

Simpkins, G. A., Holt, G., & Simpkins, C. (1977). *Bridge: A cross-cultural reading program*. Boston: Houghton-Mifflin.

Smith, F. (1973). *Psycholinguistics and reading*. New York: Holt, Rinehart & Winston.

Slavin, R., Madden, N., Dolan, L., & Wasik, B. (1996). *Every child, every school: Success for all*. Newberry Park, CA: Corwin.

Smitherman, G. (1986). *Talkin and testifyin: The language of Black America*. Detroit: Wayne State University Press.

Smitherman, G. (1991). "What is Africa to me": Language, ideology, and *African American*. *American Speech, 66*(2), 115–132.

Smitherman, G. (1995). Students' right to their own language: A retrospective. *English Journal, 84*, 21–27.

Stanovich, K. E. (1992). The psychology of reading: Evolutionary and revolutionary developments. In *Annual Review of Applied Linguistics, 12*, 3–30.

Staton, J., Shuy, R. W., Peyton, J. K., & Reed, L. (1988). *Dialogue journal communication: Classroom, linguistic, social and cognitive views*. Norwood, NJ: Ablex.

Steffensen, J. S., Reynolds, E. T., McClure, E., & Guthrie, L. (1982). Black English Vernacular and reading comprehension: A cloze study of third, sixth, and ninth graders. *Journal of Reading Behavior, 14*, 285–298.

Steffensen, M. C., Joag-dev, C., & Anderson, R. C. (1979). A cross-cultural perspective on reading comprehension. *Reading Research Quarterly,, 15*, 10–29.

Tannen, D. (1984). *Conversational style: Analyzing talk among friends*. Norwood, NJ: Ablex.

Tannen, D. (1986). *That's not what I meant: How conversational style makes or breaks your relations with others*. New York: Morrow.

Tannen, D. (1990). *You just don't understand: Women and men in conversation*. New York: Morrow.

Tannen, D. (1991). Teachers' classroom strategies should recognize that men and women use language differently. *The Chronicle of Higher Education, 37*(40), B2–3.

Tannen, D. (Ed.). (1993). *Framing in discourse*. New York: Oxford University Press.

Tannen, D. (1994). *Talking from nine to five*. New York: Morrow.

Tarone, E. (1973). Aspects of intonation in Black English. *American Speech, 48*, 29–36.

Taylor, O. (Ed.). (1986). *Nature of communication disorders in culturally and linguistically diverse populations*. San Diego: College Hill Press.

Trueba, H. T., Guthrie, G. P., & Au, K. H. (Eds.). (1981). *Culture and the bilingual classroom: Studies in classroom ethnography*. Rowley, MA: Newbury.

Wald, B. (1981). Limitations on the variable rule applied to bilingual phonology: The unmerging of the voiceless palatal phonemes in the English of Mexican Americans in the Los Angeles area. In D. Sankoff & H. Cedergren (Eds.), *Variation omnibus* (pp. 215–225). Carbondale, IL: Linguistic Research.

Wigginton, E. (1981). *Sometimes a shining moment: The foxfire experience*. Garden City, NY: Anchor/Doubleday.

Wolfram, W. (1974). The relationship of Southern White speech to Vernacular Black English. *Language, 50,* 498–527.

Wolfram, W. (1976). Sociolinguistic levels of test bias. In T. Trabasso & D. Harrison (Eds.), *Seminar in Black English* (pp. 265–267). New York: Lawrence Erlbaum Associates.

Wolfram, W. (1982). Language knowledge and other dialects. *American Speech, 57,* 3–18.

Wolfram, W. (1983). Test interpretation and sociolinguistic differences. *Topics in Language Disorders, 3,* 21–34.

Wolfram, W. (1993). Speaking of prejudice. *The Alumni Magazine of North Carolina State University, 65,* (3), 44.

Wolfram, W. (1995). On the sociolinguistic significance of obscure dialect structures: $NP_icall NP_i$ *V-ing* in African American Vernacular English. *American Speech, 69,* 339–360.

Wolfram, W., & Adger, C. T. (1993). *Handbook on dialects and speech and language assessment*. Washington, DC: Center for Applied Linguistics.

Wolfram, W., Adger, C. T., & Detwyler, J. (1992). *All about dialects*. Washington, DC: Center for Applied Linguistics.

Wolfram, W., & Christian, D. (1976). *Appalachian speech*. Washington, DC: Center for Applied Linguistics.

Wolfram, W., Christian, D., Potter, L., & Leap, W. (1979). *Variability in the English of two Indian communities and its effect on reading and writing*. Final Report to the National Institute of Education. Arlington, VA: Center for Applied Linguistics.

Wolfram, W., & Creech, K. (1996). *Dialects and Harkers Island speech* (8th grade curriculum). Raleigh: North Carolina Language and Life Project.

Wolfram, W., Dannenberg, C., Anderson, & Messner, K. (1996). *Dialects and Appalachian English* (8th grade curriculum). Raleigh: North Carolina Language and Life Project.

Wolfram, W., & Fasold, R. (1974). *The study of social dialects in the United States*. Englewood Cliffs, NJ: Prentice Hall.

Wolfram, W., & Schilling-Estes, N. (1997). *Hoi toide on the Outer Banks: The story of the Ocracoke Brogue*. Chapel Hill: The University of North Carolina Press.

Wolfram, W., & Schilling-Estes, N. (1998). *American English: Dialects and variation*. Oxford, England: Basil Blackwell.

Wolfram, W., Schilling-Estes, N., & Hazen, K. (1997). *Dialects and the Ocracoke Brogue* (8th grade curriculum). Raleigh: North Carolina Language and Life Project.

Wolfram, W., & Whiteman, M. (1971). The role of dialect interference in composition. *The Florida FL Reporter, 9,* 34–38.

Zentella, A. C. (1997). *Growing up bilingual: Puerto Rican children in New York*. Malden, MA: Blackwell.

Author Index

Subject Index

A

Academic language, 107, 127
Accent, 3–4, 16, 34
Acting White, 26
Adjectives and adverbs, 52, 216–218
African American Vernacular English, *see also* Social dialects, 68–72
Age grading, 32–33, 37
Ain't, 15, 218–219
Ann Arbor Decision, 144
Anymore, 1–2
Appropriateness, 75–84
Authority, 27, 77, 84

B

Bidialectalism, 119, 123–126
British English, 4–5

C

Classroom discourse, 24, 75–76, 88, 90–97, 106–107
Comprehensibility, *see* Dialect, comprehension of
Context, 38–40, 82–84, 91–94
Contrastive analysis, 120
Conversational maxims, 77–78
Conversational style, 5, 75, 121
Cooperative learning, 93, 128
Cultural differences, 24–25, 84–90, 145–146
Cultural group, 74–75

D

Deference, 75

Dialect
  and disability, *see also* Language deficit, 23, 100
  and job discrimination, 28, 31
  and media, 32
  and power, 19, 30–31
  and reading, 26, 141–169
  and writing, 26, 129–140
  comprehension of, 17–19, 71–72
  definitions 1–3
  regional, *see* Regional dialects
  social, *see* Social dialects
  standard, *see* Standard English
  vernacular, *see* Vernacular dialect
Dialect accommodation, 26–27
Dialect awareness, 120–121, 126–127, 175–202
Dialect contrasts
  levels of, 4–5, 177–181
  sources of, 6–8
Dialect description, 35–43
Dialect eradication, 26
Dialect groups, 8–10
Dialect leveling, 28, 32–33
Dialect prejudice, *see* Language attitudes, in society
Dialect readers, 154–155
Dialect rights, 115–116
Directness and indirectness, 76–77, 84, 93, 101–102, 154

E

Ebonics, *see also* African American Vernacular English, 20–22
Ellipsis, 14, 77–78
English language arts, 25, 31–32, 99, 119, 170–171

237